indie

FILM AND CULTURE
John Belton, Editor

indie | AN AMERICAN FILM CULTURE

Michael Z. Newman

COLUMBIA UNIVERSITY PRESS
NEW YORK

Columbia University Press
Publishers Since 1893
New York   Chichester, West Sussex
Copyright © 2011 Columbia University Press
All rights reserved
Library of Congress Cataloging-in-Publication Data
Newman, Michael Z.
    Indie : an American film culture / Michael Z. Newman.
        p. cm — (Film and culture)
    Includes bibliographical references and index.
    ISBN 978-0-231-14464-3 (cloth : alk. paper) — ISBN 978-0-231-14465-0
(pbk. : alk. paper) — ISBN 978-0-231-51352-6 (ebook)
    1. Independent films—United States—History and criticism.   2. Independent
filmmakers—United States.   I. Title. II. Series.

PN1993.5.U6N49 2011
791.43—dc22

                                                                2010039954

∞

Columbia University Press books are printed on permanent and durable acid-free
paper.

This book is printed on paper with recycled content.
Printed in the United States of America

c 10 9 8 7 6 5 4 3 2 1
p 10 9 8 7 6 5 4 3 2 1

References to Internet Web sites (URLs) were accurate at the time of writing.
Neither the author nor Columbia University Press is responsible for URLs that
may have expired or changed since the manuscript was prepared.

Portions of the following work have been published in different form and are
reprinted with the permission of the editors and publishers: "Characterization as
Social Cognition in *Welcome to the Dollhouse*," *Film Studies: An International
Review* 8/9 (May 2006): 53–67 (in ch. 3); and "Indie Culture: In Pursuit of the
Authentic Autonomous Alternative," *Cinema Journal* 48.3 (Spring 2009): 16–34
(about *Happiness*, in ch. 6).

FOR MY PARENTS

CONTENTS

ACKNOWLEDGMENTS

Portions of this work were presented to audiences at the University of Wisconsin-Madison film studies colloquium, at conferences of the Society for Cinema and Media Studies and the Society for the Cognitive Study of the Moving Image, and at the 2009 "American Independent Cinema: Past and Present" conference in Liverpool, UK. I am grateful for the feedback I got from audiences at those gatherings, as well as from the participants in my Indie Culture graduate seminar at the University of Wisconsin-Milwaukee in Fall 2008, who helped work through some of the ideas in these pages.

I benefited while writing from the smart advice of Michael Mario Albrecht, Suzy Buenger, Jonathan Gray, Michele Hilmes, Vance Kepley, Jr., Alisa Perren, Ben Singer, John Vanderhoef, Ira Wagman, and Tom Yoshikami. Bingying Liu assisted with research for chapter 2. John Belton, Jeff Smith, Murray Smith, and the manuscript's anonymous readers improved this work in numerous ways. My graduate school adviser, David Bordwell, who suggested that I write about independent cinema in the first place, shaped this project more than anyone aside from its author. The ideas in the pages to follow could never have been formulated without the influence of his teaching and writing. I would be thrilled if ever I were to approach the wit and liveliness of his prose, never mind its scholarly rigor and intellectual fecundity.

And this book could never have been written without the constant encouragement, advice, and scholarly example of Elana Levine, who gave me the idea for the book's title.

indie

INTRODUCTION

Like so many cultural categories, indie cinema is slippery. The same term refers not only to a diverse body of films spanning more than two decades, from *Stranger Than Paradise* (1984) to *Synecdoche, New York* (2008) and beyond, but also a cultural network that sustains them. This book is about American indie cinema as a film culture that comprises not only movies but also institutions—distributors, exhibitors, festivals, and critical media—within which movies are circulated and experienced, and wherein an indie community shares expectations about their forms and meanings. Its topic is the American independent cinema of the era of the Sundance Film Festival and the Hollywood studio specialty divisions. It is not especially concerned with telling the indie story as an unfolding history, but it is nonetheless historical in at least one sense: indie cinema itself is a mode of film production and a film culture that belong to a specific time. Roughly speaking, this era stretches from the emergence into wide public consciousness of this formation in American movies in the middle-to-late 1980s to the indie industry crisis and the demise of many of the indie film companies and studio divisions at the end of the 2000s.

To capture the period succinctly, we can think of indie as the cinema of the Sundance-Miramax era. Beginnings and endings are hard to mark, but two events giving shape to the history of indie cinema are the 1989 Sundance Film Festival, where *sex, lies, and videotape* launched itself improbably to commercial and cultural success, and Disney's shuttering of Miramax, which had been so influential over more than two decades in defining and promoting independent cinema, in 2010. While indie cinema has no clear moments of origin or conclusion, these two moments help to set a historical frame. Following many other critics, I am limiting my discussion to the period when the category of indie cinema began to function not just as a scattered minority practice but as a viable system that parallels that of Hollywood and in some sense has been incorporated by it.

Most centrally, indie cinema consists of American feature films of this era that are not mainstream films. Its identity begins with a negative: these films are not of the Hollywood studios and the megaplexes where they screen, and are generally not aimed at or appreciated by the same audience segments. We will soon see that this is an inadequate definition and understanding, but it is necessarily our starting point, and everything to follow in some way elaborates on indie's identity as a form of cinema that is constantly being distinguished from another one which is more popular and commercially significant, but less culturally legitimate.

The importance of its distinction in relation to Hollywood reveals a tension at the heart of indie film culture between two social functions. The value of indie cinema is generally located in difference, resistance, opposition—in the virtue of alternative representations, audiovisual and storytelling styles, and systems of cultural circulation. In many quarters, difference from Hollywood itself can be a mark of significant value. Indie film culture profits from its alterity, which sustains it and has the potential to be politically progressive and even counter-hegemonic. At the same time, this same culture functions to reproduce social class stratification by offering an elite, culturally legitimate alternative to the mass-market Hollywood offerings of the megaplex. The audience for specialty films—a film industry term which covers indie releases—is generally urban, affluent, well-educated, and fairly narrow by comparison with the audience for studio pictures. By positioning itself as artistic and sophisticated in comparison to mainstream cinema, indie culture functions as an emergent formation of high culture—or perhaps more accurately, high-middlebrow culture—inheriting the social functions previously performed by foreign art films.[1] In some cases we might also see indie cinema as a vanguard subculture, offering its youthful community a sense of insider knowledge and membership through its critical stance toward the dominant culture, which it holds in some measure of contempt. Subcultures, like high and middlebrow cultures, often also reproduce class distinction through their negation of mass or popular culture.[2] The emergence of a high-profile American cinema of theatrical feature films parallel to Hollywood that fulfills these two contradictory missions of resisting and perpetuating the dominant ideology marks indie cinema from earlier iterations of alternative filmmaking and exhibition in the United States.[3]

Economically speaking, *independent* is a relational term describing businesses that are smaller than and separate from bigger competitors. For instance, locally owned record stores are called independent as a way of comparing them favorably to regional, national, or international chains. In this sense, as in any, the term has a positive valence: to be independent is to be free, autonomous, and authentic. Calling a business independent also implies that if it is to succeed it must be more clever and innovative than more powerful competitors, like David facing Goliath, and innovation in any field is taken for an unambiguous good. In business, bold new ideas that change the way people think about an industry and its products often come from outside of more conservative established firms, from upstart independents unafraid of taking risks and trying untested strategies to fill underserved needs.[4] This dynamic of change from the outside challenging conservatism on the inside describes American cinema as well as it does many competitive industries.

The term *independent* has been used in the American film industry since before the establishment of the studio system in the 1910s and 1920s, and has undergone a series of shifts over the decades since then, though it has always referred to production, distribution, and exhibition outside of the Hollywood studios and mainstream theater chains. At different times in film history it has described varied and heterogeneous industrial and textual practices, including filmmaking of high, medium, and low budget and cultural status.[5] In every period of American cinema there have been feature films made, distributed, and exhibited by independent entrepreneurs rather than the majors. In the Sundance-Miramax era, however, independent cinema has taken on rather different meanings from those it had before. It has been transformed from mainly an economic category into one with a broader ambit, which does not necessarily hold up to scrutiny when applying solely economic criteria. If for no other reason, this is because the specialty divisions, also known as mini-majors, are divisions of Hollywood studios owned by media conglomerates and thus are not independent of Hollywood companies. In the process of shifting meanings, *indie* and *independent* have taken on connotations that are not easily encapsulated, and much of what had previously defined these terms no longer applies. Thus in the Sundance-Miramax era, the idea of independent cinema has achieved a level of cultural circulation far greater than in earlier eras, making independence into a brand, a familiar idea that evokes in consumers a range of emotional and symbolic associations. Although it is a good start, then, a definition of indie cinema centered on an industrial distinction between big and small businesses does not offer us a satisfying understanding of the concept of independence in American cinema of the Sundance-Miramax era. It does not tell us everything we might want to know and prevents us from understanding much of what people consider indie to include. In this era, indie cinema is understood according to a cluster of associations about film texts and contexts that go beyond industrial distinctions to include many facets of the cinematic experience.[6]

The shift from "independent" to "indie" is one marker of the emergence of this new cluster of associations. Although it likely originated in the world of popular music, *indie* gained salience as a more general term for nonmainstream culture in the 1990s, and applies not only to rock or pop music and feature films but also in some instances to video games, news media, zines, literary magazines, television shows, crafts and fashion, and retail businesses from booksellers to supermarkets.[7] To an extent, the diminutive *indie* is simply a synonym for *independent* with an added connotation of fashionable cool. But it also functions as a mystification of the more straightforward category "independent." This mystification diminishes or makes vague the significance of economic distinctions and injects added connotations of a distinguishing style or sensibility and of a social identity. The introduction of "indie" also allows for a separation between a strict and loose sense of the idea to which both "indie" and "independent" make reference, so that something might seem indie without actually being independent by whatever strict definition one adopts, or alternately might be independent by that definition without seeming indie. We must be sensitive to shifting and inconsistent criteria which include both textual and contextual considerations, and grant that, as a cultural category, indie cinema is the product of indie film culture's collective judgment about what counts—or does not—as indie.

This judgment depends as much on understandings of Hollywood as mainstream cinema as it does on conceptions of indie in relation to it. I consider "mainstream" to be a category that niche cultures or subcultures construct to have something against which to define themselves and generate their cultural or subcultural capital.[8] I do not believe that there is a mainstream that exists independent of this process of classification. Thus mainstream cinema is itself as much a product of expecting certain kinds of experience at the multiplex and making certain kinds of sense of Hollywood movies as it is anchored in textual practices. The mutability of mainstream classifications is confirmed in cases of crossover indie successes such as *My Big Fat Greek Wedding* (2002) and *Garden State* (2004) (or in music, alternative rock acts such as R.E.M. whose popularity threatens their authentically independent status). The appeal of a product that originates from the indie sector to a wider public potentially indicates that it belongs in the mainstream rather than the marginal alternative spheres. The "indie blockbuster," so crucial to the development of the mini-majors in the 1990s and 2000s,[9] aims to bargain away some outsider credibility in exchange for commercial reward, calculatingly nudging some indie films toward the mainstream to occupy negotiated terrain, part outside and part inside. But even in such exceptional cases as Nirvana's *Nevermind* (1991) and *Pulp Fiction* (1994), it is often possible to retain the credibility and integrity associated with independence while also appealing to a wider audience. This is evidence that "mainstream" is always a product of collective judgment no less than "indie" is.

The shifting meanings marked by the rise of indie cinema have made an industrial definition of indie (and of mainstream) cinema less descriptive and apposite. First, independent cinema is not used merely as a business term. Like independent music, independent cinema originally made its artistic authenticity contingent on the autonomy of its production from major media companies, and as such was distinctive as a cultural genre defined as much by industrial criteria as textual features.[10] But also like indie music, over time its autonomy from major media companies ceased to be so central to its identity whether because of the mainstream's incorporation of indie style or because of indie culture's greater investment in aesthetics and identity than economics.[11] Whatever the reasons, at this point indie had become recognizable as a distinct form of cinema and a promotional discourse supporting it (or, more accurately, a cluster of styles, cycles, subgenres, and promotional discourses surrounding them), and this is evident even in the simple fact of the widening currency of "indie" beyond the industry and the cinephile audience.[12] For instance, the Keystone Art Theater in Indianapolis has an Indie Lounge, and a section of DVDs in American Target discount stores beginning in 2006 used an "INDIES" sign to indicate categorization of movies for sale.[13] When media consumption is guided by this kind of categorization, indie film has become a cultural category with its own life outside of the world of people who read *Variety* or indieWire. It refers more to films than to corporate structures and interrelations in the media trade, although the origin of the term in an economic distinction is part of its wider cultural circulation. As it is used in the Sundance-Miramax era, independent cinema describes aesthetic and social distinctions as often as industrial ones. It is a matter of cultures of consumption as much as those of production.

This is not to deny that industrial or economic distinctions are part of the cluster of criteria applied in constructions of indieness. Especially among more cinephile and passionate audiences, economics might factor in quite a bit. For instance, one critic divides up indies industrially into five categories. From smallest to largest: house indies which are fully DIY operations based out of people's homes, micro-indies earning under $3 million annually in theatrical revenue, mid-indies like Magnolia Pictures and IFC, full indies like Summit and Lionsgate, and dependents like Fox Searchlight (see fig. I.1).[14] He tellingly considers all of these categories to be along the spectrum captured by the term *indie*. But economics is always considered in relation to other considerations. Even the use of the term *indiewood*, which can pejoratively mock films of Hollywood mini-majors that aim to position themselves as "indie," recognizes at once cultural and economic factors in categorization.[15]

It follows that economic and aesthetic criteria may converge, but not necessarily. Thus a film produced outside of the Hollywood studios may not be considered indie according to prevailing cultural criteria. For instance, in 1991 the independent producer Carolco made the action blockbuster *Terminator 2*, no one's idea of a 1980s indie. George Lucas financed the production of his *Star Wars* prequels himself; their

FIGURE 1.1. Indie Distribution in the Sundance-Miramax Era

DISNEY	20TH C. FOX	UNIVERSAL	SONY	WARNER BROS.	PARAMOUNT
Miramax (founded 1979) 1993–2010 (Dimension to 2005)	Fox Searchlight 1994–	Gramercy (with Polygram) 1992–1999	Sony Pictures Classics 1991–	New Line Cinema & Fine Line Features (founded 1967) 1995 with acquisition of Turner—2008	Paramount Classics/Vantage 1998–2008
		October Films (founded 1991) 1997–1999		Picturehouse 2005–2008	
		Focus Features (previously Good Machine founded c. 1991; 1999–2001 combined with USA Films) 2002–		Warner Independent Pictures 2003–2008	

Other contemporary independents of note (in alphabetical order):

Artisan Entertainment 1998–2003, acquired by Lionsgate
IFC Films 1999– (owned by Rainbow Media, a subsidiary of Cablevision)
Lionsgate 1995–
Newmarket Films 1994–
Magnolia Pictures 2001– (owned by 2929 Entertainment, a small conglomerate)
Overture Films 2006– (owned by Liberty Media, a conglomerate)
Roadside Attractions 2004–
Summit Entertainment 2006–
THINKFilm 2001–
The Weinstein Company 2005–
Zeitgeist Films 1998–

production credit goes to Lucasfilm, not 20th Century Fox. And no one considers those films indie either. But Miramax (under its Dimension Films imprint) and Lionsgate have followed strategies of combining the production of "genre" films that are not typically called indie with classier pictures aimed at the festival and art house circuits that are. If indie were being used strictly as an economic category, then Lionsgate's torture porn films like *Saw* (2004) and *Hostel* (2005) and Summit's *Twilight* series would count no less than films by Jim Jarmusch and John Sayles. But as indie is used in the Sundance-Miramax era, it might make no more sense to think of low-budget "genre" films as indie any more than it does high-concept blockbusters, though exceptions such as indie horror blockbusters *The Blair Witch Project* (1999) and *Paranormal Activity* (2007)—marketed as much on the basis of their heroic production legends as of more conventional appeals—certainly test this distinction. In any instance, factors such as style and implicit audience address and exhibition context and promotional discourse matter as much as who the distributor is.[16]

Cultural categories like indie cinema function through repeated use in multiple discursive sites, and are best understood as they are implemented by communities invested in their meanings. A good way of tracing the contours of the category is by looking at the various popular surveys of American indie/independent cinema, books like *The Rough Guide to American Independent Film* and 100 *American Independent Films* and magazine features like *Empire* magazine's "ultimate indie lineup" of fifty "greatest" films.[17] Many of these do include outlier cases. *Empire* has an action blockbuster, *The Terminator* (1984), in its top ten, and most surveys of independent film stretch back to independent cinema from before the Sundance-Miramax era, such as films by John Cassavetes, Andy Warhol, and John Waters. But the most central and recurring instances are likely those around which the category has been fashioned in the popular imagination.

Categories are often maintained by the identification of such prototypes and exemplars, those instances that are especially salient for making judgments about what the category means and what belongs or does not belong in it. Indie cinema has certain central instances, films like *sex, lies, and videotape* and *Pulp Fiction*, that have not only influenced later works but, equally important, have influenced indie film culture's conception of itself. Films find their way into the category through discursive positioning, which is partly a matter of locating a film's similarity to established central instances of indie film—whether by textual or contextual (including industrial) criteria. Thus some films might be stronger or weaker examples of indie cinema; some are more central, and some more peripheral or problematic. There is no formula for inclusion, no fixed set of textual or contextual conditions we can apply. Films like Lionsgate's genre releases might be weaker examples, while those of key indie *auteurs* like Richard Linklater or Hal Hartley might be stronger ones. Textual and economic criteria figure into these judgments, but they will not function as necessary and sufficient conditions for inclusion.

In this way indie cinema shares much with indie music, a similar cultural formation that mixes the economic and aesthetic. Some indie rock artists, like Sonic Youth, have unassailable credibility despite migrating from independent to major labels. Some, like Liz Phair, begin indie in terms both of label and aesthetic, but are eventually rejected from the category not just because of signing to a major label, but because of adopting too much of a pop sound. And other acts like Radiohead may originate on majors but gain credibility among those who identify their tastes as indie and authentic, and eventually turn to DIY distribution, the quintessential indie culture move. Judgments about indie authenticity rely on multiple and sometimes contradictory factors and are best understood within cultural contexts.

Just as independent film distributors like Summit or Lionsgate may release films or recordings that don't count culturally as independent, there are many films that do count culturally that would not be admitted to the category according to a strict economic criterion. As with indie music and major labels, distinction between films made by major studios and films made by independent entrepreneurs does not effectively mark indie cinema off from the rest of American film. This is in large part a function of the rise during the 1990s of the mini-majors, the subsidiaries of the Hollywood studios whose role is to produce and more often finance and distribute what the industry calls its specialty or niche products, lower-budget films aimed at more affluent and urban art house audiences. The cinema under consideration in these pages is to a large extent that of Miramax, New Line and Fine Line, Fox Searchlight, Sony Pictures Classics, Paramount Classics, and Focus Features. These are (or in a number of instances, were) Hollywood companies, boutique labels under the corporate umbrellas of Disney, Time Warner, News Corp., Sony, Viacom, and NBC

Universal, respectively (see fig. I.1). While *T2*, *The Phantom Menace* (1999), *Hostel*, and *Twilight* (Summit, 2008) would be "independent" according to a strict industrial definition, the numerous films released by the mini-majors over the years would not. At the same time, indie cinema also includes releases by many smaller distributors such as Lionsgate, Summit, The Weinstein Company, and IFC, and audiences and filmmakers may not distinguish very critically among mini-major films and those considered more "authentic" when considering industrial criteria. And this is not even to consider the films by artists whose work is understood to have come out of the indie movement, like the Coen brothers and Spike Lee, who have had many films distributed by majors (rather than their subsidiaries) such as 20th Century Fox and Universal. Even mini-major release and markers of "quality" may not be the right conditions for indieness, as many of Miramax's biggest successes in terms of box office revenue and high-profile awards might not seem very centrally indie within late-twentieth and early-twenty-first century American film culture (e.g., *The English Patient*, 1996; *Good Will Hunting*, 1997; *Chicago*, 2002). Determining what indie means requires that we be attentive to its cultural circulation as well as to economics, storytelling, and thematics.

In the era of indie cinema and mini-majors—which is also the era of home video and Netflix, of Hollywood as a resurgent commercial power, of intensified globalization of media, of rapidly proliferating film festivals and festival films, and of a mass culture steadily fragmenting into so many niches—there has been a fairly stable conception of what an independent film is, and this conception is distinct from those that applied at earlier moments in American film history. Broadly speaking, indie cinema is produced in the context of these various developments. Its identity comes into being in comparison to other categories of cinema contemporaneous to it, such as Hollywood blockbusters and prestige pictures, foreign imports, and avant-garde works. Indie cinema is a product of its contexts large and small. It is itself a form of niche media, a reaction against conglomerate gigantism and at the very same time, considering its mini-major producer-distributors, a symptom of it.[18] But independent cinema circulates as a concept principally within its specific institutions; it is most specifically within these institutions that its meanings and values are produced and understood. This knowledge is contextual and contingent, which is to say, it is a product of historically specific conditions.

I argue in these pages that what makes this iteration of independent cinema—the indie iteration—cohere as a cultural category is not only a set of industrial criteria or formal or stylistic conventions. It is most centrally a cluster of interpretive strategies and expectations that are shared among filmmakers; their support personnel, including distributors and publicists; the staffers of independent cinema institutions such as film festivals; critics and other writers; and audiences. All of these different people are audiences who employ these strategies, and it is only because filmmakers are also film spectators that they are able to craft their works to elicit particular responses from the audience. Indie constitutes a film culture: it includes texts, institutions, and audiences.[19] Indie audiences share viewing strategies for thinking about and engaging with the texts—they have in common knowledge and competence—which are products of indie community networks. These viewing strategies will be the subject of the pages to follow.

To think in terms of viewing strategies requires a shift away from the approach that writers, whether scholars or not, often take to analyze cultural categories or genres.[20] It is tempting to try to define a category according to its attributes, identifying essential characteristics and centering a definition on them as conditions of inclusion or exclusion. But by focusing on texts alone we miss much of what makes categories significant to our encounters with media.[21] Categories are ways of organizing experience, guides to finding order in the world. Cultural options always threaten to overwhelm, and it is only by categorizing them that producers and consumers of culture can manage to know where to pay their scarce attention. I locate media categories not only in texts but also in audiences and the institutions through which texts and audiences are brought together.

Sideways (2004) is a comedy about two friends who take a trip to a wine region of California. It stars Thomas Haden Church, Paul Giamatti, Virginia Madsen, and Sandra Oh. It was shot on 35mm color film and runs 126 minutes. The story is by turns funny and sad. It is about love, friendship, loneliness, and passion. It follows conventions of continuity editing and canonical storytelling, with clear exposition and causal narration pushed along by character conflict. Its comic style is generally subtle and character-focused, though in the final act it turns somewhat more farcical and broad. These traits are facts of the film's textuality. But its indieness is not to be found entirely by examining its textual features; indieness is the product of a judgment that we make about the film, or which comes premade for us as part of the film's promotional discourse and its contexts of consumption. Some viewers experience the film in a condition of total ignorance of the existence of something called indie cinema, and for them nothing is at stake in determining whether it belongs in this category or not, and it is simply irrelevant. Some are aware of indie's existence but refuse to allow *Sideways* entry into the category, perhaps because of textual features, but more likely because it cost more to make than was considered reasonable for a film to be indie in 2004 ($16 million) or because it was financed and released by a mini-major, Fox Searchlight.[22] And many consider it to be a very good example of indie cinema, so much so that the film won six 2004 Independent Spirit Awards, including Best Picture.[23] What made it indie might have been its storytelling and style, or the background of the director Alexander Payne (whose previous films include *Citizen Ruth*, 1996, and *Election*, 1999) in the indie movement, or its release in art houses, or its cultural positioning in trailers, reviews, and other forms of publicity and promotion. The fact that different knowledgeable and competent people can legitimately disagree about whether or not a film counts as indie suggests that this is an oft-contested category, and one that cannot be understood without considering the people who use it and their habits of textual engagement. Texts may be indie or not, but the only way of determining if they are is by looking at whether people think of them this way. Categories like indie cinema arise and maintain their significance through a process (actually a cluster of processes), and so in the pages to follow I will look at indie cinema as process as well as product.

Much of this cultural and cinematic terrain is already the subject of books such as John Pierson's *Spike, Mike, Slackers & Dykes*, Peter Biskind's *Down and Dirty Pictures*, Emmanuel Levy's *Cinema of Outsiders*, E. Deidre Pribram's *Cinema & Culture*, and Geoff King's *American Independent Cinema*, among many other writings.[24] Studies of this large field of cinematic practice have shed considerable light on some of its industrial and cultural features,[25] and Geoff King has considered indie cinema not only as an industrial designation but also as a corpus of texts, establishing general aesthetic tendencies and some contexts to which they respond.[26] King has also written about the films of the mini-majors in particular as "indiewood" rather than independent cinema.[27] E. Deidre Pribram's *Cinema & Culture* is admirable in its combination of the contextual and textual and in the array of cinema it canvases, moving from discussions of distribution to narrative to politics and thematics. Her work overlaps historically with my study, but it begins and ends earlier, covering the 1980–2001 period rather than the Sundance-Miramax era which privileges constructions of independent cinema as indie rather than, as earlier, as a more political and aesthetically adventurous challenge. It also diverges in thinking about independent cinema as multinational (including British examples) and as more intrinsically political and aesthetically confrontational in relation to classical narrative. My effort to unify indie cinema's culture through the rubric of a cluster of interlocking interpretive strategies overlaps in many ways with her analysis, though mine emphasizes indie film culture's role in setting terms through which films are understood.[28]

Jeffrey Sconce's influential essay on "smart cinema" of the 1990s and early 2000s is another work that covers some similar ground as this study, identifying a trend in American specialty filmmaking which relies on irony and nihilism as a way of distinguishing itself against Hollywood film.[29] Sconce argues that a specific "smart" tone or sensibility unifies the aesthetic interventions of many indie filmmakers to be discussed in these pages, including Todd Solondz, Todd Haynes, Wes Anderson, and Richard Linklater. He is careful to distinguish this category from indie cinema, a culture with which smart cinema overlaps. Smart cinema offers its audience a sense of distinction in relation to mainstream cinema, as I have argued of indie cinema more generally, and its ironic address splits the audience into those who get it and those who do not, which allows the ones who do a sense of their distance from the mainstream other.[30] But the smart film is a more specific category than the indie film, one that has little currency outside of academic discourse, and Sconce makes no claim that smart-ness is essential to indieness. My approach is thus more expansive than his both historically and also by considering indie films that might lack the ironic or nihilistic sensibility of a *Ghost World* or *Happiness*, such as many of the films of the strain of indie cinema I will identify in chapter 3 as socially engaged realism. And yet I do rely on some of Sconce's ideas about the Off-Hollywood audience and the functions of certain kinds of textual difference within indie contexts.

Thus as a cultural category and a film culture, indie cinema still is open to further critical analysis as a formation which includes but is not limited to the releases of the mini-majors (since indie culture does not consider an economic criterion to be necessarily above any others). Although there are many books on independent film, they often catalog rosters of savvy producers, heroic *auteurs*, and distinctive "schools" without unifying them within contexts of cultural production and consumption.[31] Independent cinema needs consideration as a corpus of works with not only underlying aesthetic conventions but also shared audience expectations. King offers a clear and persuasive overview of the industrial and formal terrain, and he also considers some of the sociopolitical dimensions of alternative cinema; I aim to consider indie film from a complementary perspective that is concerned primarily with describing the modes of engagement it solicits and encourages within the context of its institutional discourses. My project is to consider how American indie cinema is invested with significance and given unity and coherence by a cluster of assumptions and expectations about narrative form and the cinematic experience that producers and consumers of independent films share. Independent filmmakers, films, and their critics and audiences function in a circuit of meaning-making. The mode of interaction between audience and text is the product of discourses effected through a collaboration between all of the participants in constructing and maintaining "indie" as a cultural category. In tracing the contours of this category and arguing for its significance, I am most concerned with thinking about how its users make sense of it and how their sense-making is a product of cultural forces, which both enable and constrain potential meanings. Thus my approach to thinking about indie films as a coherent category is a pragmatic one, considering how it functions within the contexts of its use.[32]

This approach seizes on the nexus of film and spectator, text and audience. It is concerned with how films are experienced but not very much with how they are made. Of course, to understand everything we might want to about indie cinema, we would need to look at production practices as well. (Some scholars have done this, though much work remains to be done.)[33] But this is not a book that aims to understand everything. Its ambition is to understand how audiences and films engage one another, and it assumes that pursuing this issue is a good way of understanding how indie cinema functions as a category and concept. Thus its approach has both sociological and psychological dimensions.

In the case of independent cinema, a sociological approach can help us understand the way that the indie audience uses culture for the purpose of distinguishing itself—its taste—against the other of mainstream culture and its audiences. In this sense, indie cinema is a means of accumulating cultural capital, the forms of knowledge and experience that social groups use to assert and reproduce their status.[34] Indie culture is comparatively urbane, sophisticated, and "creative class," and it uses cinema as a means of perpetuating its place in a social and cultural hierarchy.[35] It thus succeeds art cinema in the history of cinematic taste culture in the United States as a mode of filmmaking that those aspiring to certain kinds of status adopt as a common point of reference, a token of community membership. At the same time, a psychological approach can explain how, within the audience formation that has an investment in indie cinema, text and viewer engage one another. In the following pages I will elaborate on a cluster of viewing strategies that the indie audience has in common. These strategies and the textual forms that solicit them are best understood as psychological dimensions of the cinematic experience, which arise alongside conventions of storytelling. They are means of framing the comprehension and interpretation of films. If my discussion of viewing strategies describes the phenomenon of indie cinema well, it will only be because these strategies have both sociological *and* psychological validity. That is, they are descriptive of both the audience as a social phenomenon and of the spectator as an idealization of that audience in an individual whose mind is engaged by cinematic culture and its surrounding discourses.

In this book, I first establish indie film culture as a body of works that call on shared knowledge and expectations within their institutional contexts. I then canvas three viewing strategies, relating to three prominent aspects of independent cinema in this era— character-focused realism, formal play, and oppositionality—and analyze their functioning through discussions of specific examples. The first part of the book discusses these strategies and the institutional contexts within which they are mobilized, in particular film festivals and art house theaters. It argues that in the Sundance-Miramax era, indie film essentially filled the role previously occupied by imported art cinema.

The second part considers four films as examples of how indie films represent character and make it a central aesthetic appeal. Nicole Holofcener's *Walking and Talking* (1996), Sofia Coppola's *Lost in Translation* (2003), Todd Solondz's *Welcome to the Dollhouse* (1996), and John Sayles's *Passion Fish* (1992) each illustrates some key elements of the prominence of character in independent cinema storytelling. It positions these films within a strain of indie cinema that I identify as socially engaged realism, an approach to storytelling and thematics that distinguishes character-centered indie cinema from mainstream narrative and representation.

The third part considers the viewing strategy of finding in the forms of indie films an invitation to play, of seeing unconventional or prominent formal appeals as game-like. The discussion in this section turns to the Coen brothers' films as examples of pastiche as a playful indie aesthetic, and then to *Pulp Fiction* and the many films which in various ways share some of its unconventional narrative logic, which may be said to play with narrative form itself. The emphasis on the Coens offers one significant example of indie auteurism, an ideology distinguishing alternatives from ordinary film practice, and a key approach to appreciating independent cinema. The Coens are also an excellent example of indie negotiating between the margins and mainstream, as directors whose origins in independent cinema have authorized appropriating their entire oeuvre as the work of outsiders, even as many of their films have been released by major studios to quite wide appreciation. The subsequent chapter, on ludic narrative forms, begins with *Pulp Fiction* but surveys many examples of different kinds of play with narrative conventions and expectations that function as distinction between mainstream and alternative practices.

The final part treats the topic of indie cinema as a form of opposition to the mainstream, but by looking as much at the contexts of film releases, including discourses in the popular and trade press and on cinephile Web sites, as at the film text itself. In considering the release of two films in particular, *Happiness* (1998) and *Juno* (2007), it contrasts a film whose credibility as alternative culture was constructed as practically unassailable with another whose indieness met challenges as it succeeded commercially and "crossed over." This concluding chapter about indie as anti-Hollywood argues that opposition to the mainstream is animated through the discourse of authenticity that affirms some films' indieness while denying that of others.

Although *indie* and *independent* are often terms used to describe more than just American fiction feature films, with certain exceptions I have limited the discussion in the pages that follow to fiction feature films made by U.S. directors and producers (though financing might come from abroad). Documentaries are different in a number of important ways from fiction films, especially their modes of representation and narrative exposition and their economic positioning within the American film market. Many of my claims apply to them as well, but many would not, and thus including documentaries would excessively complicate matters. The exclusion of films from outside the United States is perhaps a more contentious matter. Aesthetically, many qualities of Canadian, Latin American, European, and Asian films positioned as alternatives in local or international markets are quite similar to the aesthetics I describe in relation to American independent films, and they often call upon the same viewing strategies. American indie distributors, moreover, distribute many imports; some of the most high-profile independent releases in this era, including *The Crying Game* (1992), *Secrets and Lies* (1996), *Crouching Tiger, Hidden Dragon* (2000), *The Piano* (2002), *Once* (2006), and *The Queen* (2006), have been foreign-made indie releases. However, while I believe many of my claims do apply to films from other countries, I have still limited the discussion to American films. In part this is to make my task manageable, but also because, as chapter 2 will show, indie cinema in the United States has functioned as an alternative American national cinema. The discursive construction of American indie cinema that I have considered is largely a product of national media institutions, not only American film festivals like Sundance but also American blogs like indieWire, magazines like *Filmmaker*, trade publications like *Variety*, and theater chains like Landmark. The minimajors that control much of the cinema called indie are American companies releasing mainly American films. All of this suggests that indie culture is to some significant extent a national culture, even if it is not essentially concerned with thematizing national identity. This is not to deny that it is also a local, regional, international, or global culture, but only to defend its configuration here as American first of all. (It is also my sense that indie culture in the United States keeps imports at the periphery in its constructions of indieness.)

By describing indie cinema as a film culture, I am insisting that we think of it not just as a collection of cinematic works with similar textual features but also as a set of practices and a body of knowledge with certain privileged meanings. Our ways of thinking of indie cinema are not simply issued by the publicity departments of media companies, nor are they products merely of critical discourses in the popular, trade, or scholarly press. Indie culture is a category that belongs to all of the people who make up its community of users, which includes filmmakers and tastemakers and ordinary filmgoers. Indie can only function as a coherent term as long as there is some agreement about what it names. Only by locating indie cinema within the integrated web of text, audience, and institutions can we hope to understand this category and the concepts it calls to mind.

part 1   CONTEXT

chapter 1 INDIE CINEMA

VIEWING STRATEGIES | The key to

understanding indies is Hollywood —EMMANUEL LEVY

Several obstacles stand in the way of a unified aesthetic of indie cinema. Among the Off-Hollywood filmmaking community, evocative concepts like "independent spirit" suffice to characterize a heterogeneous enterprise that might appear to resist more specific generalizations. Filmmakers and critics insist that independent films are more offbeat or personal or character-driven than Hollywood equivalents.[1] These formulations remain rather vague. To the sheer variety of films and the difficulty posed by generalizing about them, add the problem of authenticating the very independence the name designates. Is indie cinema of the Sundance-Miramax era anything more than a marketing strategy? I believe it is, even if "independent" often does not designate what either its champions or its detractors might wish. Like all feature filmmaking, independent cinema is among other things a business. If it is undertaken for profit under the auspices of the global media empires, this complicates its status as alternative media, but it does not de-legitimate the category. On the contrary, it amplifies its salience. Since opposition to the dominant media sells to an elite niche market—which makes up in affluence some of what it lacks in size—a viable commercial logic underwrites the independent spirit. It is precisely because of its lack of true autonomy from the mainstream entertainment industry that indie cinema enjoys such prominence, that it has become such a compelling, productive *idea* in American film culture functioning in dialogue with the Hollywood mainstream.

Many filmmakers, spectators, and critics agree that independent cinema offers some kind of alternative to Hollywood, but what kind of alternative is it? What animates the "independent spirit"? In answering these questions I consider the ways that films solicit responses from viewers. In short, viewers are encouraged to see independent films as more socially engaged and formally experimental than Hollywood; more generally, they are encouraged to read independent films as alternatives to or critiques of mainstream movies. Taken together, these viewing strategies account for much of what makes the category "independent cinema" cohere.[2] They are the interpretive frame through which audiences make sense of American independent cinema, differing in several important respects from the frame through which audiences experience "mainstream" movies.

The viewer is not radically free to impose any strategy at all on cultural products. Viewing strategies, arising from critical and cultural contexts, are always constrained and closely related to textual practice. Certain kinds of storytelling solicit viewing strategies. For instance, in chapter 3 we will see that a realist mode of narration orients the viewer toward a focus on character as a specific kind of appeal of some indie films. So viewing and storytelling strategies are hardly independent of one another; but to approach indie cinema from the perspective of viewing rather than storytelling strategies one emphasizes the audience and film culture, seizing on the meanings that ultimately are most central to the coherence of a cultural category. Using films as the central site of research, an inquiry into viewing strategies can ask how the evidence of storytelling practice—in relation to a given cultural and critical context—can offer insights into the practices of viewers in making sense of narratives and their meanings. We reverse-engineer from the films, knowing something about their general appropriation by audiences and critics, to determine the patterns of meaning audiences construct through their encounter with the text.

Indie cinema is not specific enough to function as a historically stable, well-recognized genre like science fiction or a group style like Soviet Montage with clearly identifiable visual techniques shared among a movement of like-minded artists. It makes more sense to see it as a cycle or large-scale production trend within the American film industry which brings its own assumptions about cinematic form and function shared by filmmakers and moviegoers, a category in some ways similar to classical or art cinema, both of which have been systematically analyzed not only as institutions but as a cluster of storytelling conventions and a mode of film practice.[3] I am not claiming that cinema functions as a coherent narrational mode like art cinema or classical cinema, a proposition Geoff King has considered and rejected, preferring to see independent cinema as a hybrid of classical and art or avant-garde cinema.[4] I am proposing instead the concept of a film culture, which includes expectations about form which may not cohere as a distinct mode of narration clearly marked off from others, but which does include significant shared meanings within institutional contexts of what indie is and is not.

This chapter broadly outlines how indie films work. Its ambition is to describe how they appeal to their viewers and how their viewers use them. But I am not attempting to define independent films in such a way that will determine exactly which texts qualify or do not qualify for membership in the club. I assume that indie film is defined not by scholars or critics but, pragmatically and within the limits of cultural and historical contexts, by filmmakers and audiences for whom something is at stake in the designation. Indies are those films considered within the institutions of American film culture to be indies, regardless of their budget, producer, distributor, director, and cast, and regardless of their genre, theme, style, and tone. The category exists only as it is useful to the whole cultural circuit of producers and consumers that makes independent cinema what it is.[5] I discuss films that are considered by a broad consensus of filmmakers, critics, and moviegoers to belong in the category of indie cinema, regardless of who produced them or starred in them, regardless of how big or small their budgets or profits. My task, then, is to outline the contours of the category and some strong tendencies in its uses and to probe the features of independent cinema as this cultural circuit configures them.

This approach to categories assumes that they are often understood according to prominent prototypes or exemplars rather than, in the classical view, according to whether they meet a set of necessary and sufficient conditions.[6] The viewing strategies I describe in these pages are mobilized in relation to certain ideals of what indie films are like. Sometimes qualities of indie prototypes overlap, but sometimes they might be quite distinct from one another. Thus two indie films might not have much in common with one another aside from indieness. I organize these prototypes into viewing strategies, which implies that they are to be found in audiences rather than texts. But the films that call upon these strategies have qualities in common, and these qualities are what makes them prototypical. It is significant, however, that these prototypes come into being and are understood in social and historical contexts, and that indie cinema is only meaningful within these contexts.

The idea of independent cinema is hardly new, but since the 1980s it has assumed a place and function in American film culture that it never before had; connotations of "independent" have shifted according to changing conceptions of both alternative and mainstream cinemas. Although strongly influenced by the New American Cinema of the 1960s and 1970s and directors such as Martin Scorsese and Robert Altman, who serve as models for many indie filmmakers, as well as the international art cinema of the 1950s and 1960s that inspired that movement, contemporary American independent films respond to their own unique contexts and demand their own modes of engagement. These are products of a history that stretches from the present day all the way back to the days before the establishment of Hollywood, when independents helped to shape the origins of the American film industry.

Independents in American Film History

The origins of the term *independent* in cinema are old. It was applied to the producer Adolph Zukor in the 1910s when he opposed the monopolistic control of American film distribution by Thomas Edison's Motion Picture Patents Company.[7] Zukor's firm, soon known as Paramount, became the first pillar in the edifice of the American studio system.[8] "Independent" was applied to David O. Selznick, Samuel Goldwyn, and Walter Wanger in the 1930s and 1940s when they produced their own films with talent and facilities rented from the Hollywood majors and distributed through them.[9] These independents were integral to the Hollywood system, assuming risks that the majors preferred to avoid and generating high-quality product such as Goldwyn's *Best Years of Our Lives* (1946) to fill the majors' theatrical programs and earn them high profits. During the studio era there were also American productions that were genuinely separate from the Hollywood studio system, such as films made by and about African-Americans and films in Yiddish, as well as documentaries and avant-garde films such as those of the New York Film and Photo League.[10] But during the years of Hollywood's stable, vertically integrated oligopoly, genuinely independent films were seen by very few people, and independent cinema was hardly the identifiable category in American culture that it was later to become.

Following the consent decrees of 1948 that caused the breakup of the studio system, the Hollywood mode of production became centered on packages assembled by agents, stars, directors, and producers and financed through advances from the majors based on expectations of distribution revenue. The 1950s and 1960s saw a rapid proliferation of independent films in the United States, when the system of "package-unit" production still in place today was established.[11] We no longer think of this as the typical kind of independent production, but according to the terms of the studio era, it is just that. From the 1960s to the present day, the major studios (Columbia, 20th Century Fox, Disney, Universal, Paramount, and Warner Bros.) have mainly financed and distributed films produced by other companies, just as Loew's/MGM did with *Gone With the Wind* in 1939.

During the studio era and the early post-studio era, "independent" was an industrial distinction and did not designate a specific body of films that audiences would likely recognize as having shared textual features or functions. The products of independent producers like Selznick were classical Hollywood films. But since the 1960s, critics have identified a countercurrent in American cinema of films that are more widely distinguished from the commercial mainstream according to aesthetic criteria, and recognized for having cultural and textual functions and effects that are distinct from those of Hollywood films. That is, beginning in the 1960s, there is a new sense in which films can be termed independent. There are at least three major dimensions to this new entry in cinematic nomenclature: exploitation films, experimental or underground films, and art films. All of these are to some extent precursors to today's indie films.

All of these forms of cinema became increasingly prominent in the post-studio era. This prominence resulted from a steep drop in the output of the Hollywood majors, a need for exhibitors to find a product and an audience to demand it, the demise of the Production Code, and a growing interest in film as art.[12] The collapse of the studio system in the 1950s augured a binary popular conception of American cinema as Hollywood/not-Hollywood to replace the monolithic conception of the previous era wherein Hollywood and movies meant the same thing to most people. At first the term *independent* was applied to any alternative to Hollywood, a capacious category including the B movies of Roger Corman, the avant-garde works of Maya Deren, and what David E. James calls the "American art films" of Haskell Wexler, Dennis Hopper, and John Cassavetes.[13] Cassavetes' *Shadows* (1959) is a key example in this history, representing many of the era's most important independent film characteristics: a low-budget, improvisatory aesthetic similar to European art film movements; a story about a taboo subject, interracial romance; and production, distribution, and exhibition outside of the mainstream channels. In the American cinema of outsiders, *Shadows* is the ur-text. Eventually, it was the American art film that came to dominate our conception of independent cinema.[14]

Avant-garde and exploitation films were considered independent because of their distinctness from Hollywood, but each category is also distinct from what we today call indie cinema. "The precise relationship of the avant-garde cinema to American commercial film," in P. Adams Sitney's influential formulation, "is radical otherness. They operate in different realms with next to no significant influence on each other."[15] The significance of this radical otherness is that avant-garde cinema can scarcely be discussed using the same terms and concepts as Hollywood cinema. It has a very different set of determining production practices, viewing strategies, institutional bases, and critical discourses that animate it and give it meaning. The significance of independent (or indie) as it applies to today's cinema, by contrast, is that it defines a more ambiguous, give-and-take relationship between Hollywood and its alternative that supports more comparison and closer, finer distinctions between them, as we shall see. Indie as opposed to independent makes clear that the new conception of independence is in some sense less independent than some alternatives, and that more radically different work may be unsuitable for description as indie.

Over the years, the meaning of independent has become fixed on a more specific kind of film than was the case in the 1960s: the American narrative feature aimed at the alternative theatrical market.

At one point this included exploitation films, and in John Waters we have the clearest case of an indie *auteur* whose aesthetic is in this tradition. But since the 1980s, with American independent films succeeding abroad at festivals like Cannes, with Sundance becoming a high-profile event, and with the growing indie presence in annual American film awards (especially the Oscars), the exploitation component of independent cinema has been strategically, systematically downplayed, even as the companies releasing these prestige pictures, such as Miramax and Lionsgate, distribute both art house and exploitation fare. Prestige and cultural distinction have come to dominate our conception of independent cinema at the same time that this category has become prominent within mainstream American culture. The rise of the mini-major specialty divisions has been both a symptom and cause of this conceptual reconfiguration.[16] A well-known indie-branded film released by the exemplar indie distributor, Miramax, was *Pulp Fiction* (1994) rather than the highly profitable *Scream* franchise (1996, 1997, 2000), brought out by its "genre" label, Dimension Films. During the same period, American independent films came to replace foreign imports as the bread and butter of art house programming, as the next chapter will describe. Essentially, the indie movie, descendent of the American art film and of Cassavetes' maverick personal cinema, took the place once occupied by the foreign film in the imaginations of American moviegoers. It has become the cinema figured as more intellectually satisfying and culturally distinguished, and addressed to a more sophisticated audience, than the mass-market movies made in Hollywood. Art cinema and independent cinema are hardly the same thing, however, and we must distinguish between these modes in order to clarify how independent cinema functions as a cultural category.

Viewing Strategies: Independent Cinema and Art Cinema

Over the years several alternatives to classical cinema have arisen, from the European avant-garde of the 1920s to the American avant-garde of the postwar years. The most germane comparison with independent cinema, however, is international art cinema. Both are commercial modes of feature film production that have succeeded in attracting considerable business away from mainstream fare. Are independent films any different in their viewing strategies from art films? They are, though these modes also share a number of conventions. Most important, of course, is that both encourage an alternative reading; both are in some regard anti-Hollywood. But they accomplish this opposition in different ways.

Some aspects of independent film are shared with art cinema. There is an emphasis on realism in nonclassical cinema that goes back at least to the 1920s and that is an important aspect of indie film. Likewise, authorship is a key interpretive frame for both, with both being figured as "personal cinema" that demands to be read as the product of an individual's artistic expression. But other aspects are more context-specific. Art cinema was a product of a modern, bourgeois conception of art and society, in which the individual stands as a central figure whose psychological depths can never be fully explored. It is animated by the ideas and artistic currents of the time, such as Freudian psychology, existentialist philosophy, and modernist literature and drama.

One key aspect of art cinema is that it demands interpretation. Characters' goals are vaguely defined, spatiotemporal continuity is absent, and scenes slip—often with only vague signaling—from objective to subjective narration and back. The audience is encouraged to "read for maximum ambiguity."[17] Ambiguity in art cinema is typically ambiguity about an individual, and as in contemporaneous literature and drama it is driven by a modernist conception of the individual. Independent cinema is hardly as ambiguous as art cinema, and in general its style is not nearly as challenging. By comparison, indie cinema often can seem fairly classical in its narrational approach.[18] Characters often have clear goals, and events are represented legibly and are causally connected. Independent films like *Down by Law* (1986) and *Safe* (1995) end without conventional closure, but the radically challenging endings of the likes of 8 1/2 (1963) and *Persona* (1966) are seldom duplicated in recent American independent films, and indie comedies like *Juno* might not try to avoid a Hollywood ending.

Like art cinema, independent cinema is animated by the intellectual context of its era; in place of existential angst and alienation we find the multiplicity and fragmentation associated with multiculturalism and postmodernism. This is not to say that independent directors thematize these "isms" consciously or systematically, only that these ideas are in the air, and that they filter through to inform some of the basic assumptions about storytelling that are widely shared by American filmmakers and spectators of the past two decades. It is these assumptions, I argue, that distinguish independent film from the modes of cinema with which it sometimes might overlap.

Like art cinema, independent film brings with it expectations of objective realism and authorial expressiveness, but (with rare, marginal exceptions) without the more radical forms of subjectivity and ambiguity that characterized 1960s European cinema. Described thus, independent film might be seen as art-cinema-lite, taking the less challenging conventions of art films but leaving behind the really interesting ones. I reject this notion because it suggests that independent film directors seek to emulate Bergman, Godard, and Fellini but fail. Independent cinema has its own conventions, and creates its own expectations. However, independent filmmakers did not invent them out of nothing. Some aspects do come from European art cinema, but through the mediating influence of American directors of the 1960s and 1970s, themselves acolytes of the European art film *auteurs* and the models most independent directors are most eager to follow.[19] Some aspects of indie film conventions are more contextually specific. I summarize indie cinema's expectations as a set of three slogans:

1. Characters are emblems
2. Form is a game
3. When in doubt, read as anti-Hollywood

Each of these signals a distinct conception of Off-Hollywood cinema, though in practice these strategies overlap with each other, often in mutually reinforcing ways. These strategies are what distinguish independent films from classical and art films, and they are the foundation for the audience's engagement.

1. Characters Are Emblems

The first viewing strategy assumes a larger degree of social engagement in independent cinema than in Hollywood cinema, and this is the strategy clearly influenced by multiculturalism, a discourse prevalent since the 1990s, especially in education, business, and arts and popular culture, wherein liberal and especially hip, urban, affluent Americans have identified with values of tolerance and openness to diverse cultural identities.[20] However, it is not merely a matter of pointing out that some independent films thematize issues of identity. It is, rather, an implicit solicitation of audience awareness of the specificity of represented situations, and especially people, in a historical and cultural reality. With this awareness, characters become emblems of their social identities. This is the version of realism, coming from the art cinema tradition, that is of particular significance to independent film, but unlike the individual's unique interior reality in art cinema, independent film offers an engagement with *social* reality, in the sense used by Marxists to refer to relations of power among social groups such as classes. Identity in this conception is based not in a transcendent self but in group memberships and affiliations.

Many efforts to encapsulate American independent cinema come back to character. Filmmakers, critics, and audiences all seem to recognize that indie films place a special interest in character (sometimes figured as the opposite of plot), and as a result have interesting characters. Miguel Arteta, director of *Chuck and Buck* (2000), declares: "When I go see an independent movie, I want to see something totally different. I want to see characters who don't walk that predictable line."[21] According to its detractors, Hollywood cinema is often content to have characters who are one-dimensional types functioning as vehicles for other appeals, such as visual spectacle and the promotion of ancillary consumer products.[22] By contrast, the champions of indie cinema argue that its characters have more depth and complexity, are better developed, are truer to life, and are more vivid and compelling than Hollywood characters.[23] Many things might make for interesting characters, and it would be foolish to accept the naive assertion that indie characters are superior to those of Hollywood, but one aspect of this special emphasis on character is that in indie films, a certain rhetorical weight is placed on the specificity of the representation of characters as social beings.

This strategy fits best with a strain of independent film geared toward political and social commentary and criticism. Independent films as a whole cannot be said to be driven by left-wing politics, yet there is certainly more socially engaged filmmaking in Off-Hollywood than in Hollywood cinema. My point is not that independent films are generally vehicles for particular *ideas* about social reality or that they generally have a rhetorical agenda of encouraging social *change*.

It is, rather, to insist that independent cinema's characters are identified so strongly with social types that they come to represent them much more significantly than in other modes of cinema. This is as true of many independent films that are not overtly political (e.g., *Clerks*, 1994) as it is of films that clearly are political in the sense of explicitly engaging with structures of social power and advocating for a critical perspective (e.g., *Matewan*, 1987). There are also many examples that fall somewhere in the middle, incisively satirical films whose advocacy is at best indirect, combining an ironic sensibility with a keen sense of social observation (e.g., *Welcome to the Dollhouse*, 1996).

To an extent, there is value placed merely on the existence— independent of narrative content—of representations of socially marginalized identities, especially of racial minorities and gays and lesbians. At a time when few feature films of any kind were released that had African-American, Asian, Latino, or queer main characters, the release of a film that did was considered highly significant. Many of the most highly acclaimed indie films have addressed the construction of social identity as a central theme. *Boys Don't Cry* (1999) is about masculinity and femininity and the burdens of gendered identity on persons who don't fit neatly in binary categories. *Brokeback Mountain* (2005) is about the fear of being true to oneself when social structures prevent honesty and candor, and about the tragedy of prejudice against gay men, not just for them but for everyone who becomes close to them. *Dead Man* (1995) is about the cultural dislocation of both white man and Indian in the mythic Western past. (Jim Jarmusch's films in general can be characterized by their sense of cultural dislocation.) *Monster's Ball* (2001) dramatizes the relations of white and black characters in a racist world.

There is also value placed on representations *produced by* filmmakers of these identities. The 1980s and 1990s saw a series of "firsts," seized upon for publicity purposes, such as the first feature film to gain distribution directed by an African-American woman, *Daughters of the Dust* (1991), and by a Native American, *Smoke Signals* (1998).[24] As one critic of independent film writes, "Many cameras are being turned on American life for the first time, or with a fresh urgency: those in the hands of women, African-American women, African-American men, Hispanics, Asians, openly gay and lesbian filmmakers."[25] This fits tongue-in-groove with the viewing strategy that sees characters as emblems because it sees directors as emblematizers. For example, *Go Fish* (1994), a film by a young American lesbian about the experience of young American lesbians, was given authority and authenticity by Rose Troche, the film's director.[26]

We tend to think of socially engaged filmmakers as oppositional and identify them with the tradition and mode of documentary cinema (indeed, independent documentary filmmakers like Michael Moore fit this bill). Independent cinema's social engagement is animated by multiculturalism, but while multiculturalism is a self-styled progressive social agenda, in independent fiction films it is often depoliticized to the point that the goal of socially specific representation becomes reflexive rather than critical. The filmmaker is content to describe a social reality, especially its representative types, as a means of capturing a slice of life in its vividness and specificity. If not naturalizing reality, this approach does tend to see it as stable and self-sufficient. One gets the sense that the filmmaker just wants his or her world, or a particular contemporary subculture he or she finds interesting, to be thrown up on the big screen and that the spectator appreciates this representation *per se*. Thus the spectator is invited to recognize this as a socially significant act, especially when this world is rarely represented in the mass media. Yet regardless of whether or not a representation is laden with such a sense of personal-cum-political importance, a similar viewing strategy sustains it. It can be observed in films as diverse as *Clerks*, *Metropolitan* (1990), *Mala Noche* (1985), *Mystery Train* (1989), *Daughters of the Dust*, *Chan Is Missing* (1982), and *Dazed and Confused* (1993). All are social studies, microscopes on a milieu, dissections of the personalities that populate a patch of cultural turf. The subjects could as easily be alienated white kids in the New Jersey suburbs, clever Manhattan debutantes, transient workers in Portland, Oregon, or hipster Japanese tourists in Memphis as they could be Gullah islanders, a Chinese cab driver in San Francisco, or Texas teenagers in the seventies. The indie audience is primed to regard these representations as cultural or subcultural explorations.

Of course there have been Hollywood films with minorities in leading roles, mainstream films that pay attention to marginal social identities, such as *Philadelphia* (1993), and Hollywood films made by women, gays and lesbians, and people of color. Intuitively, it would seem that something differentiates such films from independent cinema that addresses the same topics. The distinction is to be found in an implicit conception of the individual in relation to his or her social identity. This conception underlies the distinction between audiences' expectations of the Hollywood and Off-Hollywood film. If the multicultural Off-Hollywood individual is recognized as a statement on cultural difference, specificity, distinctness, her Hollywood counterpart is typically defined by liberal humanism, by the transcending of difference in demonstration that we are all, at our core, the same, by the universal value of the autonomous self. This is why the gay Hollywood film promoted as a "first," *Philadelphia*, establishes such strong parallelism between the two main characters, Andrew and Joe, not only by making both high-power lawyers who dress and behave alike but also by framing, staging, and editing them in such as way as to make each one seem like the other's double. In doing so the film asserts their common humanity and makes both Andrew's homosexuality and Joe's blackness seem less significant in understanding each man more fundamentally as an individual.

Art cinema characters may differ from Hollywood's in their depth and complexity, but not in their conception as individuals. As David Bordwell discusses, its central preoccupation was "the human condition"; rather than analyzing structures of power, in art cinema "social forces become significant insofar as they impinge upon the psychologically sensitive individual."[27] To cultural critics, this kind of humanism is a means of eliding difference, of hiding structural imbalances of social and cultural power by asserting that everyone is in the same boat. By contrast with other modes of cinema, the independent film tends to have neither heroes nor antiheroes because these figures are larger than life. Emblems are exactly life-size because they are plucked from the fabric of the everyday, as realism and social engagement demand.

As Thomas Schatz has argued, characters in popular film genres are always figured in some kind of relationship to a community.[28] Mainstream cinema, in creating and sustaining popular "myths," serves to affirm the ideals of a community, which the audience recognizes to be of a piece with its own community. We are satisfied by the way a western affirms the value of maintaining legal order and by the way a studio-era musical comedy affirms the value of heterosexual courtship and marriage. Thus the function of representation of the social realm is to locate the audience's place within it. Independent cinema does something rather different. In place of appealing to us on the basis of a community that we share with that of the representation, it demands that our notions of community be redefined, reconfigured, in some cases radically reconceived. Under the sign of multiculturalism, independent cinema's audience recognizes the distinctness of cultures and subcultures within the American community, and insists on communities, plural, rather than community, singular. Rather than finding that the poor and downtrodden, the oppressed racial and ethnic minorities, and other cinematically underrepresented groups are just like "the rest of us," the indie audience sees that their difference is recognized and affirmed. Thus the aptness of the label "cinema of outsiders": if we are all in some respects outsiders, as independent films suggest, then we must question the very notion of an inside, of a universality of experience and perspective. [29] Thus is the community posited by Hollywood revealed as mere myth, or ideology. By emblematizing characters in their full specificity and distinctness, independent cinema asserts the uniqueness of identity positions while the Hollywood emphasis on transcendent human connectedness is called into question, if not demolished.

2. Form Is a Game

If the first slogan signals the potential for independent cinema to have a cultural politics, the second signals its potential for aesthetic—especially narrative—experimentation and innovation. There are several ways in which the formal features of independent cinema are figured as elements of play, in which the spectator is encouraged to conceive of the film-viewing experience as game-like. This may sound slightly odd, as the metaphor of play is most often introduced in casual descriptions of how a director or film engages with some aspect of conventional storytelling. Todd Haynes, for example, proposes that his films play with the audience by systematically arousing and betraying their expectations.[30] We say that we like the way the Coen brothers play with genre, or the way *Pulp Fiction* plays with narrative structure. But I propose this figure of speech really means that spectators are prompted to regard specific aspects of films as components of a game and to see themselves as the players.

The kind of game I have in mind is not rigidly rule-bound, like chess or baseball, but looser and more improvisatory, like charades. Furthermore, I am arguing not that film-viewing is literally a game, but that it is conceived as game-like by viewers, i.e., that it has some of the same procedural characteristics as a game such as solving problems, guessing answers, matching attributes, and having fun. This offers a pleasure in film-viewing that is distinct from pleasures offered by mainstream cinema, though this is not to say that independent cinema cannot offer those pleasures too.

Form is foregrounded when film-viewing becomes a game. Bordwell distinguishes between the classical Hollywood spectator asking plot-based questions such as "Who did it?" and the art cinema spectator asking story-based questions such as "Why is this story being told this way?"[31] The independent film spectator asks this latter question too, but has different expectations about the answer. Rather than seeing challenging form as a cue to reading for subjective realism, authorial expressivity, or maximum ambiguity—rather than construing it as an invitation to interpretation—the independent film spectator sees challenging form as a conceptual structure, such as a plot schema or character type, that defies one's convention-bound expectations. This tendency has antecedents in 1960s art films such as *Last Year at Marienbad* (1961) and in avant-garde cinema. It also has many parallels in contemporary festival cinema, and seems especially prominent in American independent films. As with much modern and postmodern visual art, the object of comprehension is not only the representation but also the artifact in its status as representation. The motivation for this divergence is located in play rather than in meanings, in a field of signifiers rather than in an authorial signified, in fun that can be had by mixing and matching conventional narrative and cinematic elements.

The payoff of narrative experimentation in films such as *Go* (1999), *The Limey* (1999), 21 *Grams* (2003), and *Memento* (2000) is not in heightened emotions, in maximized conventional suspense about what is coming next or stronger character engagement. If such films were told in a conventional linear fashion, after all, these appeals could be strengthened. It's hard to feel a connection to characters whose stories are obscure or confusing and suspense requires an understanding of causal relations among narrative events. For instance, if the story of *Memento* were told in a more canonical fashion there would be suspense over whether Leonard will kill Terry rather than confusion about his motives. Indeed, often such experimentation affords the opportunity of play only at the price of exploiting *fewer* conventional narrative pleasures. The ultimate payoff is in the spectator's appreciation of a formal achievement and in the satisfaction of overcoming confusion or lack of clarity, while the moment-by-moment appeals depend on the game and its parameters.

So what sort of play is involved? What is the object of the game? There are actually several aspects to the game that independent films ask us to play; we might call these separate games or separate processes within the larger game. Their components include conventions such as plot patterns and character types, allusions and references to films and other cultural products, and aspects of narrative design such as temporal ordering and exposition. The fun of playing is a product of engaging with these game elements and is the pleasure taken in resolving incongruities in conventions, recognizing obscure meanings in intertexts, and puzzle-solving in aspects of narrative experimentation. Two aspects of independent cinema in particular engage this viewing strategy: films encourage play by engaging unconventional genre elements and by presenting unconventional narrative structures.

Plot and character conventions are figured into a game structure most clearly in films that work both within and against genre expectations. In the spirit of Robert Altman's films of the 1970s, independent filmmakers have taken genre to be a locus of experimentation and an opportunity for critical, meta-cinematic commentary. Unlike much art cinema, which avoids adopting mass-culture forms, independent cinema is very fond of pop culture's tropes. This is an inheritance from a minority art cinema tradition represented by Godard and Fassbinder, whose love/hate relationships with classical Hollywood cinema produced films such as *Pierrot le fou* (1965) and *Ali: Fear Eats the Soul* (1974), and from self-reflexive "American art films" such as *The Last Movie* (1971).[32]

It is a commonplace of postmodernist criticism that high and low culture have collapsed on each other, that the conception of art as divided into these categories is flawed.[33] In the spirit of celebrating this collapse, artists in many media and idioms have embraced the forms and iconographies of popular culture. But in many cases, including indie cinema, this embrace is not played out in terms of practitioners of "high art" entering the mainstream of the culture industry or in terms of demolishing all distinction between mass and elite culture. One common practice is of an elite art form integrating elements of mass culture while still protecting its status. (I am using "mass" and "elite," "high" and "low" as relative terms. Independent cinema is elite/high in relation to Hollywood cinema, but it does not serve exactly the same cultural functions as traditional elite/high art such as classical music, opera, ballet, and literary fiction.)

In independent cinema as in other art forms, there is a tendency against the full adoption of the pop culture form, an effort to comment on it (however explicitly or implicitly), or a contradictory mix of forms. In independent films these forms are conventional popular film genres, and the spectator's strategy is to identify the forms, recognize and possibly resolve their incongruities, and construct a commentary on them. This might sound as though I am calling independent cinema postmodernist, which some critics have done.[34] But I am merely identifying an influence of postmodernism on the strategies audiences bring to understanding independent films.

This emphasis on play through recognition of conventional forms signals that one distinction between contemporary American indies and the European art cinema is that a different kind of connoisseurship is cultivated in American audiences, and that it must be applied to catch all the references as they flash by, like jokes in an episode of *The Simpsons*. Noël Carroll described American cinema of the 1970s as the "cinema of allusion," citing numerous instances in which the film-school generation of directors such as Paul Schrader would self-consciously rework the John Ford and Robert Bresson films that made them into cinéastes.[35] In this tradition-crazed tradition, Tarantino makes films that demand a wide sweep of world-cinema-history knowledge, albeit of a certain sort. The audience follows along in connect-the-dots fashion, recognizing the antecedents of the "Mexican standoff" in *Reservoir Dogs* (1992), the briefcase with glowing contents in *Pulp Fiction*, and numerous action, *anime*, and martial arts films in the two *Kill Bill* volumes (2003, 2004) without necessarily applying any interpretive schema to Tarantino's visual quotations.

Many of the Coen brothers' films, including *Miller's Crossing* (1991), *Barton Fink* (1991), *Fargo* (1996), *The Big Lebowski* (1998), and *The Man Who Wasn't There* (2001) are at once *homages* to classic American tough-guy, hard-boiled literature and *film noir* and brilliant exaggerations of the conventions of this genre. They work on several levels: as suspenseful storytelling, as allusive re-creations of classic forms, and as commentary on their appeals and on Hollywood representation. Their stories come wrapped in a tone of ironic cleverness, with a wink acknowledging a heightened consciousness of formal convention. There is always a strong dose of dark comedy mixed into their drama.

The game is played by applying an interpretive frame that sees the Coen brothers' films not only as tough-guy stories, but as *meta*-tough-guy stories. This reading is a product not only of textual features that reward reflexive viewing strategies, as I shall discuss, but also of the context of independent cinema spectatorship. In contrast to Hollywood's youth audience or mass audience, the audience for independent cinema is generally mature, urban, college-educated, sophisticated, and familiar with conventions of representation and reception in many various media and forms, high and low.[36] This audience might have learned reflexive readings in school, or encountered them directly in literary, art, or film criticism. Such schemas also have become familiar through dissemination in popular press discourse. When *Entertainment Weekly* routinely describes films as "postmodern," we may expect the indie crowd to be savvy to conceptions of signification and meaning suggested by that term.[37] This might seem commonplace today but it was not always so. Since at least the 1980s, the notion that rather than conveying deep symbols for scholarly exegesis, texts offer what poststructuralist theorists might call a "play of signifiers" has filtered down from academia into circles of elite cultural consumption.

Two textual cues for "meta" readings in films of the Coen brothers (and many others) are exaggeration and incongruity. In *Miller's Crossing*, one device of exaggeration is the motif of the men's hats, the icon of modern masculinity and a staple of gangster and *film noir* costuming. By returning to it so obsessively, by investing it with such importance, the Coens signal a fascination with the iconography of the tough-guy genre, constantly turning it around to appreciate its intricacies. In many of their films, exaggeration manifests itself in other extremes of mise-en-scène, from overly mannered performances to comically dark lighting. The game is played by recognizing that the conventional elements are being quoted and turned comical or grotesque.

In itself this exaggeration is incongruous, but another incongruity arises in cases in which an opposite device is employed: the insertion into a generic framework of something that clearly doesn't belong. In

Altman's early films, a war movie climaxes in a football game instead of a battle (*M*A*S*H*, 1970), a musical builds up to an assassination (*Nashville*, 1976), and a western hero is a cowardly pimp (*McCabe and Mrs. Miller*, 1971). In *Fargo*, as many critics have noted, the landscape and mise-en-scène is the opposite of that of *noir*: it is the expansive white of the Minnesota winter rather than the shadowy black of the Los Angeles night. At some point *The Man Who Wasn't There* decides to become a science fiction film as well as a neo-noir. *Barton Fink* abandons hard-boiled realism for full-blown paranoid fantasy. And *The Big Lebowski*, most audaciously, takes a Chandleresque scenario but replaces the typical private eye with an aging hippie and has the story narrated onscreen by a middle-aged cowboy. We may admire many of the Coen brothers' characters for their eccentricity and quirkiness at the same time that we may recognize their incompatibility with the narratives into which they have been mischievously dropped.

The Coen brothers are the quintessential genre-play directors, but encouragement of this kind of play actually is quite widespread. The semi-ironic tone of the Coens' films, at once respectful of their cinematic predecessors and irreverent toward them, is also found among independent filmmakers ranging from Hal Hartley to Jim Jarmusch to Quentin Tarantino to Wes Anderson to Todd Haynes. All of them, and many others, combine exaggerated conventions with incongruous admixtures to similar results.

The other main way in which independent cinema figures form as a game is through narrative structure. The most common exemplar in this case is *Pulp Fiction*, though it is neither the most original nor the most sophisticated example of a film using temporal disordering. *Daughters of the Dust* and *The Limey* are more challenging in their fluid movement among past, present, and future, while *Memento* and *Primer* (2004) are more thorough in their formal design and more demanding on the spectator. Independent films sometimes take an abstract formal pattern as a global design principle, as in *Mystery Train*. Many include significant temporal rearrangement through flashbacks or other devices. Real-time narratives such as *Before Sunset* (2004) also foreground narrative form. *Timecode* (2000) is experimental in its use of a simultaneous four-image frame. David Lynch's *Lost Highway* (1997), *Mulholland Drive* (2001), and *Inland Empire* (2006) are formally disjunctive both temporally and spatially and to a significant extent inscrutable. This makes him the independent film figure most amenable to the reading strategies of art cinema.

Of course, Hollywood films also use flashbacks and other forms of temporal reordering. Conventional, mainstream detective films and thrillers make puzzling and problem-solving central to their narrative development. The distinction here is that in independent films form becomes a game when the most important motivation for unconventional narrative structure is play. Mainstream films like *American Beauty* (1999) begin at the end for a clear narrative purpose: to cast the events of the story in a dark, deterministic light. Mainstream films like *Minority Report* (2002) use flashbacks or flash-forwards to explain important details of the narrative, to reveal key information to create a stronger emotional resonance. Temporal reordering in art cinema is also typically motivated as explorations of character, as in *Wild Strawberries* (1957), in which flashbacks dramatize Borg's reminiscences of youth. Occasionally we find an independent film that fits in this tradition. An example is John Sayles's *Lone Star* (1996), which several times integrates past and present in a single shot to show continuities between them, to show the significance of history—both the events of the past, and their figuration in storytelling—to the formation of people's identities.

In many independent films that have challenging narrative structures, there often is a weak character-based or thematic motivation carried by a stronger play-based one. It is true that viewing *Memento* is a bit like being put in Leonard's place in terms of knowledge and memory. But soon after the film is under way, we are able to remember much more than he can. The stronger motivation for *Memento*'s form is that figuring out how the film is telling its story is a fascinating activity in its own right. The means of *Memento*'s convoluted editing is so far in excess of the function of heightening our sense of Leonard's experience that we must look elsewhere for the film's formal motivation.

At first glance, *The Limey* seems to motivate its temporal narrative design as subjective narration, putting us in the head of the protagonist, Wilson. But looking more closely, we find that it is more complex than that. While many images are flashbacks to childhood scenes of Wilson's daughter, and others are flash-forwards to scenes only imagined by Wilson, many images are flash-forwards that clearly cannot be ascribed to Wilson's imagination (e.g., some proleptic images of Valentine, as during the "King Midas in Reverse" sequence, are from scenes from which Wilson will be absent and of which he will have no knowledge). Other scenes are conversations that inexplicably take place at several locations at once. On the DVD commentary track, the filmmakers suggest that these scenes play out the way people remember conversations, as composites of many encounters. But this isn't at all clear from the narration of the film, which in its flamboyant temporal and spatial shifts invites the spectator to appreciate and admire how a coherent narrative can emerge from such a jangle of images and sounds. Soderbergh encourages a play-based reading by frustrating the coherence of other approaches. It is also motivated as allusion to temporally disjunctive films of the 1960s, such as *Point Blank* (1967) and *Petulia* (1968), which cinema mavens will congratulate themselves for recognizing.

Slacker (1991) does not seem to attempt to motivate its formal principles on the level of character or story. It makes clear in its opening sequence that its design is motivated by an abstract philosophical notion of how choice and chance structure human affairs. As each sequence leads into another, one is conscious that it could have followed a different path. This is play held in balance with a thematic purpose. Similarly, in *Pulp Fiction*, the formal play of the disordered narrative sequence is held in balance with the character motivation underlying its ending with the second half of the diner scene. By ending with an emphasis on Jules's religious transformation, it might seem to amplify a character's development through its temporal manipulation. But this appeal is balanced by the novelty of the structure and the arbitrariness of Vincent's "resurrection," which has no such motivation. Thus play may be balanced with other appeals; however, the dominant reading strategy encouraged by such films is to follow the formal game.

These first two viewing strategies, characters as emblems and form as a game, can play into and feed off one another in various ways. The second strategy is a characterizing strategy too, since characters are an element of form. In many independent films, identity is a puzzle and solving it requires that both of the strategies be applied. In *Lone Star*, the constant back-and-forth between the past and the present demands an appreciation of the game of form but also an engagement with the historical and social differences that separate characters. In *Far from Heaven* (2002), the difference between Todd Haynes's characters and Douglas Sirk's, by which they are partly inspired, demands a cinema-of-allusion reading, but at the same time, the racial and sexual dimensions of the characters foreground social identities. The formal approach to characters is one way of intensifying their significance, of emphasizing that we should take interest in them. One important way of doing that is by making characters themselves puzzling, by obscuring their motivations or their backstories. These devices create complexity, which is a positive value for both formal and social reading strategies. In *Hard Eight* (1996), delayed exposition makes the old-time Vegas hustler, Sydney, into an enigma. We learn only after a long delay that Sydney is John's father, which explains much of the older man's actions. Much of the pleasure of the narrative is in puzzling over their relationship. In *Safe*, Carol White's interiority is to a large extent inscrutable. She suffers from mysterious ailments that she believes have an environmental cause, but our sympathy with her is forestalled by the distance at which Haynes keeps the audience both literally—many scenes are filmed in long shots— and in terms of allowing us to understand Carol psychologically. We are invited to scrutinize Carol without getting to the bottom of who she really is.[38] By studying such characters so intensively, we gain a greater appreciation of them in their social specificity.

3. When in Doubt, Read as Anti-Hollywood

The first two strategies suggest two prototypes of independent film, one realist and the other formalist. But the third strategy is much more general and applies to many different kinds of cinema. The practice of reading as anti-Hollywood might be as old as Hollywood, though only in recent decades has a parallel mode come into existence in the United States to make this strategy relevant to understanding a significant body of American feature filmmaking.

In his study of American avant-garde cinema, James Peterson introduces the "brute avant-garde principle," a reading strategy of last resort that allows spectators to make sense of the most confounding avant-garde films by reasoning that they sometimes reject cinematic conventions as a way "to shock viewers out of their complacency."[39] Independent cinema obviously isn't challenging to the same extent as the avant-garde, but it does often reject conventions. Rather than shocking viewers, we might say that independent cinema aims to introduce them to different kinds of experiences within the parameters of the feature film, to denaturalize aspects of conventional cinematic practice. The strategy of reading as anti-Hollywood functions as a global assumption about independent film and also as a local heuristic for making sense of specific details and devices. As Levy asserts:

> the key to understanding indies is Hollywood. Commercial cinema is so pervasive in the American movie consciousness that even when filmmakers develop alternative forms Hollywood's dominant cinema is implicit in those alternatives.[40]

Reading as anti-Hollywood also functions as a warrant for the preceding two reading strategies: social engagement and formal play can both be seen as functions of an anti-Hollywood stance, since representations of individuals and formal structures in independent cinema are viewed against mainstream norms.

Unlike the avant-garde, which is much more distinctly different from Hollywood cinema not only formally but also in the context in which it is made and experienced, independent cinema is regularly contrasted with and related to Hollywood both industrially and aesthetically. The two modes share personnel and many aspects of industrial practice (e.g., script formats, cameras, etc.) and they compete for many of the same awards. But while it is one thing to differ from Hollywood, it is another to oppose it. It is clear that some directors view independent filmmaking as antithetical to Hollywood. James Mangold describes the independent film scene as having "a good, healthy, anti-Hollywood sentiment."[41] Others see independent filmmaking as a Hollywood career-launching step. But spectators' expectations are not ordinarily dependent upon divining a director's career ambitions. If the explanation for some aspect of a film is that it departs from a Hollywood convention, it is logical that the function of that departure might be seen as an implicit critique.[42]

It is by sharing so much in common with Hollywood practice that Off-Hollywood's distinctness is thrown into relief. This is clearest in instances of generic play. In *Passion Fish* (1992), the anti-Hollywood stance is a function of the characters and situations being so typical of conventional female-friendship melodramas, then of defying our expectations. In *Bound* (1996), the classic *film noir* couple—the hero and the *femme fatale*—is a pair of women, subverting the mainstream's norms of gender roles and sexual orientation while playing out a formulaic plot. *The Blair Witch Project* (1999) presents a horror film almost completely stripped of its stylistic norms of camera placement and movement, lighting, and sound, yet completely within the audience's genre-bound expectations of affective experience.

The indie trend of "quirky" cinema, exemplified by Wes Anderson and his many admirers and imitators and part of a larger style in indie culture more generally of quirky music, fashion, and design, departs in rather minimal ways from mainstream practice.[43] Quirk is a kind of tone or sensibility that depends for its effect on a perception of its unusual, eccentric qualities, and this fits perfectly with the mission of indie cinema to distinguish itself against mainstream tone or sensibility or conventions of representation of characters and settings. Characters in quirky comedies like *Rushmore* (1998), *Ghost World* (2001), and *Little Miss Sunshine* (2006) follow fairly clear narrative trajectories in pursuit of their goals, and narration in indie films like these might seem quite classical. But even though such films might have rather conventional emotional appeals, their offbeat style distinguishes them as fresh alternatives to studio films, and their quirky, oddball characters seem especially significant in this regard.

Reading as anti-Hollywood can function on a level of much greater or lesser specificity. It can explain the pace of *Stranger Than Paradise* (1984), the lo-fi, on-the-cheap aesthetic of *Clerks* and Mumblecore, and the sophisticated dialogue of *Metropolitan*. The obscure or bleak endings of independent films like *sex, lies, and videotape* (1989), *Buffalo 66* (1998), and *The Visitor* (2007) can be understood as undercutting the Hollywood norm of leaving the audience feeling good. *Welcome to the Dollhouse, Kids* (1995), and *Thirteen* (2003) can be seen as anti-Hollywood in their approach to troubled adolescents, neither moralizing nor sentimentalizing them, and certainly not showing the way to transform them into well-adjusted young citizens. The identity politics promoted by African-American, queer, and other subaltern cinemas is anti-Hollywood as is the miniaturist approach of Jim Jarmusch, who declares that his films "concern characters who consciously locate themselves outside the zombie mainstream."[44] *Citizen Ruth* (1996) is anti-Hollywood in its unabashed advocacy of a liberal stance on the most controversial sociopolitical issue in the

United States, abortion rights. Casting choices reveal a critique of the Hollywood star system, as when character actors such as Richard Jenkins and Melissa McCarthy win leading roles (in *The Visitor* and *The Nines*, 2007, respectively). Many movies considered "small films," typically quirky comedies or chamber dramas, can even be read as anti-Hollywood by virtue of their modesty of scale and their interest in exploring character.

The notion of independent cinema as personal cinema is fundamentally anti-Hollywood, contrasting the independent artist against the soulless studio committee. The authorial reading strategy plays into this directly, as auteurism itself is historically anti-Hollywood insofar as it locates in the studio auteur (Lang, Ford, Hawks, et al.) a figure capable of communicating his vision in spite of the constraints of a studio system that by definition depersonalizes. Translated into the present-day studio versus independent dichotomy, it can even account for directors like Linklater and Soderbergh, who migrate back and forth between the modes, making their personal films as indies while paying their way taking studio projects, and for John Sayles, who supports his independent features with income earned as a Hollywood script doctor.[45] *School of Rock* (2003) and *Ocean's Eleven* (2001) are more likely to be read as commercial entertainments, made for fun and profit, while *Waking Life* (2001) and *Schizopolis* (1997) are understood to express something significant about their directors' experiences and worldviews. Any independent film that can be read as personal can be read as anti-Hollywood, since according to this scheme, Hollywood is assumed to temper personal filmmaking by putting commerce ahead of art.

The extent to which a film is judged to be anti-Hollywood can determine the strength of its candidacy for indieness. Often this takes into account more than textual characteristics, so that a film that is distributed by a major studio or that crosses over from art houses to multiplexes can be understood to be insufficiently indie based on contexts of production and reception. In making judgments about what counts as indie and what does not, the culture of indie cinema asserts the values of autonomy as a marker of indie authenticity and uses this to maintain its distinction in relation to studio filmmaking. Thus it is even possible to read as anti-Hollywood in relation to a film that is not considered authentically indie. (This topic will return in the final chapter in regard to *Juno*.)

This last viewing strategy is the ultimate justification for independent cinema as a category. It defines it against the other of the mainstream, commercial industry to show it off to its best advantage—as more honest, artistic, political, realistic, personal, intelligent, or whatever else its audience wishes it to be. As a strategy of both first and last resort, it always allows for the tradition of independent cinema to be maintained, for the independent film to be understood within the context of film culture. For as long as Hollywood exists, so will the desire to oppose it.

Conclusion

These three slogans make up a system of protocols in the sense that they operate sequentially and in a hierarchy of generality and significance. The first slogan is the most specific and easiest to apply. We look for characters (in situations) to be representative of real-world types in a way that is distinct from our engagement with characters in other modes of cinema. The second slogan is more general and calls on operations that are cognitively more sophisticated because they require a more active kind of problem-solving or puzzling. This step comes into play only in the presence of challenging form, and since some independent films are formally highly conventional, it is not necessarily activated in all cases. The last slogan is the most general and versatile. It is both a blanket assumption that guides global expectations about independent cinema and a precise tool for interpreting devices that cannot otherwise be assimilated under the preceding two slogans.

I have argued that this mode of film practice coheres around a set of conventions, and although I have spoken of films and directors encouraging certain reading strategies, the conventions are best thought of as belonging not to films or directors, but to all of indie culture. The films offer evidence of these conventions and are part of our education in them, along with cinematic institutions and reading strategies imported from other art forms and media. Taken together, these three slogans cover the lion's share of American independent cinema. They should not be taken as a recipe for making an independent film, though, or as a set of necessary and sufficient conditions. These slogans reference ways of understanding certain exemplars of independent cinema. Some films are closer to the exemplars than others, and some films are exemplary of more than one slogan. Some independent films are more peripheral according to this scheme, fitting Hollywood viewing strategies more than may be typical of independent cinema. Others, such as the films of David Lynch, are limit cases that function as anti-Hollywood by being challenging in unusual ways, but which also seem to demand their own means of interpretation. While the periphery of the category may be a fuzzy area, the center is where we find films such as *Blood Simple* (1984), *Do The Right Thing* (1989), *Slacker*, *Passion Fish*, *Lost in Translation* (2003), *Sideways* (2004), *Pulp Fiction*, and *The Limey*, which encourage the modes of engagement that are central conventions of American independent cinema. Such films typically reach their audience through the institutions of the film festival and art house theater, within which these viewing strategies are mobilized, and it is to these indie institutions that we will turn next.

chapter 2 HOME IS WHERE THE ART IS | Indie Film Institutions

| What I'd like to do here is make art the core, and see if business can get around that. I don't know if it's going to work, but that's the way I want to go.—ROBERT REDFORD (1983)[1] | Alternative commercial cinema lives.—NEW YORK TIMES (1989)[2]

In the Sundance-Miramax era, indie has assumed a role in American culture as *the* alternative cinema. At different times, *independent* has referred to everything from Monogram westerns to Otto Preminger prestige pictures to exploitation and drive-in movies to the products of the indie mini-majors. The meaning of independence in the indie era has a specific relation to the other term in its pairing—Hollywood—which was not central to any of its previous connotations. In particular, independent cinema has come to signify a parallel American cinema of feature films for exhibition venues that are alternatives to mainstream first-run exhibition. In this sense, indie in cinema and music are facets of the same cultural phenomenon, positioning modes of popular culture in opposition to a mainstream other. American independent films and the alternative venues where they screen are constructed not only as a taste culture to distinguish non-mainstream movies as more artistically serious and legitimate than mainstream films but also as mature in comparison with multiplex fare and audiences. These are not meanings that "independent" very often had previously.

Even if their films had content deemed mature, Preminger and other independent producers would not have adopted such a rhetoric of opposition in contrasting independents and Hollywood studios as we observe in the indie era. Hollywood's standard system of production after the Paramount case consent decrees of 1948 came to rely on packages put together by producers or agents (the package-unit system)[3] and distributed and often financed by major studios. This was independent production by name in the 1940s, '50s, and '60s, but despite the fact that few changes have occurred in the premises of this system in the years since, Hollywood no longer calls package-unit production "independent." The shift in the term was engendered by a new popular conception of American feature filmmaking that has room for more than just Hollywood movies. In the 1940s and '50s, there was no well-established American alternative to Hollywood in the realm of narrative feature films. Independent prestige pictures did not appeal to audiences or critics on the grounds of opposing Holly-wood-as-mainstream, and the independence of low-budget exploitation films in the years to come was hardly to be made into a mark of distinction. There were foreign imports, most notably European and Asian art films, but these were not "independent" by name in the discourse of American movies and culture then any more than they are now. What occurred to bring about the contemporary era was a rise in American feature film alternatives to mass-market, mainstream cinema—which were also an alternative to foreign films, whose market share has declined since their postwar heyday—and a new configuration of sites of film-viewing, especially new film festivals and new art house theaters and chains, to be constructed as the alternative to the suburban or exurban megaplex and its standard commercial fare. What is new about indie in the history of independent cinema is its status as a distinct, American, alternative cinema of narrative feature films that have a cultural and commercial presence much greater than that of the cinematic underground or avant-garde. Even as it opposes Hollywood as mass-culture commercialism, indie is a thoroughly commercial endeavor and could not have reached its level of cultural currency without being viable as a business.

Whatever its commercial status, the cultural mandate of indie cinema is to be legitimated in comparison to Hollywood. This legitimacy in turn produces cultural distinction for indie cinema, and the institutions of independent cinema are the site within which this legitimacy is maintained. This chapter is about these institutions as productive entities, as cultural resources for the exploitation of the indie community. If culture, as the sociologist Ann Swinton writes, is a toolkit for social interactions, then the institutions of indie cinema offer specific utility to those who pass through them.[4] Among these tools are the strategies of socially engaged characterization, formal play, and oppositionality.

These strategies, which make possible an understanding of independent cinema as textual experience, are themselves made possible by the institutions through which they circulate. The discourse of independent cinema moves through various institutional channels to form a set of common conceptual frames shared among filmmakers and support personnel, distributors and marketers, cultural gatekeepers such as film festival programmers, tastemakers including journalists and scholars, and many ordinary filmgoers. This makes a community of the different persons and groups for whom indie is a meaningful concept; they form this community around their investment in ideas of what indie is and is not.

This understanding is informed by the institutional theory of art of Arthur Danto and George Dickie, which holds that art consists of whatever an art world considers it to be.[5] It gives the power of definition to the participants in the community, essentially substituting a sociological understanding for an aesthetic one. "To see something as art," Danto writes, "requires something the eye cannot decry—an atmosphere of artistic theory, a knowledge of the history of art: an artworld."[6] This assumes that even though the art world does not produce a formal statement indicating rigorous conditions for inclusion and exclusion in the category around which it is constituted, it still follows fairly reliable habits of reasoning to determine what counts and what does not. Such heuristics might not always be logically sound or empirically valid. Categorizations might defy traditional canons. But this is less important than the fact that these judgments are common to members of the community, and that one member is likely to apply the same heuristic and in the same manner as another. Indie cinema is not the exact same kind of category as art (actually it is a subset), but the same kind of social process obtains in making the category cohere through shared meaning-making.

This notion of indie as communally rather than critically defined is also informed by Howard S. Becker's sociological study of artistic practice, *Art Worlds*, which is itself a transposition of the institutional theory of art from philosophy to sociology.[7] Becker identifies an art world as a network of cooperation that includes not only an artist producing an artwork but also everyone from the person who brews the artist's tea to the public who experiences the artwork to the state whose laws or absence of laws make possible certain kinds of action and prohibit others. Art worlds have their own systems of meaning, conventions of artistic practice and experience shared among constituents.

As an art world, American independent cinema in its current configuration depends on all of the parties I mentioned above to determine how it evaluates its works. Some of these have more of an active role than others, but all are crucial. The roles that I want to consider most centrally in this chapter are the institutions through which independent films are most directly accessed: the venues of the cinematic experience and the discourses through which they are experienced. Considering these institutions at the nexus of independent films and their audience is a way of establishing the sociological dimension of indie cinema.

"Art" and "indie" are both cultural categories, and cultural categories exist in the minds of the participants in a culture. One of the most significant heuristics used in understanding a category is to match instances—in our case films—to familiar examples. Within the community of an art world, members can identify new items as candidates for the category by matching them to those already recognized as exemplary. For American independent cinema in the indie era, the most salient exemplars tend to be films whose success arrived through alternative institutional channels, especially those of the film festival circuit and the alternative, independent, or art house theater. The community's notion of what an independent film is follows the examples of notable independent films like *sex, lies, and videotape* (1989), *Slacker* (1991), and *Pulp Fiction* (1994). This notion is not a strictly textual one. A film comes wrapped in layers of paratextual discourse, from posters and reviews to theatrical experiences (which include elements both social and architectural) and word-of-mouth. These layers have an essential mediating effect that shapes the viewer's construction of the text. In the case of *Slacker*, a location-shot film depicting denizens of Austin, Texas, news of the film's success in an engagement at an Austin alternative theater functioned as advance publicity to assure potential audiences of its credibility as a document of an alternative scene.[8] It also had the boost from the word *slacker* itself becoming part of a constellation of terms and associations applied to a generational trend (it was paired at the time with "Generation X"). In the case of *sex, lies, and videotape*, the film's bonanza of positive reception and top awards at Sundance and Cannes shaped publicity, while the director's status as a totally unknown novice gave the film the added mystique of being original and new. It also helped to have a title, trailer, and poster pushing risqué images and adult themes. *Pulp Fiction* was the follow-up to *Reservoir Dogs* (1992), an indie standout by a twentysomething *auteur* self-fashioned as a California Godard. It was much publicized after winning the Palme d'Or at Cannes (a later American successor to *sex, lies* in taking this honor) and was eagerly anticipated for its promise to redeem the career of John Travolta, beginning Tarantino's practice of giving Hollywood back aging stars it had prematurely relegated as has-beens. All of these films arrived through the mediating power of exhibition contexts and their surrounding discourses that are distinct from those of standard commercial exhibition even if some of these films (*Pulp Fiction* in particular) crossed over from festivals and art houses to suburban megaplexes.

There are ways in which categorization and institutions feed back into one another. Exhibition in festivals and art houses is an institutional characteristic of some films and can be used as criteria of categorization; the community can deem films that play these venues indie given that other criteria match that judgment (e.g., they are low-budget American films, described a certain way in the media). But institutions also are sites for the construction of other criteria, such as the textual and contextual terms like form, style, genre, nationality, star, author, and theme. The institution is thus at once a criterion and a context for categorization, and the characteristics of films that are often included within the institutions will likely become fixed as criteria of resemblance used in sustaining the category.

By endowing the film festival circuit and the upscale, alternative theater with an aura of worthiness, the indie community articulates its validation of a certain conception of cinema and culture. Of course, there are many institutions supporting and circulating the reigning conceptions of indieness in American cinema. These would include specialist magazines such as *Filmmaker* and *The Independent*, the boutique cable television channels Sundance and IFC, indie blogs such as indieWire and Indie Movie City, and events like the Independent Spirit Awards and the IFP's (Independent Feature Project) Independent Feature Films Market. Although I will have occasion to include some of these in this chapter, the focus will be on the most significant institutions of indie film circulation and cinematic experience—the film festival and the art house theater. These are more than venues of exhibition. Film festivals and art houses are cultural sites and social spaces, and they generate and benefit from a rhetoric of distinction. They function to set apart both cinematic forms and the audiences who consume them.

Film Festivals

In the years after World War II, the film festival became one of the most essential institutions in securing and maintaining for commercial cinema a status above mass or popular culture.[9] Although the first film festivals were held in the 1930s, it was the debut of Cannes in 1946 that properly launched the international film festival in its function of annually surveying the best of each country's film output. André Bazin wrote of the first Cannes festival that it would serve "to establish comparisons," to offer a sampling of recent cinema from around the world.[10] In addition to the other European festivals of mid-century vintage, including Venice, Berlin, Locarno, San Sebastian, Edinburgh, Moscow, and Karlovy Vary, Cannes offered its cultural sanction as a validating institution beyond the national film industry and separate from commercial success (though a festival competition prize might spur box office revenue). At festivals, writes Marijke de Valck, films were "not treated as mass-produced commodities, but as national accomplishments; as conveyors of cultural identity; as art and as unique artistic creations."[11] Addressing this sense of collecting national accomplishments, Thomas Elsaesser has dubbed the film festival circuit a "parliament of national cinemas."[12] Film festivals offer examples of each national film industry's output that are not merely representative but exemplary of the nation's culture. The indie movement has used this same institution for similar ends, to validate and legitimate, to nominate exemplary works and artists, and to offer its best to the global film community as American national cinema.[13]

For the first few decades, entrants in film festivals, like Olympic athletes, were selected by each nation's film committee, and in this way films at festivals were officially national, formally representing each participating nation as its own choice. This changed in 1972 when Cannes made the festival director rather than the national committee the one responsible for selection, a move quickly followed by the other events.[14] As of that time, inclusion in the festival would be a product of independent curatorial judgment rather than of a national culture policy. This selection process became one of the key legitimating elements of the festival as an institution, as inclusion as an "official selection" would be taken to be evidence of a film's worthiness and seriousness according to criteria applied by international connoisseurs. The directors of film festivals are thus accorded a large measure of respect; they function as both gatekeepers and tastemakers.[15] Selection committees do the work of determining what kind of cinema will be consecrated and what kind will not. They are critical nodes in a network of legitimation.

In the case of indie cinema, depending on the nature of a given festival, its selection committee has the power to nominate films as indie or, more importantly, to establish which indie films and artists will be considered exemplary. The slate at Sundance each January represents the year's fresh crop of American indie talent, and from this harvest the community expects to find outstanding or "breakout" artists and films. But being selected for the two main competitions at Sundance, for dramatic and documentary films, is the first coveted honor that a low-budget film by a novice director can hope for. Festivals also function to place indie films on a level equal to the highest artistic echelon of international filmmaking. The slate at Cannes each May represents the state of the global cinematic art, and makes room for only the eminences of each country's film culture. The inclusion in the main competition program of films by Jim Jarmusch, the Coen brothers, Spike Lee, and Michael Moore has positioned the most respected indie *auteurs* as the American peers of Pedro Almodóvar, Claire Denis, Wong Kar-wai, Abbas Kiarostami, Hou Hsiou-hsien, Michael Haneke, and Apichatpong Weerasethakul. As much as the French might admire Steven Spielberg or Clint Eastwood, the festival's official selections tend away from filmmaking that might be seen as commercial even as the event also includes a huge film market and plenty of opportunities to promote big-budget releases. It is true of festivals in general, actually, that cinema perceived as "too commercial" is a structuring absence, an Other. Thus Kenneth Turan, in his survey of the world's festivals, praises Sundance for the opportunities it affords independent films to find large audiences, but complains of its selection process, accusing it of favoring "films that feel as if they're making the cut because they will never reach a wider audience."[16]

Festivals have a complicated relationship to the marketplace, both stimulating commerce in films and avoiding the taint of the mass audience whose attention guarantees successful films a commercial windfall. Feature filmmaking tends to be commercial, but in the mid-century, postwar period, for commercial cinema to be consecrated as artistic and legitimate it needed a means of establishing valuation of artists and artworks outside of the terms of the mass market. Everyone knew that films were important as mass culture, and artistically literate cinemagoers knew of the 1920s cinematic avant-garde and of certain outstanding Hollywood filmmakers such as Charlie Chaplin, Frank Capra, and Walt Disney, but whether sound feature films made within commercial industries could be taken seriously as art was not yet a matter of consensus. Critical judgment within a discourse of artistic respectability would be one way of achieving this status. Canonization of *auteurs* and masterpieces by critics like Bazin and his acolytes was essential for the establishment of international cinema culture as an art world. And film festivals in turn were essential for critical capital to be mobilized, as the attention they attracted from the press not only helped them solidify themselves as institutions but also helped their product, the films, gain the artistic validation that would in turn confirm the cultural importance of the festival. So many of the narratives of *auteur* and national cinema "discoveries" and milestones hinge on festival moments: booing, cheering, prize-giving, recognizing that something new has come to claim its rightful place. *Rashomon* (1950), *Ugetsu Monogatari* (1953), *Pather Panchali* (1955), *The 400 Blows* (1959), and *L'Avventura* (1960) are a few of the films to benefit from this phenomenon in the heyday of international art cinema. American independent cinema has reproduced this dynamic with its annual Sundance "discoveries" that become the following summer and autumn's art house micro-hits or crossovers.

Indie cinema has been helped enormously in its arrival as a parallel to Hollywood by the validation of its films at festivals and of certain fests themselves. This is most evident in the rise of Sundance as a major event, but also in other American fests identified with the indie movement, such as South by Southwest, Telluride and Tribeca, and other international fests that are main stops on the circuit for films of whatever provenance. The status of American cinema in the international community of festival followers has been bolstered by the prominent inclusion of indie films in top-shelf festivals around the world, including Cannes, Venice, Berlin, New York, and Toronto. Independent cinema has given festivals the opportunity to program American films within the context of a parliament of national cinemas and at the same time avoid the mass-market, commercial, cultural-imperialist taint of the Hollywood blockbuster.

In essence, the film festival circuit is a distribution network parallel to commercial, theatrical distribution. The circuit is not merely a small number of high-profile events recurring seasonally and annually. It has exploded since the 1970s to the point that there are always festivals going on, probably several at any given time. They come in many varieties, with some devoted to themes or genres (e.g., short films, Queer films, Jewish films, environmental films), some focused on competitions (e.g., Cannes, Venice), and some that are overviews of world cinema, which Julian Stringer calls "universal survey festivals" (e.g., Toronto, New York).[17] Virtually every city and many resort towns have one, and there are too many to keep track of or even to tally up. For this discussion, the high-profile events are most significant, but the existence of so many festivals around the country and the globe has opened up a world of films to new audiences and a world of audiences to new films. However, the terms on which films and audiences are brought together are different in the case of festivals from the standard commercial mode of film distribution. The film festival works according to different principles of funding, different protocols of criticism and cinema-going, and with different paratextual discourses structuring the encounter of film and audience. All three of these differences are significant in determining how indie films are positioned within the American media industries and within American film culture. They are a significant part of how indie films come to be seen as such.

The Film Festival as Arts Institution

In the history of American culture, many forms have undergone a process of legitimation that elevated their status and consecrated them as high art and their patrons as members of elite society. In the nineteenth century the art museum and symphony orchestra became the model arts institutions. Both visual arts and classical music have long, illustrious traditions, but in the United States their status was affirmed in the mid-nineteenth century by their institutionalization outside of the sphere of commercial trade, in trustee-governed, nonprofit organizations such as the Metropolitan Museum and the New York Philharmonic. When new candidates for legitimation arose within the sphere of the arts in the twentieth century, they tended to follow the template set forth by the museum and orchestra. Paul DiMaggio writes about the rise in cultural value of theater, opera, and dance between 1900 and 1940.[18] Among other developments, some of the most crucial for distinguishing these forms came from applying what DiMaggio calls the "high culture model." These arts approached the status of painting and concert music by being presented within nonprofit organizations, often connected with education programs, such as the Metropolitan Opera's. By 1929 there were 1,000 noncommercial theaters in the United States, and by the 1940s, outside of New York, the only way for theater companies to survive was by being not-for-profit.[19] In the early twentieth century, commercial mass culture was on the rise, with cinema replacing the stage as the most popular form of public entertainment. In order for theater, opera, and dance to become sacralized as high art, DiMaggio argues, they had to "free themselves from the grip of the marketplace."[20]

The film festival shares some of the same institutional characteristics as museums, symphony orchestras, and opera, theater, and dance companies. These arts organizations receive various forms of essential support from outside of the commercial marketplace. Cinema is often a lucrative commercial enterprise, and one without the kind of cultural legitimacy accorded opera and ballet. It is only by distinguishing some kinds of films from others that the cultural logic of the arts institution can be made to apply to cinema. And it is primarily through the institution of the film festival that this cultural logic is applied.

The financing of American arts institutions in the post–World War II era comes from a number of sources. One of these is the federal government's support through the National Endowment for the Arts. The NEA also passes along funding to state and local arts organizations to supplement their budgets. Much of the expenditures of these governmental agencies at all levels goes to support musical and theater companies, museums, and other arts institutions (as opposed to being offered directly as grants to artists). Some of it funds film festivals. But a much larger share of funding for the arts comes from donations and sponsorships. It is only by registering for nonprofit status that arts organizations in the United States are able to accept tax-deductible donations from foundations, corporations, and individuals. In addition to monetary donations, arts organizations such as film festivals receive substantial donations in volunteer time. Festival volunteers staff screening committees, sell and take tickets, organize crowds, introduce films and moderate discussions afterwards, and work behind the scenes to make sure events run smoothly. Although there are festivals, such as Tribeca, which are run for profit, the vast majority could not exist without the support of the public in its various forms.

It might not be explicitly articulated or the product of government's clear intentions, but a state cultural policy produces the nonprofit film festival and supports its functioning.[21] Public policy establishes the value of arts as an end in themselves, and also instrumentalizes arts to produce desired secondary outcomes, such as increased cultural tourism and economic investment. Many urban planners and local government officials believe that a lively arts scene is critical to attracting or maintaining a "creative class" of desirable citizens to a city or region. The American cultural policy of incentivizing donations to nonprofits through tax deductibility is an enormous boon to the arts and comes at a sacrifice to the government treasury of between $26 and $41 billion each year.[22] European governments do not offer similar incentives, but do support the arts through direct subsidies to a much greater extent. Thus European and American film festivals are both beneficiaries of national cultural policies, but each region's policies produce different streams of revenue. The American film festival, like the American art museum and symphony orchestra, supports itself through a combination of government subsidies, corporate and individual donations including donations of time, and revenue from selling tickets. None of these are typically in business to make money.

An additional form of public support for film festivals comes from their affiliation with universities. Major fests are not typically campus events, but many festivals are affiliated with campus film societies and university arts organizations. The Wisconsin Film Festival held annually in Madison is supported by the university's Arts Institute and university-administered foundations for arts support. Many American campuses program annual film festivals large and small, many of which are thematic and associated with academic departments, e.g., an Asian-American Film Festival produced by a department of East Asian Studies or a Jewish Film Festival from a Jewish Studies department. These fests harness the resources of campus communities, including not only funding but also personnel, to bring independent cinema (among other things) to students, faculty, and community members.

But campus and college town festivals are not the only ones with an educational dimension. Many high-profile film festivals legitimate their mission by proclaiming it educational and combine classes and workshops with screenings and parties as part of the official festival program. The Sundance Film Festival has its origins not only in the Utah/U.S. Film Festival but also in Robert Redford's Sundance Institute, a program for training young filmmakers. The Institute's programs continue to this day, and have been the breeding ground of several of Sundance's most illustrious alumni, including Quentin Tarantino. The San Francisco Film Society, which is part of its Film Festival organization, defines its mission as educational and offers year-round programming both in filmmaking and film appreciation. The inclusion of education within the film festival mandate further elevates and legitimates it as an institution.

Many of these educational programs function within the natural extension of a festival into a film society or cinematheque like Wisconsin's. The Toronto Festival Group sponsors not only the annual festival but also TIFF Cinémathèque (formerly Cinémathèque Ontario), a year-round series of retrospectives screened in an auditorium in the Art Gallery of Ontario. It has also published several scholarly books in connection with its series, including volumes on Robert Bresson and Shohei Imamura.[23] The Toronto Festival Group also has a film reference library for public use in researching cinema, again linking festival culture with scholarship.

The New York Film Festival is part of the larger Film Society of Lincoln Center, which puts cinema squarely within the cultural institutions of high art, sharing its space with opera, ballet, symphony, and theater companies, as well as the Julliard School. The Film Society also runs regular retrospectives at the Walter Reade Theater and publishes *Film Comment*, a highbrow bimonthly. All of these are non-profit cinema institutions that depend on public funding and are thus legitimated by their freedom from the marketplace, their affiliation with museums and other fixtures of high culture, and their scholarly or educational endeavors. The fact that American independent cinema, but not contemporary Hollywood cinema, comes to the public through the mediation of these institutions positions indie cinema within a sphere of rarefied culture rather than one of mass commercialism. The meanings behind the institution distinguish not only its audience but also its art forms.

Even as film festivals have come to be recognized by the mainstream industry as a crucial venue for discovering new talent, launching prestige pictures, and attracting media attention for their stars who offer themselves up to photographers on the ski slopes of Utah, they maintain their status as arts institutions by remaining noncommercial and nonprofit. The Sundance brand would seem to have extended itself far beyond the mission of making space for new and marginal voices. It has given its name and Robert Redford's entrepreneurship and investment to a boutique cable channel partly owned by two media conglomerates, CBS Corporation and NBC Universal, and a nascent chain of alternative for-profit cinemas. But the institute and festival remain nonprofit, as do all of the major North American events. Redford's Sundance Group oversees both nonprofit and for-profit endeavors, the Sundance Film Festival and the Sundance Channel, but their business models remain separate, allowing the educational and artistic missions of the institute and festival to be unhampered by an agenda for commercial success.[24]

One way of consecrating a culture as artistic is by locating it within institutions that eschew the marketplace model of popular or mass culture. A more prominent strategy of legitimation is the adoption of categories and concepts for identifying works from already legitimate art worlds. Richard D. Christopherson has written about the development of photography from commercial to artistic culture and notes that among other strategies, art photographers sought to make their practice appear similar to an already-legitimate form: oil painting.[25] The established art forms take different categories for identifying works than commercial media forms, like the name and nationality of the artist. As film progressed from mass medium to legitimate culture, one central development was the rise of authorship criticism and the discourse of auteurism to discriminate among greater and lesser instances of cinematic art.[26] It was joined by a concern with establishing film history as a history of national cinemas associated with national cultures and their long histories of artistic and cultural achievement. Photography, according to Christopherson, was made into a legitimate art form by being associated with an artistic tradition. Popular culture is ephemeral; art aspires to the status of classic. American independent cinema comes to its audience through the mediation of the film festival as an arts institution that adopts art world categories rather than mass culture categories to classify films and identify their significant traits. Festival paratexts such as catalog descriptions and press materials articulate a discourse of legitimacy that contrasts them with the paratexts surrounding popular cinema.

Popular cinema identifies films for spectators through a variety of paratextual discourses, such as newspaper and television ads, promotional magazine articles and talk-show segments, and showtime listings in a variety of media. Since the formation of the Hollywood studios, the categories popular cinema has adopted for discriminating among films have invariably been genre and star. In the blockbuster age, another central category is now the franchise. Audiences fasten on films and identify which they want to see primarily according to these terms. Of course there are exceptions when source material such as a novel or true story or a celebrity director like Hitchcock or Spielberg claims special attention. But the typical instance is of categorization by star, genre, and franchise.

By contrast, like works in a museum, films in festival catalogs are identified by artist (director), nationality, medium, and year of release. Festivals adopt the categories of already legitimate art worlds to legitimate themselves and their entrants. By establishing these categories as central ones, festivals have influenced world cinema's canon formation by indicating the relevant criteria for judgment and evaluation of films *qua* artworks and encouraging these criteria to be taken up in the popular press. Just as museums sort their collections by movement, nationality, and oeuvre, festivals and film societies see cinema in the terms favored by art worlds rather than mass-media institutions.

Festivals are thus essential to the discourse of both national cinema, a central category for ordering the world cinema canon, and *trans*national cinema, wherein a global cinephile culture makes its discoveries and assigns value.[27] Festivals began as projects for the promotion of national cultures. Venice was to be a showcase for fascist society; Berlin was begun under the Allied occupation in 1951 to be a site for a spectacle of democracy; Sundance began as the Utah/U.S. Film Festival in 1978 with a retrospective program paying tribute to portrayals of "Landscapes of America."[28] As they accrue prestige, festivals have the power to establish *auteur* reputations, elevating some directors and not others to pantheons of national and world cinema authors. As Liz Czach has written, the Toronto festival has been essential for the formation and perpetuation of Canadian national cinema at home and abroad, and it has done so by promoting its own directors such as Atom Egoyan as international *auteurs* by giving them prominent places in the festival schedule among their international peers.[29] American indie *auteurs* benefit from the same process at domestic events such as the New York Film Festival, which had few homegrown entries even by 1987, when the *New York Times'* Vincent Canby complained about its lack of American content.[30] A decade later, many of the festival's slots were being claimed by fall releases from indie *auteurs* such as P. T. Anderson, Harmony Korine, Todd Solondz, and Todd Haynes, filling the American seat in the cinematic parliament.[31]

Film festivals have also, like museum exhibits and other similar institutions in the history of the arts, been instrumental for identifying movements within national cinemas. The French New Wave was a discovery of the 1959 Cannes Film Festival, when Truffaut won the Palme d'Or for *The 400 Blows*. The New German Cinema gained attention and momentum from its Oberhausen Manifesto of 1962. In more recent times, the Danish Dogme 95 movement made its splash at Cannes to claim the attention of the international press in attendance. The 1990s' most acclaimed new cinemas, those of Iran and Taiwan, would hardly have existed if not for the festival circuit as its own distribution network for global art cinema.[32] Indie cinema is itself a kind of mega-movement with many American festivals that cater to it, from Sundance, Telluride, and the Independent Feature Project's Independent Film Week held in New York City, to many smaller fests whose main American content is independent cinema. Within the indie phenomenon are smaller clusters of artists being named as movements, such as the Mumblecore group of the mid-2000s. These filmmakers, including Andrew Bujalski and Joe Swanberg, have been closely identified with the South by Southwest event in Austin, Texas, and its programmer, Matt Dentler, whose blogging helped the Mumblecore label stick.[33] Before them were groups such as the New Queer

Cinema, identified with up-and-coming directors of the 1980s such as Haynes and Gregg Araki.

Sundance, Telluride, and the History of the Indie Festival

Of course, the festival with the strongest influence on independent cinema is Sundance, and its origins and development are worth considering as a way of demonstrating its significance as the institution that first connects many independent filmmakers and films with critics, distributors, and ultimately, audiences. Sundance is now as much brand as festival, offering its name not only to movie theaters and a cable channel, but a DVD box set of some of its "greatest hits" to commemorate the festival's 25th anniversary, most of them films from the 1990s and 2000s.[34] The festival itself is the main subject of a number of books and its name appears in the titles of several others, including Turan's *Sundance to Sarajevo*, James Mottram's *The Sundance Kids*, and Peter Biskind's *Down and Dirty Pictures: Miramax, Sundance, and the Rise of Independent Film*.[35] It is a commonplace to call Sundance synonymous with indie cinema, and some also call it America's Cannes.[36] Amy Taubin, a longtime champion of American indies, named Sundance the most crucial of all of independent cinema's institutions.[37] When the festival turned twenty-five, *Entertainment Weekly* produced a top ten list of its most influential movies, canonizing recent indie cinema for consumption by the mainstream publication's wide readership and further consolidating a roster of indie *auteurs*. These films were *Stranger Than Paradise* (1984), *sex, lies, and videotape* (1989), *Reservoir Dogs* (1992), *El Mariachi* (1992), *Clerks* (1994), *Spanking the Monkey* (1994), *The Blair Witch Project* (1999), *Memento* (2001), *Napoleon Dynamite* (2004), and *Super Size Me* (2004).[38] Like the DVD box set, the Sundance being canonized is largely that of the post–*sex, lies* period—in other words, the Sundance that proved to Hollywood that it was a worthy object of attention as a source of potential investments to promise potentially substantial returns.

The standard story in the popular accounts of independent cinema is that Sundance was a fledgling festival in the 1980s until *sex, lies, and videotape* came along at the 1989 event and went on to win the Palme d'Or at Cannes and gross $25 million at the domestic box office.[39] *Variety*'s Todd McCarthy wrote in 1995 that Sundance "can be divided into two eras, before and after 'sex, lies, and videotape.'"[40] The film is the turning point, the catalyst remaking a sleepy festival into a hot spot. The new era in indie cinema is epitomized by the Sundance scene that combines annual discoveries of unknown talent and anxious deal-making among the suits chattering into cell phones.[41] The independent film business in general was regarded as troubled in the late 1980s, with distributors losing money and critics complaining of a lack of originality and fresh perspectives in the indie sector. The film critic John Powers complained in *Film Comment* in 1987 that indie cinema had "settled into a complacent mediocrity whose axiom is 'Play it safe.'"[42] In 1989 the *New York Times* rounded up the Sundance festival at which Soderbergh debuted under the headline, "Independent Films Get Better But Go Begging," noting that after the 1987 stock market crash some independent production and distribution companies went bankrupt, that video stores were generally unwilling to carry nonmainstream titles, and that small distributors had been enduring a string of bad luck at the box office.[43] But independent cinema was never the same after Harvey Weinstein and Miramax established *sex, lies* as a new, bold exemplar of indieness in terms both aesthetic and economic—what Alisa Perren calls the "indie blockbuster."[44]

Even if 1989 was a major turning point for Sundance, as well as for Miramax, there were also significant continuities in Sundance as an institution that held over from the 1980s to the 1990s. As is often the case, the representation in popular narratives of a watershed event might miss the wider context and diverse forces that produce change. To begin with, in order for this turning point to have occurred, there had to be a festival devoted to American independent cinema in the first place, and this existence was a product of several historical forces. In the heyday of the European film festival and the European art cinema, there were no major festivals devoted primarily to showcasing American movies. American cinema, and in particular Hollywood cinema, was actually a structuring absence of film festivals whose function was implicitly to offer an alternative to Hollywood, to stand face to face with the institutions of commercial, mass-market cinema. From its origins as the Utah/U.S. Film Festival, Sundance was already to be a specifically American event, primarily promoting the history of Hollywood classics and supplementing its retrospective series with a small number of new films in a competition.

The first Utah/U.S. Film Festival in 1978, held in Salt Lake City, programmed only eight recent independent films in competition. Its mission was to celebrate American moviegoing. The competition films might have been called independent, but at the time they were as often called *regional* films, films not made in New York City or Los Angeles but in the middle of the country, in places like Utah. Like many American festivals that have tried to imitate its success, Sundance was funded in part by a public film commission (the Utah Film Commission) as a way of bringing talent to the area and stimulating film production there. It was hardly anticommercial in its aims of bringing independent cinema to Hollywood and Hollywood to independent cinema, but it did so under the rubric of a cultural as well as an economic policy. When the festival eventually moved to Park City in 1981, thirty miles from Robert Redford's Sundance ski resort, the agenda was to attract more visitors from Los Angeles eager to mix business and pleasure. Like many European film festivals, Sundance was located in a resort town just off season (late January is a lull time for ski resorts) to boost tourism and also to piggyback on the cachet of the classy setting.[45] Redford already had bought the ski resort near Park City and apparently intended to create his own version of Aspen, Colorado, in the Utah Rockies—an upscale artists' colony adjacent to his resort, only substituting cinema for the more traditional arts.[46] By the early 1980s, Rocky Mountain ski slopes had become a favorite vacation destination for Hollywood power players; Sundance hoped to benefit from their attention.[47]

The focus on American cinema was essential to the festival's identity from its inception, but this alone was not sufficient to make it the event it was to become. And more than the move from the city in early autumn to the mountains in midwinter, and also more than Robert Redford's involvement *per se*, the most significant developments in the history of Sundance before 1989 were the combination of the Utah/U.S. festival with the Sundance Institute, the shift in the festival's orientation from the old to the new, and the ability of the festival to attract attention from the national press. These developments were not just significant for the establishment of a successful annual event; they set the terms by which independent cinema would circulate as a discourse beyond its immediate context of film production and distribution.

The Utah/U.S. festival had the good fortune to emerge just at the same moment as home video, and as Kristin Thompson and David Bordwell observe in their survey of world cinema history, the new technology functioned to encourage the spread of festivals devoted to new films because it facilitated the screening of multiple entries.[48] At the same time, the festival was running at a deficit from the first year and needed strategies to cut costs. Running retrospectives has the virtue of potentially attracting major talent who will appear if they are being honored, and this is good publicity, but it can also be expensive because the festival needs to pay rental fees. Focusing instead on the competition films shifts the expense of supplying films from the festival to the filmmaker.[49] And according to the festival's competition programmer in its early years, Lory Smith, the audience for the festival was most eager to see the new films.[50]

At the third Utah/U.S. festival in 1981, the first one held in Park City, the emphasis shifted from retrospectives to the competition, following the lead of the newly formed IFP Independent Feature Films Market, which held its first event in 1979 in New York City. The Market, another institution supported by a regional film commission (the New York City Mayor's Office for Theater, Film, and Broadcasting) combined screenings of independent films for distributors with seminars about independent filmmaking.[51] It was at this point that programmers and filmmakers alike recognized a potential for American festivals to nurture American filmmakers outside of the Hollywood development system.[52] The IFP event's inclusion of practical discussions with filmmakers about how to get movies made and seen was also a template for the way the Utah/U.S. festival combined with the Sundance Institute, making the festival more than just an exhibition of films to be an educational resource for filmmakers.

The Sundance Institute, which began in June 1981, was supposed to be a laboratory for nurturing talent in American cinema in a different atmosphere than conventional film schools.[53] Redford told the *New York Times* in 1983 that he had been concerned that the "alternative voice was being driven out of American films."[54] Like the IFP, the Utah/U.S. festival, and virtually every other alternative cinema institution, Sundance was modeled on existing successful nonprofit arts institutions (in particular the American Film Institute and the

Eugene O'Neill Theater Center in Waterford, Connecticut).[55] Rather than establishing itself as a for-profit business, it drew on state and private support (from the NEA, the Ford Foundation, the Utah Film Commission, and corporate donors including several Hollywood studios).[56] Its centerpiece was a summertime laboratory in which young artists workshopped scripts and scenes with the help of directors, actors, and cinematographers who had worked in Hollywood, including Redford, Sydney Pollock, Laszlo Kovacs, and Frank Daniel.[57] The aesthetic agenda of the Institute was to provide an alternative system for the development of talent and films, focused less on commerce and more on art. It was not oppositional, and Redford has always maintained that his position is not at all anti-Hollywood. But it was aimed at addressing a perceived deficiency in Hollywood at the time, which is captured in this chapter's epigraph, but also in the independent cinema of the time, which Redford perceived to be lacking in technical skill, even if brimming with personal passion.[58] Redford, like so many figures of the independent movement, wanted American filmmaking to do better at balancing art and commerce; many believe his guilt over having found such success in a highly commercial industry prompted him to try to give something back to the creative community. (He was also undoubtedly eager to establish local attractions to bring business to his resort.)

Film festivals like Sundance are not merely exhibition venues and nodes in a distribution circuit. Like any successful cultural institution, they encourage production of appropriate works, give artists the incentive to create, and cultivate an audience. As the Sundance Institute and the Utah/U.S. festival progressed, they encouraged the production of the kind of cinema they championed—low-budget films made independently of the industry. Whereas once only a small number of feature films were made each year by such artist-entrepreneurs, by the mid-1980s hundreds of such works were being financed on credit cards and by generous parents and friends. Eventually the number would climb into the thousands. The institutions of independent cinema gave these artists an opportunity not only to have their work seen but also possibly to be acquired for distribution and shown beyond the festival circuit. The production of films outside of an industry is by nature a different sort of endeavor from production financed by a studio or distributor, typically pursued out of passion for creativity and expression as well, undoubtedly in most cases, out of a desire to win some measure of fame and fortune. This is a matter of a relative balance rather than a strict either/or.

In 1985 when the Sundance Institute and Utah/U.S. festival joined forces, a rhetoric of "symbiosis" between the two events suggested that together they could better accomplish the mission each had been pursuing individually of shifting the balance between art and business in American filmmaking.[59] The year 1985 happened to be especially strong for the festival's entrants, screening *Blood Simple*, *Stranger Than Paradise*, *Brother from Another Planet*, and a number of documentaries that went on to have successful theatrical releases including *The Life and Times of Harvey Milk*. The *auteurs* behind these films, especially Joel and Ethan Coen, Jim Jarmusch, and John Sayles, would soon be seen as not just fresh alternative voices but as central figures in a movement, a generation of American filmmakers after the Hollywood Renaissance generation, whose name was to be made by going outside of the usual Hollywood channels, and whose identity as mavericks, a favorite term of indie champions, was to be guaranteed by this outsider quality. At the same time, the festival had an impressive program of international films screening outside of the competition, including Wim Wenders's *Paris, Texas*, Woody Allen's *The Purple Rose of Cairo*, and new films by Werner Herzog, Stephen Frears, Sally Potter, Andrzej Wajda, Roland Joffe, and Lina Wertmuller.[60] And yet by keeping the dramatic and documentary competitions strictly American, the festival was able to accomplish one of the central aims of independent cinema in the United States: establishing its specificity as a national cinema and its legitimacy on equal terms with the international roster of *auteurs* and national cinemas producing films for the festival and art house circuits. In 1986, eleven of fourteen dramatic competition films were picked up for distribution, the highest percentage ever at that time. Attendance was 30 percent higher than the previous year, and publications with national readerships were paying attention to the festival.[61]

The films shown at Sundance were not simply independently made by passionate young novices. They were perceived to have certain textual features in common as well, especially an alternative sensibility eagerly casting its light on themes and topics and characters not often seen in Hollywood cinema, and a sense of risk-taking that would be impossible in a mainstream industrial context of production. The mid-1980s competition included films such as *Desert Hearts* (1985), a film about lesbians set in Nevada; *Dim Sum* (1985), about Chinese immigrants in San Francisco; and *The Killing Floor* (1985), about black slaughterhouse workers in the 1910s. The indie cinema's agenda of multiculturalism in dramatic films was matched by the political advocacy in much of its documentary slate, as in *The Atomic Cafe* (1982), about American nuclear-testing propaganda. Documentaries might also advance the notion of a personal cinema, as with Ross McElwee's *Sherman's March* (1986), a film ostensibly about the Civil War that turns out to be about the filmmaker's idiosyncratic interests. By being perceived as personal and political, the Sundance film was firming up an identity that would be defined as something more specific than just an independently made feature. Thus when John Powers complained in his *Film Comment* article that the festival had started playing it safe, he was comparing the new independent films at Sundance not just with certain predecessors but with exemplars. He mentioned *Stranger Than Paradise* (1985), *Kiss of the Spider Woman* (1985), *Salvador* (1986), *Re-Animator* (1985), *Trouble in Mind* (1985), *She's Gotta Have It* (1986), *True Stories* (1986), and *Blue Velvet* (1986) as the movies to emulate (though several of these were not Sundance competitors) and wrote that he still awaited films with their passion and purpose, their "personal, political and aesthetic agendas that could fire an indie movement, define it against existing cinema, and give it some sass and subversive energy."[62] In blaming that year's Sundance indies for playing it safe, Powers was articulating a powerful conception of the values Off-Hollywood filmmakers—and their public—should adopt. *Sex, lies, and videotape* emerged within this context.

In the years after *sex, lies*, the festival crowds grew and Hollywood started to pay more attention. Attendance at the festival in the early 1990s increased by 30 percent each year in spite of the festival's efforts to rein in growth.[63] An audience of about 400 in 1984 had increased to roughly 6,000 a decade hence.[64] Annual entrants in the festival competitions exploded from dozens to thousands.[65] Innumerable media reports would sound the familiar refrain that Sundance was being sold out or co-opted as deal-making vied with filmmaking as a locus of interest. Distribution rights were regularly paid in the millions of dollars, and even some documentaries fetched impressive prices. It was certainly true that independent cinema was now big business, as was evident in the attention Hollywood was paying. And yet it was in the 1990s that Sundance firmly established a reputation for reliably turning up the talent that would become fixed as the "Sundance kids" of James Mottram's book and the "rebels on the backlot" of Sharon Waxman's, the directors like Soderbergh, Tarantino, Linklater, Kevin Smith, and P. T. Anderson, whose mini-major pictures became central to conceptions of indieness in the 1990s.[66] It was only by attracting the attention of the film industry that the independents were able to make their name and gain the widespread notoriety and acclaim that made them into a movement that the world outside of film festivals would recognize. The alternative and the mainstream exploited each other to connect movies with the audiences that made them a success.

Lory Smith's history of the festival marks this period as one of "synthesis of . . . clashing cultures," alternative and mainstream. As evidence he gives the appearance of "Sundance" in a clue on the game show *Jeopardy!* and in a line of dialogue from Robert Altman's Hollywood satire *The Player* (1992). In that scene Griffin, the murderous studio executive played by Tim Robbins, asks John Cusack (as John Cusack) if he will see him at Telluride, and Cusack replies no, he is going to Sundance.[67] As these examples attest, the festival and the movement were gaining recognition and this was, of course, something many would face with ambivalence. But the festival as institution proceeded as before, cultivating its identity as a—relationally—artistic and alternative space. Hollywood was eagerly buying in to its promises of authentic personal and political filmmaking to fill its mini-major distributors' slate of films destined for the new art house theaters that would arise in the 1990s to satisfy the explosion of indie cinema on the American marketplace (more on this in a moment). But it was only because Sundance and indie cinema were perceived according to the terms established within the institution that this buying in was potentially to Hollywood's advantage, as the terms had been projected outward from the festival to the audience through the intermediaries of the press and the promotional discourses touting festival reception, selections, and awards—including the promotional discourses involving festival deal-making. From their beginnings, the Sundance institute and festival had the mission of making a space for independents, for their distinctive values and energy, that would gain them visibility and viability in American film culture by exploiting Hollywood's power to reach audiences.

Indies at Telluride and New York

While the Telluride and New York Film Festivals are not as important in the history of independent cinema in the United States as Sundance, their development expresses one especially significant point about indie cinema as a product of its institutional contexts: that beginning around the time of *sex, lies*, the American independent film rose to the status not only of a parallel and alternative to mainstream Hollywood film but also of a parallel and equivalent to global art/festival cinema. This shift is apparent from considering media coverage of indies in the late 1980s. Only two years after lamenting the absence of American films at the New York Film Festival, Vincent Canby declared in the fall of 1989—the season of *sex, lies*—that "alternative commercial cinema lives."[68] Nineteen eighty-nine was not just Soderbergh's year; *sex, lies* was joined in the competition at Cannes by Spike Lee's *Do the Right Thing*, and together they represented the American independent movement as a new and significant development in world cinema that would offer both personal and political perspectives typically absent from Hollywood movies. In the years to follow, many festivals opened up to more American cinema, and in this regard Telluride and New York may be seen as typical. The history of these festivals' programming of American cinema sheds light on how this transformation in American film culture took place, wherein American films came to occupy the place once reserved for foreign films.

The Telluride Film Festival began in the mid-1970s as a highly selective and exclusive event in another off-season resort town.[69] It was founded by film programmers from San Francisco and Rochester, New York, and was intended to be a true festival, a celebration of cinema. It had and has no competition; selection in the festival's small slate would be honor enough for new films. Its audience in its early years was made up of only a small gathering of filmmakers, critics, and film buffs.[70] Like Sundance in its first years, much of the slate at the early Telluride festivals was devoted to American cinema. But also like Sundance, the retrospective programs of American films were thoroughly Hollywood. Early festivals paid tribute to studio-era personages including Gloria Swanson, Henry King, King Vidor, Sterling Hayden, and Chuck Jones. The film historian William K. Everson was a regular at Telluride, bringing programs of B-westerns and silent comedies. To attract Hollywood names and their attendant publicity, Telluride honored contemporary heroes like Francis Ford Coppola, feted at the inaugural fest in 1974, and Jack Nicholson, the subject of a tribute in the second year. Its American focus was mainly historical, treating Hollywood history as a great tradition. It also included programs of avant-garde and documentary cinema, with regular appearances by Stan Brakhage and Les Blank, but little that we would recognize as indie according to the terms set in the 1980s and 1990s.

At the same time as it offered retrospective programming, the festival regularly presented the best of recent world cinema, especially European and Japanese films by the international *auteurs* of the day. Werner Herzog was a perennial presence. The 1976 festival included new films by Louis Malle, Akira Kurosawa, and Eric Rohmer. In 1979 there were recent films by Rainer Werner Fassbinder, Alain Tanner, and Jiri Menzl, and just about every festival in the 1970s had some Czech New Wave titles. It also included American features such as Errol Morris documentaries and Robert Downey's experimental feature *Two Tons of Turquoise to Taos* (1975), but it certainly did not have a mission of presenting recent Off-Hollywood feature films seeking commercial distribution, as Sundance soon would.

In the same period, the New York Film Festival, founded in 1962, had an almost exclusive focus on European cinema. Like Telluride, New York is a prestigious and noncompetitive festival with a small program of recent films, and selection by New York is as great an honor as winning prizes at many other events. For both of these fests, as for the competition at Cannes, the annual slate is taken to be a bellwether of world cinema. In his roundup of the 1977 festival in *American Film*, Jonathan Baumbach reflected on new films by Agnès Varda, Luis Buñuel, François Truffaut, Claude Goretta, Herzog, Pier Paolo Pasolini, Bresson, Wenders, Bernardo Bertolucci, and the Taviani brothers (Paolo and Vittorio). The only American film mentioned was Jonathan Demme's *Handle with Care*, a B movie about the CB radio craze that bombed in its release under the title *Citizens Band* and which Baumbach noted hardly belongs on the same program as *1900*. "For the chic Lincoln Center audience," he wrote, "to whom the CB craze must seem like a Martian folkway, this ordinary film is a cultural exotic."[71] Demme was again the sole American (with *Melvin and Howard*) at the 1980 NYFF, an event that as ever took European art cinema to be the only form of legitimately artistic contemporary feature filmmaking. It must have seemed natural to Vincent Canby, rounding up the festival in the *New York Times*, that an American film festival would be made up of foreign films almost exclusively, as this fact passed without remark.[72]

In 1987, the year of Powers's denunciation of the "safe" Sundance slate, Canby summed up the New York festival again, but this time took the angle of comparing foreign and domestic cinema as candidates for inclusion. He noted that although at the time the festival was founded it had studio-era Hollywood producers on its board (David O. Selznick, Samuel Goldwyn, Daryl Zanuck, Jack Warner), it had never been a festival of American films.[73] Old Hollywood, Canby remarked, had viewed American festivals as competition for moviegoers rather than promotional opportunities, and always had disdained anything perceived as arty. Occasionally the studios would send the New York festival a film that was judged to have little in the way of commercial prospects (e.g., *Mickey One*, 1965; Demme's films). And American cinema by confirmed talents of other highbrow art worlds were always welcome (e.g., works by Susan Sontag, Norman Mailer, and David Mamet). But in spite of some exceptions (e.g., *Badlands*, 1973), Canby proclaimed, "As it was in the 1960's, it is today: The good foreign film is more likely to be the work of a single sensibility than the good American film."[74]

Just two years later, Canby had evidently reversed his opinion. For his roundup of that year's Cannes film festival the headline was "Home Is Where the Art Is," noting that among that year's impressive offerings were a number of American films by young directors, including *Do the Right Thing*, *Mystery Train*, and *sex, lies.*[75] And in introducing the fall prestige films, some of them Cannes winners, the headline proclaimed, "Rejoice! It's Independents' Day." The lead read, "Alternative commercial cinema lives."[76] The article discussed *sex, lies* and *Roger & Me* in greatest detail, and identified the rise of a viable American alternative with its "especially evident" presence at the 1989 New York festival, which included Moore's documentary as well as Jarmusch's *Mystery Train.*[77] In the years to come, American indies would prove to be a mainstay of the New York Film Festival.

Ten years after Canby's 1987 denunciation of American cinema, the festival's opening night feature was Ang Lee's *The Ice Storm*, and the festival program also included *Boogie Nights, The Apostle*, and *Fast, Cheap and Out of Control*. The 1998 festival's roster of American films included *Rushmore, Happiness, Gods and Monsters*, and *Velvet Goldmine*. And in 1999, New York showed *Dogma, Boys Don't Cry, Julien Donkey-Boy*, and *Being John Malkovich*.[78] In the 1990s, the films of the mini-majors and the new generation of American outsider directors claimed spots in prestigious events that had previously been reserved mainly for international art films. Inclusion in the club proved their legitimacy.

Likewise, Telluride was transformed in the late 1980s and 1990s into a showcase for independent cinema alongside the international films it had always screened. Some of the landmarks of the 1980s American indie scene played there, including *Stranger Than Paradise, Blue Velvet*, and *River's Edge* (1986). In 1990 the festival paid tribute to the films of New York indie Jon Jost. And throughout the decade to follow, Telluride premiered new indies for the American audience, including *Roger & Me* (1989), *El Mariachi* (1992), *Sling Blade* (1996), *Swingers* (1996), *Gummo* (1997), and *Rushmore*. By 2001 virtually all of Telluride's films were premieres rather than revivals, and the festival's inclusion of American cinema had thus shifted from a focus on past glories to new triumphs presented in parallel to those of the global circulation in festival films, and destined for the art house screens which had also once been the domain of the foreign film, which is where our attention turns next.

Art House Theaters

The American art house emerged in the 1950s as a vital institution for the circulation of alternative films and as the venue where American audiences typically encountered the forms of cinema that were to gain cultural legitimacy in the period in which auteurism, the international trade in movies, and an awareness of Hollywood history came to be central to an emergent cinephilia.[79] As Barbara Wilinsky and Douglas Gomery have written, the postwar art house, largely in major urban centers, distinguished itself from the typical first-run or neighborhood theater in various ways.[80] It showed different films from different contexts and attracted a clientele of high-income, well-educated spectators.[81] The art house was likely to have modern and sophisticated design and décor and to serve coffee and tea with fancy candies rather than popcorn.[82] Its social function was to promote distinction for both movies and their audience, offering the latter participation in a quasi-highbrow taste culture.

The art house theater in its heyday from the 1950s to the '70s offered two kinds of programming. Some houses specialized in the revival, especially of studio-era Hollywood movies but also of international classics. Along with movies seen on television and on college campuses in classes and at film societies, the repertory cinema functioned to canonize Hollywood stars like Fred Astaire and Ginger Rogers and *auteurs* like John Ford. Retrospectives at the Brattle off Harvard Square fed the cult of Humphrey Bogart. The preservation of film history as a fecund tradition was essential to its elevation to the status of art, as art claims its status by rising above the ephemera of commercial culture to become immortal and timeless. At the same time, many art houses were first-run theaters specializing in foreign films, including recent festival-winners from Cannes, Venice, or Moscow and new work by confirmed *auteurs* like Truffaut and Fellini and featuring international stars like Brigitte Bardot and Marcello Mastroianni.

In the same period as the founding of the Utah/U.S. Film and Telluride festivals, major American cities like New York had numerous art houses with both revival and first-run policies. But beginning in the 1980s, many of these old theaters started to close. In New York City, the New Yorker and St. Marks cinemas both closed in 1985, prompting the *Village Voice* to ask in a headline, "Is New York Losing Its Reps?"[83] The Metro closed in 1986, the Thalia and the Embassy in 1987.[84] The Regency, once anointed "Manhattan's premiere revival house,"[85] was transformed that same year when Cineplex-Odeon bought the Lincoln Center neighborhood theater and reopened it as a first-run venue for Hollywood films.[86] In 1990, Cinema Studio closed its doors, to be replaced at Broadway and 66th Street by Capital Cities/ABC headquarters.[87] And in 1991 the Bleecker Street Cinema, long a fixture of Greenwich Village's counterculture, closed as well.[88] In 1987 *Newsweek* reported that the revival house was dying out across the country, a result of a "relentless one-two punch . . . from cable and video cassettes."[89]

Some film historians in the early 1990s misidentified this decline of a certain kind of theater with the decline of the art house as an institution. Tino Balio writes in his study of the American market for art films in the 1990s that "the number of specialized theaters in the U.S. declined steadily during the 1980s."[90] And Douglas Gomery writes of the "end of the art house" in his history of American film exhibition, prematurely declaring that "the art house phenomenon came to an end" with the closing of these repertory theaters and a decline in the American market for foreign films.[91]

While America's market for foreign films did decline in the 1980s and 1990s, and video did kill most commercial revival theaters (though not the nonprofit film society and cinematheque venues, as we have seen), the art house didn't stay dead. In the late 1980s, 1990s, and 2000s, there have been scores of art house theaters operating in the United States in big cities and college towns. But just as the American film festival changed over this period, so did the art house theater. In particular, its bread-and-butter programming substituted one kind of alternative cinema for another. The art house became a site not necessarily for "art films," and less and less for foreign-language ones, but increasingly for what the Hollywood trade press calls "offbeat," "niche," and "specialty" fare, often released by mini-majors, and very typically American and indie. (In a 1997 article, *Variety* defined "specialized" fare as "pictures that play on a limited number of screens and have genuinely upscale appeal.")[92] Although we might hesitate to call it an "American art cinema," the indie phenomenon has basically fulfilled that function, replacing the mid-century's dominant conception of alternative cinema as serious, intellectually demanding, high modernist, and Continental with a new conception that was a product of the multicultural and postmodern currents within elite Western culture of the 1980s and 90s. The art house of this period has not been the same institution as the art house of the 1960s, though it still performs a similar social function. Its distinction now comes through the audience's identification with a new generation of filmmakers and a new set of parameters for making sense of their work. It is within this iteration of the art house as institution during the Sundance-Miramax era that most audience members have encountered indie film culture. It is within this space that our viewing strategies are mobilized.

Indieplex: The Art House of the Sundance-Miramax Era

The market for specialty cinema has always depended to a large extent on New York City. New York is an important launching pad for such films because, like any cultural capital, it has the support of a large audience base for sophisticated culture. Foreign and independent films are routinely opened first in New York, where a profitable run indicates the potential for a film's success in the rest of the country. New York is home to many of the country's most influential critics, who are especially powerful when it comes to the prospects for elite culture.

In the 1990s, New York lost many of its favorite old theaters, but it also gained several new ones. The ones that closed were revival houses; those that opened were first-run houses. The old art houses were single-screen edifices, many from the picture-palace era of cinematic architecture. Some had been converted to duplexes or triplexes following the trends of the 1960s and '70s. But the new theaters followed the exhibition trend of the 1980s and '90s: multiplexing. The new art house theaters followed the same commercial strategies of the mainstream theater, maximizing their investment and minimizing their risk by showing five or more films in each venue.

At the same time that the revival houses were closing, the Lincoln Plaza Cinemas on Manhattan's Upper West Side was opening and soon thereafter expanded from three screens to six. This theater, owned by Dan Talbot of the art film distributor New Yorker Films, was launched as part of a strategy of vertical integration, giving Talbot an exhibition outlet for the imports he was handling as distributor. But over time it became a significant venue for independent film exhibition beyond Talbot's own titles as American films shared space with European imports on the multiplex marquee.

But the more significant new art house multiplex development in New York City came in 1989 when the six-screen Angelika Theater opened in a location straddling Greenwich Village and Soho in downtown Manhattan, a part of the city historically underserved by movie theaters. The Angelika was the first indie multiplex, with six screens devoted to Off-Hollywood fare. In 2003 the *New York Times* described it as the originator of "a whole new genre of movie house: the indieplex."[93] Throughout the 1990s the Angelika was the model followed by emergent art houses and was the top-grossing art house theater in the country.[94]

Like Talbot's theater, the Angelika was founded by a film producer-distributor, Joe Saleh, eager to create a venue for his own films, which he had been having difficulty placing in theaters.[95] From the start, Saleh's ambition for the theater was to attract to it "upscale people," as he told the *Village Voice*. The theater's upstairs café featured "a very long, 40-foot bar area . . . serving cappuccino, espresso, all the with-it drinks, and finger food. This is to serve our people, the yuppie audience."[96] In another interview, he said that

> [the] Angelika will be catering to better-educated, more sophisticated moviegoers, offering them better-quality films. "We're ready to play anything, but not *Chainsaw Massacre* or *Rambo IV*, not the mass, mass-market product," Saleh says.[97]

The theater's identity was thus a product of its association with communities of downtown hipsters and cinephiles and their habits of consumption. It was also a product of an attempt to make the Angelika into an indie brand by expanding to other cities (Dallas and Houston) and by lending its name to a television series on the Independent Film Channel called *At the Angelika* (1997–; and, later, *At the IFC Center*), in which directors and actors from newly released indie films appear in interviews, using the two New York theaters' lobbies as the show's set. As the flagship theater is described in the company's Web site,

> The Angelika plays an impressive and diverse mix of independent films, and is the definitive cinema of choice for filmmakers and film lovers alike. Since its opening, the Angelika New York has become the most successful and recognized arthouse in the United States. . . .
> The Angelika offers a dynamic and sophisticated atmosphere. The theater is a great place to meet your friends or hang out by yourself, and patrons who come early can enjoy a gourmet snack at the café or browse our InFocus newsletter.[98]

The terms the company chooses to describe itself indicate the indie art house's positioning in relation to the mainstream theater. The films are independent rather than Hollywood. The theater is an art house rather than a multiplex. The atmosphere is sophisticated rather than common. The concessions are gourmet and come from a café rather than being standard junk from a candy counter. And the reading material available is the theater's own newsletter promoting its films and their creators rather than the type of in-house publication available in regular theaters promoting Hollywood movies and their stars. Although there was scant discourse of "independence" surrounding the Angelika in the moment of the theater's opening (this is just on the cusp of the *sex, lies* transformation), the theater's identity was to be defined most of all by the indie movement and its audience. As Christine Vachon, the producer of films by Todd Haynes among others, describes it, in its early days, the Angelika was

> the kind of movie theater that other movie theaters pay close attention to because it triggers tsunamis of word of mouth. . . . In the late 1980s and early 1990s, the Angelika was like a Grauman's Chinese Theater of independent film. . . . Playing at the Angelika meant you had the best shot of entering the conversation.[99]

I often saw movies at the Angelika in the mid-1990s, and typically these were American independent films such as *Amateur* (1994), *Smoke* (1995), *Kids* (1995), and *Safe* (1995). The theater's atmosphere of edgy cool was unmistakable and unparalleled in any venue in the city.

While the Angelika was establishing the indieplex template—hip urban location, sophisticated interior and amenities, American Off-Hollywood films—it was another chain that took the indieplex to the largest number of viewers around the United States. Landmark Theater Corp. began as a chain of repertory theaters based in Southern California in the 1970s and over the years shifted to a first-run policy as home video emerged, endured several ownership changes, expanded its properties and opened new ones to become, by the mid-1990s, the biggest and most profitable art house chain in the country. Among its theaters are art houses in Los Angeles, San Diego, Sacramento, Seattle, Dallas, Houston, Denver, Minneapolis, Milwaukee, Boston, Detroit, New Orleans, St. Louis, and New York City.

Although the Angelika is the quintessential indieplex, many of Landmark's theaters are of a different sort. Angelika's New York flagship theater is notorious for requiring that patrons suffer its small screens, uncomfortable seats, and the unpleasant racket caused by regularly passing subway trains (the theater auditoriums are on a basement level). The Landmark indieplexes that opened in the 1990s took the Hollywood megaplex as a partial model, with not only multiple screens but also comfortable stadium seating, ample parking, and of course the requisite fancy coffee drinks and snacks.[100] As its former president, Steve Giulia, described the chain, Landmark theaters developed into "the boutiques in an industry of megamalls."[101] As the mainstream multiplex construction boom of the 1990s progressed, many observers hoped that these new theaters might set aside one or two screens for niche films, and some did so. But according to a *Variety* report in 1998, the audience for specialty films avoids seeing them in megaplexes, preferring "dedicated cinemas" and the atmosphere they offer.[102] Since the 1990s, Landmark has most often provided these cinemas to the American audience for independent film.

Among the theaters Landmark opened in this period is the five-screen Sunshine Cinema (in 1999), just down the street from the Angelika in downtown Manhattan. The Sunshine was built in the shell of an 1898 Yiddish theater, with its marquee and signage restored.[103] Its interior was an improvement on the Angelika, with stadium seating and digital sound. Around the same time, across the East River at the Brooklyn Academy of Music cultural center, another new specialty theater with multiple screens was debuting, the BAM Rose Cinemas. It opened its doors in 1998 and was heralded as part of a resurgence in art screens in New York City.[104] And in 2005, the three-screen IFC Center opened in what was formerly the Waverly, a Greenwich Village art house on the Avenue of the Americas, to be "home to the indie film community," according to IFC's president, Jonathan Sehring.[105] It is owned by Rainbow Media, the parent company of IFC and subsidiary of Cablevision, which also owns the Sundance Channel. As the "undisputed capital of specialized filmgoing," New York was to be well served by a number of theaters with multiple screens dedicated to independent cinema.[106]

The company identity at Landmark depends on the combination of its programming policy and its theatergoing experience. It aims to show edgy, controversial fare and boasts of its own courage in showing films such as Todd Solondz's *Happiness*, dumped by its distributor because of its problematic content, and Catherine Breillat's *Romance* (1999), a sexually explicit French import.[107] In this way it inherits the "adult" art house's tradition of promoting the raciness of its films.[108]

The fact that *sex, lies, and videotape* is the pivotal independent film places the movement squarely within this tradition. And by boasting of its embrace of controversy, the chain sets itself apart from the bigger, more mainstream companies that must keep their multiplexes safe for audiences of all ages. This positioning of the indieplex as uncompromising is ultimately ideological, validating itself as adult and sophisticated at the expense of the purveyors of mass culture. It also bespeaks the notion that the indie film comes from an artistic, rather than merely commercial, source, and has the validity that art brings no matter the salaciousness of its content.

In addition to its programming policy, the chain prides itself as well on the architectural distinction of its theaters. Many of its new theaters are designed to be a contrast in appearance from typical suburban multiplexes, while others inhabit old picture palaces, including Milwaukee's Oriental and St. Louis's Tivoli. The company touts the awards its theaters have won from local media polls that rate municipal attractions, such as *Time Out New York*'s award for "#1 Art-House in New York City (2003)" to Sunshine Cinema and *Entertainment Weekly*'s "'One of the 10 Best Movies Theaters in America (2005)" to the Oriental.[109] The company describes the Kendall Square Cinema in Cambridge, Massachusetts (opened in 1995), as "among the most successful, beloved and architecturally intriguing homes for independent film, foreign language cinema, restored classics and documentaries in the nation."[110] Of the Magnolia, a Dallas art house opened in 2003, Landmark boasts that it not only has an "acclaimed theater design [which] has been profiled in numerous publications," but that "exuding the beauty and warmth of an upscale restaurant," the theater "attracts a mixture of sophisticated, intelligent, upscale adults seeking an alternative to the megaplex madhouse."[111] These strategies promoting the theatergoing experience become enmeshed with the experience of independent cinema as culture and as community. Until 2007 the Landmark chain published *FLM*, a magazine ("The Voice of Independent Film") distributed for free in the lobby of every theater. *FLM*, like the Angelika's InFocus newsletter, functioned as a crucial node in the network of indie ideas, establishing the director as a focus of paratextual discourses by providing interviews with *auteurs* of upcoming releases and encouraging the viewing strategies that make indie cinema cohere as a category, especially the notions of social engagement and oppositionality. Many Landmark theaters, including Seattle's Egyptian, are also venues for annual film festivals, further solidifying the connection between independent cinema, art house theaters, and the festival circuit. And Landmark's theaters are central to the release strategy of any specialty film opening in America. The distinction offered in these theaters has been "a crucial part of the success of the independent film business," said Tom Bernard, co-president of Sony Pictures Classics, to *Variety* in 1999.[112]

In 2003 Landmark was acquired by a pair of Internet entrepreneurs, Mark Cuban and Todd Wagner. Among their other holdings are Magnolia Pictures, an independent distributor; Rysher Entertainment, a library of television and film programming; and HDNet, a television channel. All of these are under the corporate umbrella of 2929 Entertainment, which also includes 2929 Productions, a film production company. Like so many before them, Cuban and Wagner's investment in exhibition is part of a strategy of vertical integration in the movie business. Although they are not Hollywood, they are continuing the tradition of making independent cinema into big business, and a business of cultivating status by opposing the mainstream industrially, culturally, and socially.

They are joined in this by Robert Redford, whose Sundance Group, the for-profit side of his enterprise, also launched a long-in-the-works exhibition venture with architecturally distinguished art house multiplexes showing indie films and selling upscale foods in Madison, Wisconsin, and San Francisco, both of which opened in 2007.[113] This brings us back to the nexus of film, festival, and art house, the connection of institutions and texts that brings the community of independent cinema into existence and gives it meaning. Sundance as a brand and as an institution extends to every level of the independent film process: creation, distribution, promotion, and exhibition. Making Sundance synonymous with independent film means that the ideas associated with the institution—individuality, authenticity, progressive politics—are products not just of texts but of a wide and encompassing context of American cinema culture. Sundance and the other institutions of indie culture propose a conception of an alternative American national cinema, a national cinema based on putting (or appearing to put) artistic expression before commercial profit.

Indie cinema depends on the festival and the art house to establish its significance as a distinct form of culture. The festival fixes a film's worthiness as artwork rather than commodity and is the occasion for the first paratextual ideas to begin to circulate, strongly influencing subsequent discourses. And the art house allows for an audience to be constituted for indie cinema—an audience not in the sense merely of those who come to watch and listen, but in the sense of a community of like-minded cinemagoers who share more than just their presence in the space of a theater.

The films to be discussed in the following chapters are the products of filmmakers, but also of contexts. Contexts come in many varieties. Some, like the zeitgeist, are vague and loose and hard to pin down. Others, like the film industry, are more specific. The industry is more than just producers and creative personnel and distributors, some of whom will appear in the pages to come. It includes the institutions of contact between the product and the audience for which it is intended. The independent film industry crafts its wares to fit the demands of these institutions—of the festivals which are the first to get and screen films, and the art houses whose projectors are the next stop for the cream of the festival crop—and it is within these institutions that films' meanings are produced, aided of course by paratextual discourses such as publicity and word of mouth. What those meanings are and how they are realized in the encounter of the cinema and its audience will be the concern of the rest of this book.

part II CHARACTER

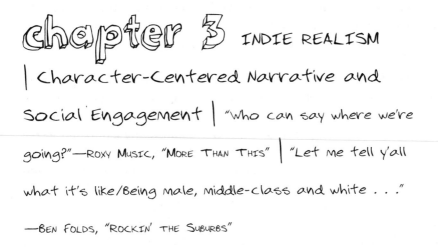

chapter 3 INDIE REALISM

Character-Centered Narrative and Social Engagement | "Who can say where we're going?"—ROXY MUSIC, "MORE THAN THIS" | "Let me tell y'all what it's like/Being male, middle-class and white . . ."

—BEN FOLDS, "ROCKIN' THE SUBURBS"

One distinction at the heart of indie culture is between mainstream and alternative aesthetics, which includes not only patterns of textual representation but also conventions of understanding these patterns and their significance. Different films and filmmakers, and different contexts of production and reception, offer different versions of these aesthetics, such that they appear in different configurations historically and according to differences within indie culture. Indie cinema is thus clearly not one genre that can be understood according to a unified set of widely shared and recognized formal and interpretive conventions; but within the discursive construction of indie culture,[1] a number of strains of filmmaking do cluster around such conventions, and this chapter is concerned with one strain in particular, which has a long history in alternative cinema: dramas and comedies that tell stories about fairly ordinary people in recognizable places and situations (like the suburbs in 1996's *Welcome to the Dollhouse* and 1998's *Happiness*), typically in the present day or else in a familiar nostalgic past (*Dazed and Confused* [1993], *Slums of Beverly Hills* [1998], and *Adventureland* [2009] capture the years of their creators' fairly recent coming-of-age, which presumably were also the same years for many in the audience). Conventions of representation of setting and human behavior in this kind of film are typically naturalistic. Characters have no magical powers, no exaggerated bravery or intellect or sexual attractiveness, and the world they live in follows the same rules as the world we know from real human experience. A significant objective of the narrative representation seems to be capturing recognizable, typical lived experience.

One kind of prototypical indie film is this kind of personal, "small" film, and this kind of cinema occupies much of the idea of indie in the popular imagination. In 1989, *sex, lies, and videotape* set an example for many to follow; despite a marketing campaign heavy on suggestiveness, the film is mainly about people talking about themselves and each other. But it had many antecedents in realism and modesty of means in prominent films by the likes of John Cassavetes, and in art cinema imported from Asia and Europe. Films in this realist mode have been essential in the careers of many more indie directors in the Sundance-Miramax era such as John Sayles, Todd Solondz, Miguel Arteta, Allison Anders, Ang Lee, Gus Van Sant, Jim McKay, Kevin Smith, Wayne Wang, David O. Russell, Neil LaBute, Susan Seidelman, Richard Linklater, Alexander Payne, Sofia Coppola, Noah Baumbach, Nicole Holofcener, Terry Zwigoff, Whit Stillman, Wendy Reichert, Tom McCarthy, Rahmin Bahrani, and the Mumblecore group. And the cultural prominence of indie cinema is increased every time a film in this style such as *You Can Count on Me* (2000), *Lost in Translation* (2003), *Sideways* (2004), or *Precious* (2009) is nominated for a major award, as happened regularly in the late 1990s and 2000s when the mini-majors pushed their "quality" offerings with festival buzz and late fall release dates on nominating committees. Films about ordinary people's day-to-day lives can be relatively cheap to produce and lend themselves to the kinds of performances that win accolades and impress festival and art house audiences.

Such comedies and dramas fit into a mode of storytelling and representation that we ordinarily call realist, a difficult and ambiguous designation but one which best captures the value of representation in such films. A great many widely admired indie films have mined this territory, offering their audiences representations of life as it is lived—through adolescence, young adulthood, marriage, family, school, home, work, romantic relationships—the stuff of ordinary people and their indiscretions, foibles, and minor-key victories. And it is precisely this quality of ordinariness—of human life as a daily adventure just as worthy of our interest as the heightened spectacles of the megaplex—that gives this strain of indie films their value in relation to studio films. The ending of *Lost in Translation*, a bittersweet embrace before the final parting of a mismatched romantic pair, captures this emotional register well. There might be elements of quirk (a railroad-obsessed dwarf protagonist in *The Station Agent* [2003], Natalie Portman's "manic pixie dream girl"[2] in *Garden State* [2004]) or profound trauma (sexual assault in *Boys Don't Cry* [1999], paralysis in *Passion Fish* [1992], HIV infection in *Kids* [1995]), but the narrative plays fairly straight by engaging with the emotions at the heart of people's relationships and daily struggles.

Sometimes narratives like these might seem to be devoid of genre conventions such as those found in more recognizable popular entertainment forms such as the horror or action film or musical comedy, and this lack of generic framework is a significant part of their appeal. These films have no diabolical villains and virtuous heroes, no high-stakes plotting (certainly not in early, tone-setting expository sequences), no supernatural interventions, and little of the "eye candy" that sustains the summer blockbuster market. Comedies lack the outrageous dimension of more studio-initiated efforts as the typical Adam Sandler or Will Ferrell vehicle; indie comedies such as *Sideways* and *Kissing Jessica Stein* (2001) offer more low-key and sophisticated, or at least less broad, forms of humor. But indie realism still encourages its own expectations and patterns of meaning, and we can understand its appeal by examining these as they function within the culture of indie cinema to produce distinction in relation to the studio film. One way in which this distinction is often framed is within a comparison between Hollywood and Off-Hollywood in terms of plot and character, and the relative centrality of each of these, with indie cinema's investment in realism aligning with an interest in character, and in particular with certain kinds of characters and characterizations.

Each of these two categories can be conceived of using vivid prototypes. On the Hollywood side is the big genre blockbuster with high-concept visuals and heroic, conventionally attractive protagonists played by bankable stars. On the Off-Hollywood side is the small drama or light comedy about ordinary lives filmed on a modest budget with less expensive talent (or with mainstream stars building acting credibility while publicly forgoing the perks and wages of Hollywood production) and less aggressive combinations of sounds and images. In the collective imagination of indie culture, this difference spells a significant gain for indie culture when considering its implications for character. Whether or not these prototypes effectively capture the range of Hollywood and indie cinema—they leave out Hollywood's modestly budgeted dramas and comedies and also visually and aurally high-concept indie films like Tarantino's—they stand for a powerful way of thinking about American cinema in general, and about indie cinema in particular. So even if a distinction between plot-driven blockbusters and character-driven indies is a somewhat misleading and unsophisticated simplification, it still has an important rhetorical function, encouraging us to think about different films (and kinds of films) in certain different ways, and it holds up more than a little bit to critical scrutiny when properly qualified and thoughtfully considered.

The first part of this chapter offers a model for understanding indie realism as distinct from canonical, mainstream narrative practice in terms of character superseding plot, i.e., as a style of storytelling; and as a rhetoric, appealing to the audience according to certain acknowledged terms of address. This first part considers *Walking and Talking* (1996), a typical realist indie comedy, as an example of character-focused indie storytelling. The second part of the chapter covers three films in depth in terms of their characters and characterizations, analyzing the ways in which indie realism works to foreground and emphasize character: *Lost in Translation*, *Welcome to the Dollhouse*, and *Passion Fish*. These four films are not necessarily representative of all indie realist works, but they are intended to illustrate some of the most important principles of narrative construction, thematic meaning, and rhetorical appeal in this strain of American cinema.

Studio vs. Indie as Plot vs. Character

Many attempts to encapsulate indie cinema in a brief, succinct definition have resorted to some variation on the notion of Hollywood films suffering for being plot-driven while indie films, by positive contrast, are valued for being character-driven.[3] Filmmakers and critics alike point to the heavier investment of independent cinema in characterization as a means of distinguishing Off-Hollywood from Hollywood narrative practices.[4] Indie filmmakers are thought to devote more of their interest to character, and to make films whose characters are thus more interesting (whatever that might mean: perhaps more thought-provoking, lifelike, or surprising), than those of main-stream cinema. Whether this is true or not—and I'm not sure how one measures the comparative interestingness of characters—a rhetoric of difference on the level of plot and character sustains the construction of indie cinema as a distinct alternative to studio filmmaking. Along with this distinction runs another, between plot-driven filmmaking as a technically sophisticated mode of spectacle subordinating nar-rative, and character-driven filmmaking as by contrast technically re-strained, grounded more in traditional storytelling values than whiz-bang computer-generated effects and sensational excesses of sound and imagery. The films that emphasize visuals are positioned accord-ing to this dichotomy as less invested in a cluster of narrative values: not just in character as its own kind of narrative appeal but also in verisimilitude and social engagement. According to the terms of West-ern film culture, we expect much of Off-Hollywood cinema to be the antidote to the expensive spectacles that please the large, young mul-tiplex audience, and one means of distinction from such offerings is in forms of storytelling, in this putative emphasis of character over plot.[5]

This contrast between plot and character is an oversimplifying di-chotomy to be sure; the Hollywood formula—to the extent that such a thing exists—cannot really be fairly described as giving character short shrift. [6] As David Bordwell argues in *The Way Hollywood Tells It*, conventions of studio storytelling include elaborate character jour-neys such as the one he describes for *Jerry Maguire* (1996).[7] Main-stream screenwriting advice always puts great emphasis on character as a key element of a good story, and the canonical scripts offered as models, such as *Chinatown* (1974), *E.T.* (1982), and *Tootsie* (1982), obviously have vivid, well-developed characters.[8] But whether or not textual scrutiny of Hollywood films bears out the contrast, a sense of indie cinema's comparative character-centeredness persists and re-mains a central facet of the rhetoric that sustains the category of indie cinema, a rhetoric that thrives on dichotomy.

One central function of character-centered kinds of storytelling in indie cinema is to orient attention—within the critical context of indie culture—to topics or themes raised in indie films, and in particular to issues of social experience and identity, which returns us to the sig-nificance of realism in the mainstream/alternative cinema dichotomy. Characters in such films are understood to stand as emblems for their social identities, and within a larger cultural and artistic discourse of multiculturalism, indie cinema's representations of the specificity of character experiences illuminate the distinctiveness of these social identities. This was a central part of the construction of independent cinema when it emerged in the late 1980s as an alternative not only to Hollywood's forms of production and narrative structure but also in terms of its ideological function of normalizing the dominant male, white, middle-class identity position. Thus in addition to the ubiquitous auteurism of independent film discourses such as articles and books in the popular press, the value of indie cinema is often located in the ethnic/racial and gender/sexual identities of filmmakers and characters. The title of John Pierson's *Spike, Mike, Slackers & Dykes* makes clear this emphasis on identity, combining the auteurist approach to identity (Spike and Mike) with the multiculturalist (Lee represents African-American and Moore represents working-class culture, while slackers and dykes are themselves terms marking identities one would not find represented in mainstream cinema).

Social identities are those identities shared among significant and well-recognized groups of persons, such as sexual and gender identities; racial, ethnic, national, and regional identities; and identities of age or generation. To say that narratives make characters emblematic of their social identities is simply to identify how characters are made to stand for who they are within a narrative representation: working-class postadolescent white men in *Clerks* (1994); bohemian Austin oddballs in *Slacker* (1991); a bourgeois East Coast family in *Rachel Getting Married* (2008); a suburban middle-school girl in *Welcome to the Dollhouse*; sexually precocious, lower middle-class young teen girls in *Thirteen* (2003); upper-crust Manhattan trust fund kids in *Metropolitan* (1990); a rich Southern California housewife in *Safe* (1995); middle-class heterosexual men in the films of Neil LaBute. The whole Mumblecore cycle of the late 2000s has taken as its central subject the interpersonal dynamics of the milieu of its creators, post-college young adults adrift among the creative class.

It might seem as though the emphasis within a multiculturalist discourse on social identities would produce an indie cinema with an emphasis on underrepresented groups such as ethnic or sexual minorities, which we sometimes find in films such as *Chan Is Missing* (1982), *She's Gotta Have It* (1986), *Daughters of the Dust* (1991), *The Living End* (1992), *Mi Vida Loca* (1993), *The Wedding Banquet* (1993), *Go Fish* (1994), *Smoke Signals* (1998), and *Boys Don't Cry*.

In the 1980s and 1990s, independent cinema was more closely associated, especially in critical discourses, with multiculturalist "outsider" voices and the challenge they offered to a white, straight, male-dominated mainstream society and culture. But while the centrality of this socially marginal position might have lessened over time in indie culture, as independent cinema became more visible and firmly situated within art house film culture, the interest in identity as such continues to be a key focus of indie cinema and culture's meaning-making. Indeed, the focus on the identities of filmmakers, the largely white, urban, and middle-class identities of much of the writers, directors, and other creative personnel active in American filmmaking, is still of central significance to indie culture. The interest in identities transcends the specifically political agenda of increasing representations of the underrepresented, and as much of the community of filmmakers and audiences is hegemonic rather than subaltern, we find a preponderance of films about the identities of the relatively socially privileged in the indie cinema of the 1980s, 1990s, and 2000s.

Thus to say that indie culture is socially engaged can mean different kinds and degrees of interest in the social world. In some instances, such as John Sayles films like *Passion Fish* and *Lone Star* (1996), it means the specifically progressive, political forms of social engagement that we ordinarily think of in relation to artistic representations called "socially engaged," such as the German New Objectivity and French Popular Front movements, and protest music and culture of the 1960s-era counterculture. This is part of the "cinema of outsiders" tradition, one integrating regional (non-Hollywood and non-big-media-city productions) film, feminist film, and new black and Queer film, all of which are given chapters in Emmanuel Levy's *Cinema of Outsiders*. But more fundamentally, social engagement as a focus of storytelling and its reception implies no necessary critical political content or progressive cultural agenda. In the realist strain of indie cinema, one focused on character and the appreciation of how identity is explored in narrative, social engagement might more often be drained of much of its political meanings and impacts and thus fail to pose any challenge to hegemonic social institutions and roles.

Of course Hollywood studio films are also in some sense about social identities. Romantic comedies are about relationships between male and female characters, and action-adventure films typically focus on masculine hero/villain dyads, often with a component of ethnic coding for good and bad characters as in the *Rambo* and *Indiana Jones* films, heroicizing white American heroes by contrast with ethnic others.[9] Mainstream culture can also engage socially, and reflect on the politics of identity, though this seems hardly central to its usual agendas. The distinction between character-driven and plot-driven constructions of characters, realism, and social engagement has to do with the relative emphasis and dominance of meanings within critical and cultural contexts rather than with clearly marked territories of textual conventions and production practices. It is crucially within reception practices that the dichotomies sustaining indie culture are most centrally established and circulated, in the emphasis on interpretive thematic meaning alongside the conventional pleasures of entertainment.

Even if it is drained of the progressive political implications usually associated with the term *social engagement*, indie cinema's realist, character-focused strain still does function to produce and sustain notions of differential value Thus a character/plot dichotomy implicitly carries a political valence in a certain sense of cultural politics, of opposing one form of cultural power (mainstream Hollywood cinema) with an alternative: because characters are positioned as emblems, and mainstream plots are by contrast seen as merely the vehicles on which to hang spectacle, the investment of indie cinema in character is not merely a matter of formal distinction from a different mode of filmmaking, not merely a textual tendency, but a kind of advertisement of moral virtue. Being character-centered thus connotes engaging with life as it is lived in historically and geographically specific contexts, and perhaps being concerned with dynamics of power and inequality therein. This does not necessarily mean that character-centered indie films are didactic, preachy, or overtly political in their rhetoric. Some of them are sometimes, but for the most part they emphasize characters in their social specificity without making this too obviously part of a political or moral agenda—as is true of subtle, artful narrative generally.

Thus this chapter is concerned not so much with defending the idea of indie films' characters as superior to those of studio films as with understanding this rhetoric of indie cinema's character-centered storytelling and its functions both textually and in indie culture. This is a rhetoric of difference that works to position different forms of

American cinema in relation to each other in order to establish their relative value and appeal.

I say a rhetoric of difference, rather than simply a difference, not because I mean to cast doubt on whether indie films are really, truly, adequately different. Rather, by addressing this chapter at a rhetorical process I mean to seize on the importance of differentiation for the construction of indie cinema as a film culture. Indie culture generates this rhetoric of difference around storytelling and makes it a salient detail of film aesthetics that works to maintain categories of film production and reception. One way this rhetoric works is by positioning a certain mode of storytelling in cinema as realist. (Other, more formalist, ways this rhetoric works are addressed in chapters 4 and 5.) This means that producers and audiences alike think of this type of film as realist (whether or not they use the term/concept *realism* as scholars might), and that realism is central to these films' cultural circulation even if it does not function as an industrial genre label along the same lines as comedy or drama. Understanding character-centered realism as a rhetorical appeal rather than a genre defined strictly by textual characteristics allows us to see the functions of the realist text in relation to its audience's appreciation of it, and more generally of the cultural circulation of media. At the same time, of course, there are textual characteristics that encourage a mode of appreciation we can call realism, and identifying these characteristics in relation to this mode of appreciation will be one task of what follows. It will be helpful at this point to clarify what we mean by realism, and what kind of relation to the real and to other forms of narrative deemed comparatively less real we might find in indie cinema.

Indie Realism as Realism

Realism has a long history in the arts. Naive observers might think of realism as those representations which are somehow closer to being real than other, more stylized ones, a notion demolished in structuralist and poststructuralist cultural theory.[10] The standard approach to realism in cinema studies is well summarized: "Realism is now considered to be a matter of form, with a very debatable relationship to the real."[11] Although one might think of realism as an absence of style—as the capture and representation of reality in artistic media—most serious critics and historians of the arts take the opposite position and think of realism as a style, or rather as a series of historical styles in various media. For example, Jeanne Hall argues that the Direct Cinema of the early 1960s Drew Unit, far from offering an unmediated representation of reality (whatever that might be), was actually a style of documentary with its own typical employment of camera and editing techniques.[12] At the time of its creation, Direct Cinema appealed as having greater realism than other modes of cinema, but seen in its historical contexts we can understand how specific applications of technique encouraged the audience to appreciate these films as concerned with the representation of reality. Such films today seem hardly more true-to-life in their treatment of actuality than many other forms of mediated representation.

The realism of past eras can appear to viewers at later times as highly conventional, losing its connotations of immediacy and the effect of verisimilitude. For instance, method acting of 1950s cinema, such as James Dean's "You're tearing me apart!" performance in *Rebel Without a Cause* (1956), looks and sounds more melodramatic than realist when judged next to contemporary performance styles. This is evidence that what appealed as fresh, bracing realism at one time will likely seem stylized, even trite, by the standards of another. It's hard now to see how realist painting of the nineteenth century might have any closer resemblance to reality than many other styles, from Impressionism to Photorealism. Cinematic movements called realist such as Neorealism and Poetic Realism are encapsulated in film historiography as styles, with conventional visual and narrative attributes. As Kristen Thompson writes of *Bicycle Thieves* (1947), realism is closely tied to the conventions of the times.[13] To the 1947 spectator, Vittorio De Sica's film might have appealed as realist because of its difference from certain prevailing conventions, but a film adopting the same style a decade later would have had a harder time appealing as realist. Realism is the product of a rhetorical process—within given production and reception contexts, certain artworks may appeal as realist—rather than a necessary relation between reality and representation, which is naturally greater in realist than in nonrealist artworks.

We can consider indie cinema's character-centered strain as a style that appeals as realism, understood as character-focused storytelling set in recognizable, familiar locales, within the context of indie culture. But from the standpoint of narrative analysis we must be careful to avoid seeing character-focused storytelling as a self-evident category, especially given the positive moral and aesthetic valence that indie culture places on this dimension of cinematic narrative. Any cursory consideration of how narrative really works must conclude that character and plot can hardly be so easily divided as appeals, given how tied up they are in one another. Indeed, the character/plot dichotomy recognizes implicitly that character and plot work as a dynamic pair, that one is essential for the other and that they are always bound together in the most basic work of storytelling. But it also implies a sort of see-saw effect whereby an emphasis on character can mean a de-emphasis on plot; an emphasis on plot can mean a de-emphasis on character. They still require each other, however, as Henry James's famous formulation makes clear: "what is character but the determination of incident? what is incident but the illustration of character?"[14] This is to suggest that incident has a function reducible to another (characterization), and that character should ultimately be the agent of any significant narrative development. But it also bespeaks the impossibility of reducing one narrative element to the other.

Because the rhetoric of indie culture is dichotomous, positioning indie as an alternative, the distinction between Hollywood's plot-driven storytelling and indie cinema's character-driven alternative functions rhetorically. It is precisely by diminishing the importance of a certain kind of plotting that indie realism gains its advantage. This is a clearly relational conception of realism—realism means little and has little cultural value absent a comparative context. Realism thrives on difference, within a given context. Thus the rhetoric of realism, the appeal of texts as realism, meshes with a cluster of textual techniques and conventions to distinguish one kind of cinema from another.

In the case of indie films that emphasize character over plot, the point is not that the films have no plot or little plot, or that the audience treats the plot as somehow extraneous to characterization. It is, rather, a matter of dominance and subordination.[15] When character is dominant, plot becomes relatively subordinate. The best model for how plot drives the construction of narrative in popular cinema is that of classical Hollywood as theorized by Bordwell, Staiger, and Thompson.[16] Note, however, how much of this model requires certain conceptions of character: goal-orientation, for instance, is a description of plot in terms of character. Events of the narrative are in service to the character's pursuit of a goal. Deadlines and appointments structure the character's time along this pursuit. Causality in classical Hollywood is understood to be character-centered: if the movie culminates in a dramatic chase, the hero is the one who prevails by dint of his wits and skills. But all of these characteristics, which balance plot and character to some extent in Hollywood storytelling, function well with characters who can be relatively thin and generic. The clarity and redundancy of classical narration require characters with small numbers of traits. But this does not mean the characters of classical cinema are uninteresting. After all, we have to care about them enough to keep watching the movie they are in. It means, rather, that the narration tends not to emphasize characters in relation to the plots whose actions they typically drive through their actions.

Character is emphasized, though, in an absence of—and at the expense of—hard-driving plot with clear, high dramatic stakes, and without the forward-driving tricks of classical plotting such as suspense-building scene-to-scene hooks and goal deadlines.[17] In films with a slack time frame, in which characters pursue goals without fixed time frames or goals without clear markers of fulfillment, the audience's attention is managed differently than it is in the classical, mainstream movie. As Kristin Thompson observes, "one thing that sets art-film narratives apart from classical-style ones is that often the protagonist in the former is under little time pressure to accomplish his or her goal."[18] In this regard, indie realism may often be closer to art cinema than classical style. Many of the most beloved independent films fit this description: meandering narrative, built up out of well-observed scenes pitched as straightforward realist drama or light comedy, episodic in construction, often beginning and ending to some extent in medias res. That is, the plot has a beginning and an end, but the world of the narrative seems merely to go on independent of its narrative representation. These films have conventional exposition and several more degrees of closure than more challenging or experimental films like *Inland Empire* (2006). They have endings: lovers part, a trip ends or begins, someone gets married. But they also leave things loose at the end, suggesting that life goes on.

David Bordwell says of realist postwar international art cinema that films often "trace an itinerary,"[19] and the realist strain of indie cinema often functions in similar ways to realist art films from De

Sica and Rossellini to Bergman and Truffaut, to more recent examples from Iran and Taiwan. In *Lost in Translation* a pair of Americans feeling alienated by travel in Japan connect across a series of encounters. It seems they might be falling in love. After a few days, one of them leaves for home. In *Away We Go* (2009), a couple soon expecting their first child traipse from city to city across North America, from Colorado to Montreal to Miami, in search of a place to settle down. In *Sideways* a pair of friends meander from winery to winery, chatting up women and arguing. Some films follow a "slice-of-life" formula by focusing on a single day (*Clerks*, *Kids*). Films about weddings concentrate their action around a weekend of family drama in which everyone knows the plot—the couple marries, everyone celebrates—and in which the interpersonal character dynamics are our central focal point (*Monsoon Wedding* [2001], *Margo at the Wedding* [2007], and *Rachel Getting Married*).

Walking and Talking: Realism, Narrative Form, and Character Emphasis

Whatever their temporal scheme, character-centered, realist indie films typically connect their events loosely. *Walking and Talking* describes not only much of the action of the Nicole Holofcener film of that name (as well as her later film *Lovely and Amazing* [2001]), but countless "small" films about ordinary people. Other films might better be called "Walking and Not Talking," especially if they are about lonely solitary figures like the protagonist of *Wendy and Lucy* (2008).

Walking and Talking is a good representative of the kind of narrative development and form to be found in indie realist films. It is a film about two straight women struggling to maintain a friendship as they pass through the typical events of their late twenties adulthood—in particular, romantic partnership and marriage, which serve to distance female friends from each other and divide them. By considering its dramaturgical shape we can see the way the realist idiom of indie cinema foregrounds—and backgrounds—various elements of its narrative, in particular character emphasis as its own appeal.

This film has a meandering plot centered around women, Laura (Anne Heche), who is in training to be a psychotherapist, and Ameila (Catherine Keener), who works at a newspaper in the classifieds department. Laura's life is more organized, and in an early scene this contrast between the women is cemented as she gets engaged to her boyfriend, Frank (Todd Field). One of her first thoughts after accepting his proposal is about her best friend and the effect that the engagement will have on her feelings. She thinks aloud, "Shit, how am I going to tell Amelia?"

Amelia reluctantly goes on a couple of dates with the clerk from her video store, Bill (Kevin Corrigan), who she and Laura nickname "the Ugly Guy," a moniker reflecting more on Amelia's character than on Bill's—Amelia is so hapless she must lower her standards and date men she hardly finds attractive. The first third of the film alternates between Laura's happy relationship and Amelia's more lonely, desperate single life. Amelia's cat has cancer, and news of her best friend's impending marriage, the film suggests, launches her into demoralizing self-pity. Though she has recently decided to quit therapy, she reverses course after hearing Laura's news and tells her therapist she wants to return, only to hear that he has already given her hour to another patient.

Amelia takes Bill home one night after a date and has sex with him. Afterwards while she is in the bathroom with the faucet running, the phone rings in the living room and the answering machine picks up. Bill, standing shirtless in the living room, hears Laura's voice recording a message in which she says she can't believe Amelia is still out with "the Ugly Guy" (fig. 3.1). Amelia is unaware that he hears this message or even of the message's existence—he deletes it and leaves abruptly without saying why. The next part of the film concerns Amelia's worry over why Bill never calls her, and Laura's frustrations with Frank. He has some obnoxious habits and their sex life is predictable. She starts seeing a coffee shop waiter on the side.

Amelia asks her ex-boyfriend Andrew why they broke up, and he says she made him too important and relied too much on him. This upsets her so she storms out of the grocery store where they are shopping. She proceeds unsuccessfully to stalk Bill. She gets angry at her therapist in her final session. Laura counsels her to put the sick cat to sleep. Amelia's life seems seems to be falling apart: her pet is dying, her best friend is getting married, she feels abandoned by her therapist even though it's her fault for quitting therapy, and an "ugly" man she barely even likes much won't call after they sleep together once. She finally goes into the video store and makes a scene. She asks Bill why

FIGURES 3.1 Bill, "the Ugly Guy," discovers how Amelia thinks of him when he hears Laura's telephone message, which she cannot hear. She will not know why he stops paying attention to her.

he hasn't called her. She yells in front of everyone that they had sex. On the street outside he tells her he had heard her friend's message and erased it. Amelia realizes she is to blame for the failure of this relationship. This deepens her pathos and self-loathing.

The setup of the film, approximately its first half hour, articulates clear character traits and relationships and situations, but those goals that are presented are rather general and their pursuit is hardly systematic. The expository portions of any film set up the audience's expectations for everything that is to come after and give us indications of what to pay attention to. In the first act of a canonical Hollywood screenplay, the characters are presented not only in terms of their traits, relationships, and situations but also in terms of specific goals and subgoals with well-defined helpers, obstacles, and antagonists, not to mention deadlines. These techniques focus the storytelling and the audience's attention and function to drive narrative forward and engage interest and suspense. In *Walking and Talking*, the goals such as they are are largely internal (to be happy or fulfilled) and vague (to be successful romantically while also maintaining friendship). Events are linked by patterns of action and reaction, cause and effect, but loosely and without the tight focus on clear goals and obstacles of more canonical narratives, such as the pursuit of a villain seeking to harm a victim, defeating a rival at a contest or competition, pulling off a deception or scheme (a common romantic comedy device), or making it to a certain place at a given time.

The canonical classical film, with its organization into acts with their patterns of rising action, raised stakes, dramatic reversals, and shifting goals, is typically tightly causal. Scenes advance goals or sub-goals, answer questions posed in earlier scenes, and convey new narrative information. Perhaps the most essential task of the canonical storyteller is constantly winning back the attention and interest of the audience, which tightly causal narration effectively accomplishes. Causality in classical cinema and canonical story formats more generally is character-centered.[20] Events do not merely happen to our protagonist; he or she initiates actions central to narrative events, reacts to events to bring about new ones, and ultimately is the agent of many of the narrative's most central events. In her study of storytelling in recent Hollywood cinema, Kristin Thompson argues that the most significant large-scale structure of classical narration, the act, is defined by character goal-orientation.[21] Thus narrative structure in mainstream cinema is constructed around active central characters in pursuit of specific and well-identified goals, and shifts from one act to another are accomplished through the achievement, deferral, redefinition, and introduction of these goals. Every scene ideally functions to propel narrative forward, which means pushing characters along their pursuit of goals and their overcoming obstacles to achieving them. One metaphor often used for this element of classical cinema is the "causal chain": an earlier scene leads into a later scene through devices of linkage. B occurs because of A, C occurs because of B, D because of C (or A), and so on. An act is made up of a series of linked scenes all of which lead toward a common goal. This gives classical cinema a sense of forward-driving momentum most evident in high-impact sequences such as chases and confrontations.

The character-centered narration of much art and indie cinema often diminishes the centrality of this kind of causality, and while hardly absent—characters are still goal-oriented; narrative events are still causally linked—the structures of the classical film are less significant. Goals are less clearly articulated and may seem vague by comparison with those of mainstream cinema, as is the case in *Walking and Talking*. Events are often linked by temporal succession (this follows that chronologically) as they are by linkage in a causal chain (this follows that as a necessary outcome of one from the other). Episodic narration, as in picaresque tales of heroes encountering situations seriatim in which one does not necessarily follow from or build upon the last, offers a succession of events. One marker of episodic narration is that the basic meaning of a story would still be comprehensible if some of the events were rearranged, as Thompson argues is the case in the classical Neorealist film *Bicycle Thieves*, especially in its later scenes after Ricci has seemingly given up on finding the bicycle and turns his attention to his relationship with his son, Bruno, after the scare in which we fear Bruno has fallen into the river. Scenes following this have a more episodic quality than the earlier sequences of pursuit and chase. Tightly causal narration, by contrast, cannot be so manipulated without a loss of sense. In television series, for instance, serialized narratives such as soap operas are typically more tightly causal than episodic narratives such as sitcoms. Sitcoms can often be viewed out of order without a loss of sense. There is no natural propensity of either episodic or tightly causal narration to be more character-centered—it's not as though sitcoms have a greater purchase on reality than soap operas. But in art and indie cinema, as in other narrative genres, a rhetoric of realism has attached to episodic narration as a function of distinction between classical or mainstream storytelling and alternatives to it.

The action of *Walking and Talking* rarely proceeds according to necessary linkages of tight causal unity, and when there are links from one sequence to the next they are often de-emphasized thematically. Part of the film involves Amelia's pursuit of the Ugly Guy, a fairly conventional pattern of goal-orientation. But after finally getting Ugly Guy to talk to her again, he tells her he is seeing someone else and that ends that, and the causal chain merely ceases midway through the film. On a number of occasions Laura gets angry at Frank and they part, and she even has an affair with another man, and yet at the end of the film they are about to get married though we have seen no reconciliation between them. Near the film's end, Amelia goes back to sleeping with her ex-boyfriend Andrew, though this is not the

FIGURE 3.2 Laura and Amelia recognize each other's feelings, reinforcing the film's emphasis on female friendship.

outcome of any pattern of pursuit and active anticipation between these characters, who are friendly throughout the film, yet we hardly hope they will become a long-term couple. Although it ends on the day of Laura's wedding and seems to be anticipating this event more than any other, the film's most dramatically resonant and powerful scene is shortly before that, between the two women. After Amelia's cat dies, Amelia confronts Laura for shutting her out, for putting distance between the two of them. They recognize each other's feelings, apologize, say they love each other, and embrace. This makes clear that the friendship between the women, rather than their relationships with men, is the film's real dramatic core (fig. 3.2). Yet there was never any clear sense in the film's expository scenes that the goal-orientation of Amelia, as the film's most central protagonist, was around the reinforcement of her friendship with Laura. The narrative stakes are never presented in such a way as to make us fear for the continuation of the women's friendship, which is often presented as secondary to the women's relationships with men. This is part of the film's message about female friendship and gendered identity—that women, who invest so much in their friendships with one another, ultimately wind up sacrificing these relationships for conventional heterosexual pairings.

Realism in a film like *Walking and Talking* is thus as much a product of narrative form as it is of locating the action among recognizable character types and settings. It relies on the delay and attenuation of forward-driving, suspense-generating character goals, which are general and interior, having to do with the happiness of characters with their lives rather than any particular external achievement (though success in a romantic relationship would be welcome for Amelia, its nonachievement is as much a positive resolution as the opposite might be). *Walking and Talking* thus demonstrates how patterns of temporal design are a central feature of the rhetoric of realist drama and comedy. Temporality, as one aspect of narration, can be ordered and represented in various ways, and *Walking and Talking* exemplifies how many indie realist films approach narrative time as linear and fairly episodic as a function of their realist rhetoric.

Although it does not necessarily have a present-day setting, the typical realist indie film is a product of the here and now, a portrait of characters in a definable present moment. *Walking and Talking* is set in a recognizable contemporary New York City. Verisimilitude is a central value. "Genre" films can more easily depart from representing times and places that seem familiar. They are more likely to jump around in time, to complexify their storytelling with convoluted plot structures and the mind-bending storytelling tricks that often make up part of the appeal of noir and science fiction. The indie realist idiom, however, is marked by a general linearity of narration. Consider two of the most influential and paradigmatic indie films, *sex, lies, and videotape* (1989) and *Pulp Fiction* (1994). *Pulp Fiction* is a good example of another tendency of indie narration: play with form. Its genre foundations are in crime fiction and cinema. Although set in a recognizable present-day Los Angeles, it makes little attempt to capture life as it is lived in the here and now. Part of its narrative sophistication is its jumbled storytelling (a topic to come up again in chapter 5). *Sex, lies, and videotape*, by contrast, exemplifies the "little" indie film that exceeds expectations, a realist drama about "the way we live now" in which characters are portrayed with psychological depth—they talk at length about their own feelings and psychology—and verisimilar detail in diction, costume, and setting. A central part of the appeal of indie cinema as an alternative cinema springs from the idea promoted through the successful launch of films such as *sex, lies* that "small" stories about ordinary people's lives can be just as engaging and worthwhile as more lavish big-budget spectacles. One way of capturing this sense of the representation of the ordinary is by focusing on the linear and relaxed flow of events in a setting recognizable in place and time and thus familiar to audiences. This of course follows a long tradition in storytelling arts of distinguishing serious, literary, and elite forms from those of mass and popular culture.

Canonical Narration, "Good Stories," and Artful Variations

Researchers in narratology and related fields argue that in the Western tradition, qualities that make for a typical story, and more importantly for a good story, include a central protagonist, the pursuit of a goal, the overcoming of obstacles, and narrative resolution. This "canonical" story format, moreover, conforms to the Aristotelian division of narrative into three parts, which go by different names in different accounts, but which obviously align with the three-act structure of mainstream screenplay advice manuals and industry conventional wisdom. We might call these the beginning, middle, and end; or exposition, complication, and resolution. In experimental research, subjects have been found to comprehend stories better when they conform to this canonical format, and to remember stories in this format even when their events are represented differently.[22] A crucial aspect of Western narrative aesthetics is thus the problem-solving protagonist and the focus of the story around this character's highly focused activities. According to such aesthetics, every episode in a narrative should function in relation to this problem-solving agenda. The idea of a schema, moreover, implies that this format is not merely a common structure in narrative texts but a mental structure, a set of expectations common to Western narrative audiences which shapes experience of narratives. Narratives in a given culture conform to schemata, which audiences apply in making sense of them. Narrative schemata are as much cognitive as textual.

In its commercial imperative of appealing as widely as possible, popular story forms such as those of classical Hollywood cinema build on expectations about storytelling with deep cultural roots. Western traditions of storytelling have a history thousands of years old, and it is from this tradition that the basic building blocks of specific popular narrative forms emerge. The divergence of "realist" narrative modes such as those of indie cinema can serve multiple functions in departing from orthodox canonical storytelling. Thus one simple and straightforward value of episodic narration can be located in marking indie cinema as alternative, in the value of differentiating Off-Hollywood from Hollywood. But other functions can explain the loosening of causality. One is to give the effect of narrative hewing more closely to a shared perception of human experience rather than to an artificial story format. An effect of realism can be the product of loosened causality if it helps to convey the rhythms of everyday life. Episodic narratives might seem to have some of the qualities of the quotidian in which events seem to be "one damned thing after another" rather than a tightly plotted drama of cause and effect. If character-centeredness is itself a point of pride for indie cinema, and if part of the realist rhetoric of indie culture is socially progressive, then the loosening of causality can function to direct the audience's attention to character as socially emblematic and intensify the connection between character and identity.

Narrative researchers further describe qualities that make people ordinarily more likely to judge a story to be good. Studying child language development and storytelling skill, Nancy L. Stein finds that narratives of increasing complexity are often judged to be "better" examples of stories than simpler narratives.[23] Stein argues that complexity in this context means not intricate plotting or extensive intermeshing of character relationships, but merely the inclusion of certain canonical elements that make for something more elaborate than mere description. In order from less to more complex, Stein moves through a number of dimensions of narrative: centering on an animate being (character), temporal and causal relations of events, goal-orientation, the presence of an obstacle to the goal, the inclusions of an ending to the story, and the inclusion of "complete and multiple episodes." Thus a narrative with only an animate being and temporal and causal relations is judged less complex, and thus a less likely candidate for being a "good story," than a narrative that also includes goal-orientation and obstacles.[24]

In the case of indie cinema in a realist, character-centered mode, we have to shift our conception of "good story" to understand the function of loosening of causality and attenuation of goal-orientation. In the context of research into real-world oral storytelling, "good story" might mean a good example of a story, or a story well worth telling or hearing in a social setting. Meandering, slow-paced, low-conflict, or episodic stories might not function well as stories in social settings compared with more canonical examples. But within the institutions of commercial cinema, difference from canonical story formats—however incremental and circumscribed—can function in a number of significant ways as an appeal in its own right. Conforming less to the standard notion of what makes a "good story," realist dramas and light comedies offer themselves as more lifelike and less formulaic (perhaps less storylike) than mainstream cinema. They also position their own aesthetic in counterpoint to that of mainstream cinema, making narrative form into a point of difference and distinction in relation to a dominant other.

And yet the realist indie film is not without its own kinds of causally linked, suspenseful plotting. For instance, *sex, lies, and videotape* eventually turns from a loosely plotted character study into a story of betrayals and confrontations, with suspense raising the pitch of the drama significantly compared with early sequences (will John find out that his wife Ann has made a tape for Graham confessing her innermost sexual urges and experiences, and will Ann find out that John has been sleeping with her sister Cynthia?). *Kids* starts off with slack-paced observational scenes aiming for a slice-of-life, real-time portrayal of its subjects. There is much walking and talking. After the film's initial mood- and tone-setting sequences, however, and especially in the film's second half, rather conventional plotting kicks in. We learn that Telly (Leo Fitzpatrick), the boy who aims to have sex with many pubescent virgins, is HIV positive, and a girl he has infected, Jennie (Chloë Sevigny), is trying to find him to let him know before his next conquest harms another innocent girl.

One variation that we often find, then, marking realist indie narration off from classical Hollywood is the delay or retardation of the suspenseful, high-stakes plot. Mainstream screenwriting emphasizes quick and strong narrative hooks, first acts that introduce conflict early on and seize the audience's attention forcefully. Indie films in the realist mode are typically much more elliptical early on, more likely slow-paced, and oriented more around establishing characters, settings, and moods than around clarifying the conflict and the narrative stakes.

There are two distinct but interrelated rhetorical strategies of indie realism to be traced in the analyses to follow. One is the relaxation of canonical narrative structure by the use of devices such as delayed exposition and lower-stakes plotting to lessen the impact of forward-driving suspenseful narration and thus orient attention more on setting and especially character (which is defined in part in relation to setting). The other is the emphasis, within this special focus on character, on the social identity of the protagonist (or protagonists) as a central theme of the narrative, anchoring the meaning of the film. The two are connected, insofar as the relaxation of narrative structure in less canonical stories functions in certain contexts to orient attention on characters in all of their social specificity.

Lost in Translation: Parallel Lives and Loose Plotting

Sofia Coppola's second feature, *Lost in Translation*, offers an example of how patterns of exposition and conflict shift interest from the causal chain of classical, "good" storytelling, to characters (and settings that help define them), shifting the attention of the audience from the hard-driving forward momentum of suspenseful canonical storytelling to the more slack, day-by-day existence that can seem typical of real-world experience. The filmmaker herself has testified to the character-centered dominant of her film, telling an interviewer that "the story has no plot."[25]

Lost in Translation follows a number of patterns in its narrative unfolding. It traces a series of encounters between two Americans in Tokyo, the middle-aged fading Hollywood star Bob (Bill Murray) and the aimless recent college graduate, Charlotte (Scarlett Johansson). It begins by forming its narrative around alternation. The iconic opening shot sets the film's title against the reclining form of the film's female lead, shot from behind to frame her lower torso and legs but withholding her face from our view. After fading to black for a few seconds, our next view is of Bob, his eyes closed, en route from the airport to

FIGURES 3.3 AND 3.4 Parallelism between Bob and Charlotte is established compositionally, by framing both characters with closed eyes against nighttime Tokyo cityscapes with moody, colorful lights out of focus.

his hotel in downtown Tokyo, and after opening his eyes he wordlessly takes in the bright-lights imagery of the nighttime cityscape.

The film's expository sequences reveal each character in turn: Charlotte is bored and alienated, as well as sometimes sad and lonely. Her young husband, a photographer, has come to Tokyo on an assignment and pays too little attention to her; she seems to have few friends in Japan and little purpose to fill her time. In one early shot she is awake from insomnia and sits in the window of her hotel room, the colorful lights of the city out of focus in the background. Bob is likewise lonely and alienated. We see this clearly in an early shot on an elevator, as his gloomy, jet-lagged face contrasts against those of the Japanese businessmen, all of them much shorter than he is, who fill the space. Bob suffers the self-inflicted humiliation of selling his image for a big payoff from a Japanese whiskey company, Suntory, for use in their advertising. He is also seemingly at an emotional

distance from his wife and children back in the States—in one opening scene he is handed a fax from his wife which tells us he has for-
gotten his son's birthday. In the opening scenes, Coppola alternates
between each character's solitary pain.

Another narrative rhythm established early on is parallelism.
Both Charlotte and Bob are lonely and frustrated, and the patterning
of alternating scenes functions to establish the congruity of the two
protagonists and their journeys. Both are Americans in Tokyo, both
have trouble understanding the local culture, both seem unable to get
enough sleep (perhaps a consequence of adjusting to the time difference), and both, the film frequently suggests, are turned off by the
vapidity and superficiality of show business. They are also paralleled
visually, as both are framed with eyes closed and away from the camera against a window through which we see the colorful Tokyo lights
in moody bokeh shapes (figs. 3.3 and 3.4).

Charlotte's husband wants to spend time with a young American actress in Japan to promote her new movie, and Charlotte obviously considers this woman to be beneath her. Bob is faced with an arrogant young director shooting his Suntory commercial and whose lengthy verbal notes to Bob are barely even translated to him. This darkly comical sequence establishes at once the debasement of the aging Hollywood star selling his image for an ad campaign, the fish-out-of-water sense of the American stuck in a place where he cannot understand anyone, and the specific self-loathing of this character who finds himself unable to connect meaningfully with any person in his social environment. Both characters seem to be stuck in somewhat unsatisfying marriages and both seem to need the attention and affection of another person who will understand them.

Flouting our canonical schemata, the film establishes no clearly defined, specific external goals for either character to drive the narrative forward. At one point Bob tells someone over the phone, "I've gotta get out of here as soon as I can," meaning Japan, we are to suppose. But he never seems eager to return to his family in the States, and he agrees to stay on longer to do a television interview, suggesting that he is just as happy to be away from his family as with them, even if he suffers the social dislocation of being a foreigner in Japan. A typical scene is one in which we observe behavior which, while goal-directed, might have no significance to the long-term trajectories of the characters. For instance, in one scene reminiscent of Chaplin in *Modern Times* (1936), we see Bob struggling to slow down an elliptical trainer exercise machine on which he seems to be stuck moving much too fast. This functions to symbolize his frustration, and the fact that no one is ever around who understands his needs and can help him, and it encourages our sympathy with him. But the scene is of little relevance to other events of the plot.

What goals there are function more as psychological clues to understanding the characters than as plot devices to motivate causally linked actions. Rather than following from cause to effect in a tight chain, the film is highly episodic, moving along a series of encounters and excursions around Tokyo which lead mainly in the direction of the characters growing closer. As spectators we formulate questions about the characters, and this motivates our continued interest. We wonder if each character will stay with his or her spouse. We wonder if they will really fall in love with each other, as seems possible (and desirable to us). But there is no scene in which these outcomes are posed as questions with absolute answers or deadlines by which time decisions must be arrived at.

Compared with canonical narratives such as the typical classical Hollywood film's, there is not even all that much conflict or drama in the first half of the film. There are arguments between Charlotte and her husband, and tense conversations between Bob and his wife. But the relationship between Bob and Charlotte, as it begins to be established, consists of a number of casual conversations and outings. There is one scene in which events push in a specific direction more than any other. In the hotel's lounge, Bob is sitting alone while Charlotte across the room is suffering the company of people she doesn't like. He catches her eye and she walks over to his table. He jokes that he is organizing a prison break and asks if she is in. She agrees to go off with him, but they make no specific time or place to leave, and the plans hardly seem to go beyond the common desire they articulate to escape their figurative prison. This leads to the characters going out later to bars and to sing karaoke. Essentially, the goal articulated in the "prison break" scene is for the two characters to do things together, which leads toward their series of excursions in the second half of the film. To the extent that this is goal-orientation, the goal is achieved right away and there are no evident obstacles to it.

Only in the final scenes of the film does anything like conventional conflict and drama appear. Bob goes to bed with a woman more his own age, the chanteuse from the hotel's lounge. Charlotte appears at his door to see if he wants to go to a restaurant and hears the other woman. This provokes her jealousy, and when they eventually do go out for dinner together she speaks to him sarcastically, mocking his age and his has-been status in show business. Soon afterwards it is time for Bob to leave Tokyo, and his goodbye with Charlotte is rather cool. She is still, seemingly, mad about his tryst with the older woman, and she leaves him quickly, the elevator doors closing behind her right away as she parts. As Bob is driving away toward the airport, he has his car stop so that he can return to find Charlotte, who happens to be walking outside in a busy street. They embrace and Bob whispers something in Charlotte's ear, which the audience cannot hear (fig. 3.5). He kisses her on the lips and then on the cheek amidst the crowd of city dwellers moving about the city. This is the emotional culmination of the characters' relationship, their final

FIGURE 3.5 The ending of *Lost in Translation* is moderately ambiguous.

connection, their mutual realization of deep friendship. Although they kiss, and although it is clear in this moment that they love each other and recognize each other as soul mates, the scene never has anything like an erotic charge, and the ambiguity around the words spoken leaves open several possibilities of closure, none of which the narration fixes as a concrete meaning. Whatever the words, the characters' connection to one another is expressed in an embrace which brings them together as deep friends rather than passionate lovers. There is no note of frustration over the failure to consummate the relationship sexually. This is the film's closure: Bob and Charlotte part as the closest of friends, but also likely recognizing that they will never be together.

Unlike more romantic films such as *Before Sunrise* (1994), another meandering, episodic character-focused narrative, *Lost in Translation* does not make a parting of lovers the least bit tragic, and the mood of the ending of *Lost in Translation* is hardly even marked by pathos. Rather, one feels the satisfaction of seeing characters recognize a common bond. The ending is hopeful but not triumphant, and although the characters must part despite their love, they do so without overwhelming sorrow. The ending mixes complicated, conflicted feelings about friendship, love, and human connection. It is not so outlandishly ambiguous or open-ended like more radically challenging art films; rather, it is negotiated in its stance toward the characters. Perhaps they cannot be together, but that's life sometimes, and it's good that they had the time together that they enjoyed.

This means that *Lost in Translation* functions as a representation principally of characters and their relationship with one another rather than of characters' actions in pursuit of external goals. Whatever their external goals may be, the film never makes them explicit, never addresses them directly. Whatever goals we can infer pertain more to internal than external states. They want to be happy, to feel the pleasures of real human connection, perhaps to find fulfillment in life. It can be hard to pin these desires down, when no clear textual evidence determines what they may be. Unlike more plot-heavy canonical narratives, films like *Lost in Translation* focus the audience's attention on expressive moments. A number of these that reveal the characters' interiority especially well are performances of songs. The Hollywood actress claiming Charlotte's husband's attention is represented in a negative light when she performs an inauthentic drunken rendition of a cheesy pop song. By contrast, Charlotte's choice of karaoke, the Pretenders' "Brass in Pocket," gives her more credibility, and her vulnerable but campy performance in a pink wig endears her to Bob. She articulates her own self-importance but also her interest in Bob when singing to him, "I'm special, so special/ I gotta have some of your attention, give it to me."

But the key moment of karaoke is Bob's pained, tone-deaf warbling of Elvis Costello's "(What's So Funny 'Bout) Peace, Love, and Understanding" and Roxy Music's "More Than This" (fig. 3.6). This musical performance solicits our sympathy for Bob and encourages us to feel, with Charlotte, that he is a man worth caring for—that he suffers alone, but is capable not only of introspection but also of raw self-expression. In the Elvis Costello song, he sings of "searching for light in the darkness" and of "pain and hatred, and misery." And in "More Than This," he sings to Charlotte, showing her his vulnerable, pained face, earnestly hoping for her affection and understanding. He sings of the present moment, defining himself: "More than this—there

FIGURE 3.6 Characterization by karaoke, effective as realism because the context is not so goal-directed.

is nothing." Also of his uncertainty, which he shares with Charlotte, about the future: "Who can say where we're going?"

Precisely because these scenes of character expression and revelation do not function as nodes in a tightly causal and focused goal-directed plot, they draw our attention to character as its own narrative appeal. Realism, and character-centered realism in particular, thus appeal to the indie audience by contrast with another form of narration, and by adopting its own storytelling form that lends itself to emphasis on vivid, lifelike characters whom we are made to feel we know and understand intimately.

Welcome to the Dollhouse: Emblematizing the Outsider

Todd Solondz's *Welcome to the Dollhouse* offers us some of the same lessons as *Walking and Talking* and *Lost in Translation*. It too begins with expository sequences that are less focused on defining clear major goals and obstacles and more centered on characterizing a protagonist, in this case Dawn Wiener, a troubled, pathetic, and mistreated middle-school girl in suburban New Jersey. Like many films of the indie realist strain—and unlike *Lost in Translation*—*Welcome to the Dollhouse* eventually abandons its slack, episodic pattern of narration for more goal-oriented suspense. Even though it does eventually find a fairly conventional melodramatic plot in late segments, however, it's important to remember that the audience's expectations and their understanding of the characters are set early on, during more character-focused sequences which establish the mood of gloom and frustration surrounding the protagonist, while the action unfolds in a linear succession of naturalistic scenes. In the case of *Welcome to the Dollhouse*, the plot kicks into a higher gear when Dawn's sister Missy goes missing more than halfway through, and Dawn disappears as well looking for her. But rather than focus only on the expository and narrational aspects of its realism, I want to isolate *Welcome to the Dollhouse* as an example of a film that encourages a reading of its main character as an emblem of her social identity, in Dawn's case the awkward adolescent alienated from all of the social institutions within which she has no choice but to live, especially school and family. One point that seems especially significant about *Welcome to the Dollhouse* in terms of its emblematizing identity is how thoroughly white and middle-class this identity is, while at the same time the film aims for a sense of universal adolescent angst to resonate with a largely adult indie film audience. This film also shows the necessity of balancing two storytelling imperatives while pursuing the rhetoric of indie realism: the central character must be presented as a unique individual to be a vivid, interesting character, but she also must be in some important ways typical of her role and social position. *Welcome to the Dollhouse* thus balances the particular and the universal, the person and the group, the specificity of one character's suffering with the humanist recognition that coming of age has its inherent traumas.

A Hollywood genre film might make the situation of *Welcome to the Dollhouse* into the foundation for a teen makeover comedy in which any awkwardness is easily overcome, or a horror film literalizing the metaphor of adolescence as grotesque hell. A typical realist indie film makes the exploration of social identity itself, within its usual settings, central without resorting to working up fantasies of transformation or transgression. Solondz told an interviewer that his

FIGURE 3.7 The opening scene of *Welcome to the Dollhouse* establishes Dawn's outsider identity.

inspiration in making *Welcome to the Dollhouse* was the success of the nostalgic television series *The Wonder Years* (ABC, 1988–93), which he said "didn't speak to anything real in my experience. I hadn't seen an English-language film that dealt with this material in an honest way that captured that period of life."[26] *The Wonder Years* was a mainstream representation of adolescence and coming of age depicting children's formative years in the upbeat, lessons-learned tone of prime-time network television. *Welcome to the Dollhouse* is a more frank and disturbing portrait of youth, thus distinguishing indie cinema against mainstream media culture by its eagerness to engage with reality rather than idealize or mystify it. It aims to portray a darker portrait of the middle-school years, and it does so principally through its characterization of the central character.

The opening shot of *Welcome to the Dollhouse* scans a school cafeteria with a slow pan, surveying the space, resting on the image of Dawn duplicating its gaze out into the crowd (fig. 3.7). In subsequent shots, we see several vacant seats being claimed by other kids. No one notices Dawn or offers her a place. Then she asks to sit at a table at which a sullen girl, Lolita, is eating alone. As the scene progresses, a group of popular girls—cheerleaders—approach and taunt Dawn by calling her "lesbo," and Lolita, who might have seemed possibly sympathetic, reverses our expectation when she joins in their cruel talk. This brief sequence of shots is a remarkably rich bit of expository narration. These first moments give us the character and her world. This is accomplished by the casting of Heather Matarazzo, an awfully gawky-looking adolescent, but also via other details of the mise-en-scène such as décor, facial expressions, and costumes. The film encourages us to fill in Dawn's psychology, to imagine her thoughts and feelings when faced with such a situation. Immediately, then, the film solicits our sympathy for Dawn as an outsider, and cues us to understand her character in opposition to the hostile world she faces. Our assumptions about middle school as filled with in some ways troubled or uncomfortable youth, as a site of the routine humiliations of adolescence, are confirmed by the abjection of Dawn's pathetic gaze out into an environment in which she finds no good place for herself. All of this is conveyed in an exchange of looks within a recognizable social context.

We also encounter Dawn in the setting of her suburban family home, especially after school and at family dinners. A pair of dining room scenes function to establish her character especially well, making clear that her alienation in the school setting is easily matched by her experience at home (fig. 3.8). In one scene her mother demands that Dawn tell her little sister, Missy, that she loves her. When Dawn refuses she is punished by having to sit alone at the table all evening. In another her parents demand that Dawn dismantle her backyard clubhouse to make room for a party, and when she refuses they withhold dessert from her and she has to watch as her share of chocolate cake is divided among her eager siblings. In both scenes, Dawn sits stubbornly, defiantly, showing no signs that she considers capitulating to make her life easier. She is a sympathetic antagonist, always pitted against someone she irritates or upsets or enrages.

The film makes clear that, in some ways, Dawn is no different from the rest of the cruel and selfish kids depicted, suggesting situational causes for Dawn's suffering. As a running motif, she is often shown treating others in ways she personally finds hurtful. The cheerleaders call her "lesbo," and at dinner that night she calls her younger

FIGURE 3.8 The dinner table, another site of alienation for Dawn.

sister Missy "lesbo." Brandon, the bully who later becomes her friend, mouths "fuck you" at her during detention, and at dinner that night she mouths "fuck you" at Missy. Late in the film she also insults her only friend, Ralphie, repeating the other kids' taunts of "faggot." Dawn's brother, Mark, treats her brusquely, ordering her out of his room. In turn, Dawn tries to treat Missy the same way. Watching the film, every time you start to sympathize with Dawn's suffering, she turns and tries to inflict the same treatment on Missy or Ralphie, the only two characters who are smaller and weaker than she is, neither of whom seems to suffer as Dawn suffers. The film implies that name-calling, taunting, insulting, and teasing are normal behaviors among middle-school students, opening up the most unpleasant aspects of this age for the audience's consideration.

However, the film constantly isolates Dawn and makes her seem to be in some sense responsible for her own suffering. The situations in which Dawn teases and bullies others are different from those in which she is teased and bullied. She never does any of these things in school. Furthermore, despite this behavior, Dawn is still more of a victim than any other character. Only Dawn has her locker vandalized and only she is given an insulting nickname, "Weiner dog," that even the other social outcasts use against her. This suggests that on the school's social ladder she is at the very bottom. She is the only one without a seat in the cafeteria, the only one taunted by the cheerleaders, and the only one victimized by spitballs during the class assembly.

She is also portrayed as uniquely hapless. She is given a detention when Brandon tries to cheat by looking at her test, and then gets a D-minus because, she says, of being upset by the incident. She asks the teacher if she can retake the test, and for that is assigned as punishment a 100-word essay on the subject of dignity, which in a scene of painful indignity she is forced to recite before the class. She is showered with spitballs during the assembly, but the one spitball she fires back is the only errant one, finding its way into a teacher's eye. When the family watches a video of the parents' anniversary party, everyone is impressed by Mark's amateurish musical performance and at Missy's cloying cuteness, but they all laugh at the one image of Dawn—a bit of cruel physical comedy in which she is shoved into a wading pool and falls splashing on her backside. Everyone worries when Missy is kidnapped, but when Dawn disappears for a night to search for her sister, no one seems to miss her.

Dawn has a strong desire to be popular, to fit in, to be liked, to have friends, and to have a romantic relationship with a boy. But she lacks self-knowledge in certain important respects, which contributes to her misfortunes. She fails to see that her backyard "special people's club" is laughable and that she would not make a suitable romantic partner for the much more mature Steve. When she tries to look sexy for him by wearing tight pants and a skimpy top, she seems to have debased herself in a way that she doesn't recognize. She also can't see that her dinner-table battles against her parents are doomed to fail. Any punishment only seems to strengthen her defiance, while as spectators we wish for her sake that she would just capitulate. As one who suffers constantly, she often fails to take opportunities to ease her own suffering.

Being socially awkward and being a social outcast obviously feed into each other, and if nothing else this film is a study of this character type, the unfortunate preadolescent outsider. Dawn's lack of self-awareness also feeds into her social status and vice versa. At the same time, however, some of her personality traits seem to defy her situation. Why is she hopeful of having a romance with the older and more mature Steve when she has never had a romantic relationship with any boy, when the boys in her school either ignore or taunt and tease her? In the film's final scene, why isn't she happy to be part of a class trip to Disney World that gets her away from her family and her school environment? On one level, Dawn's lack of self-awareness is a facet of her social outsider identity. If she were more aware, she would be able to fit in better. On another level, though, this trait is a hindrance to her ever escaping herself, which would be her only possibility for change. It cannot be explained only by her situation, but functions to maintain her personal hell of adolescence. In other words, Dawn is presented in some ways as a unique individual, and in other ways as emblematic of a whole class of persons—a group identity. But I argue that her unique individuality makes her a more vivid exemplar of the group identity. It makes her stand out as an especially acute type of unfortunate suburban, white, female middle-schooler, and the audience can fasten onto her and identify their own experiences with hers without necessarily having ever been quite—or nearly—so outcast and depressed themselves.

There is tension at the heart of the social rhetoric of realist indie cinema between the unique individuality of characters on one hand, and the impulse to regard characters like Dawn as emblematic outsiders and representatives of a whole class of persons (suburban adolescents and social misfits). It is only by making characters well individualized that they can function as a central appeal of indie aesthetics, because character-focused narratives need boldly individualized protagonists to appeal to their audience with a rhetoric of realism. And it is by being so well drawn and individualized that characters can function rhetorically as emblems. Dawn Weiner can stand for every preteen misfit, especially for the idea of adolescence carried as memories of challenging coming of age as recalled by an older indie audience. This despite her clear differentiation from the rest of the film's characters, for the sake not only of clarifying her own significance and emblematic status but also of telling a good story about a compelling, unique individual.

During the film's final scene, with Missy recovered and order restored, Dawn is on a school trip with her singing group, the Hummingbirds, en route to Disney World. The children sing together as

FIGURE 3.9 Even on a trip to Disney World, Dawn is a figure of pathos.

their bus rolls along, and Dawn sings their cheerful theme song along with her classmates without expressing any joy or enthusiasm in contrast to the lively body language of others (she is still an outcast, never overcoming her situation), which underscores the pathos of her character and the centrality of the struggle to fit in to her characterization, and to our idea of adolescence as a social identity (fig. 3.9).

Even at the moment that ought to seem like a final respite of pleasure, of upbeat hope and even modest improvement for such a troubled character, Dawn still, as ever, suffers. In considering this concluding image it pays to consider again Solondz's reaction to *The Wonder Years*, a representation of childhood that evokes quite different feelings from *Welcome to the Dollhouse* with its halcyon days nostalgia, its yearning for a lost, innocent happiness. The social realism of Solondz's bitter note amidst an ostensibly positive scene of this ending on the bus is offered as the antidote to the idealization and distortion of reality in one mainstream other, the sitcom, with its routine of problems solved, of weekly happy endings. Dawn's affect emblematizes the adolescent outsider who, amidst the comforts and joys of an American, middle-class, suburban upbringing, finds little about which to be genuinely happy. This film thus distinguishes itself as social realism not only by subverting a formal expectation of canonical Hollywood storytelling, a certain kind of ending and a thematic note of hope and community (another narrative device indie realism shares with art cinema), but also by emphasizing a telling moment of character psychology and not an achievement of a narrative-spanning, suspense-driving goal. The film ends as it begins, picturing Dawn Weiner as a prototype of the tortured middle-school outsider.

Passion Fish: Marginal Identities and Pleasant Surprises

John Sayles's realist drama *Passion Fish* focuses, as does *Walking and Talking*, on female friendship, but unlike the other examples thus far, *Passion Fish* does make more marginal identities central in its thematic configuration. In Sayles's typical fashion, in *Passion Fish* we see more of a progressive, multiculturalist agenda at the heart of realist indie aesthetics than in our previous cases. This exemplifies the possibilities within indie realist aesthetics for a mode of representation to be considered socially engaged in the more typical, political sense.

The use of cinema as an instrument for the promotion of civic engagement—rather than "mere entertainment" as in the masscult Hollywood mode disdained by indie's champions—requires a mode of representing the issues that matter to the artists eager to promote their causes. Since the 1980s, one of the central tropes of progressive social activism in general has been identity politics, and in particular the promotion of multiculturalism, diversity, and tolerance as liberal-humanist virtues. Sayles's oeuvre announced its commitment to the left side of American politics from the beginning with *Return of the Secaucus 7* (1980), a nostalgic and wistful baby-boomer film about the alumni of 1960s-era counterculture movements, reflecting on their missed opportunities and post-coming-of-age struggles. In subsequent films he turned his eye on labor history in *Matewan* (1987), race relations in *Brother from Another Planet* (1984), and urban politics in *City of Hope* (1991). *Passion Fish* continued his interest in leftish topics, this time regional and racial identity politics (which he would go on to explore further in *Lone Star*, among others), making his approach more personal by considering a quiet, domestic, and regional topic, painting on a deliberately small canvas, as a way of exploring gender and racial social structures and their limitations and possibilities for the individual. The characters in *Passion Fish* have on them several burdens: of standing for their respective and various identities, and also of transcending them so that they do not come across as thinly drawn symbols. Sayles has the task of distinguishing his characters from those of typical mainstream cinema to gain the distinction of independence, but also a complementary task of making his characters speak for roles they take from a society in which identity is a matter of struggle and negotiation. *Passion Fish* is thus a film about gender and ethnic and regional identities, not just a film about a black woman and a white woman set in rural Louisiana. It is also about physical ability and disability and about the identities that are products of various kinds of physical and psychological impairments. Its setting in the Louisiana bayou is a constant contrast against the northeastern big city where one main character, May-Alice (Mary McDonnell), a paralyzed soap opera actress, has previously lived. Femininity and female friendship is also a persistent theme. But the relationship between the white and black women, and between the disabled patient and the able nurse, who turns out to suffer from her own kind of disability in the form of addiction, makes race most central in the film's constellation of thematic meanings.

Passion Fish appeals as realism in a number of related ways. Like *Walking and Talking*, *Lost in Translation*, and *Welcome to the Dollhouse*, some of these have to do with narrative structure. The plotting in *Passion Fish* is quite slack, and especially in the first half or more of the film, goals are loose, deadlines are nonexistent, and storytelling is episodic. Parallelism often substitutes for forward-driving plotting. This of course works to emphasize character and setting at the expense of plot, and functions within the rhetorical appeal of realism as character-focused. But narration also functions to withhold certain key bits of narrative information, details of character background that change our perception of the central figures in the film. Narration also delays plotting, as in *Kids* and *Welcome to the Dollhouse*, so that more melodramatic sequences are held off until later in the story. In combination with these narrative strategies, *Passion Fish* allows us to consider its characters' identities in unpredictable ways—just as the storytelling surprises us, so do the characters as emblems of their identities. Like *Welcome to the Dollhouse*, we see a tension between unique individuals and social identities, which enriches our sense of the latter.

Passion Fish also marks itself as realism, as did *Welcome to the Dollhouse* in relation to *The Wonder Years*, by taking familiar thematic material and working to move it in an unfamiliar direction as a point of contrast against mainstream representations. The scenario of female friendship between a rich white patient and her black nurse might seem like material for a sentimental Lifetime movie or soap opera, but in the indie realist version we find something quite different. In differentiating itself from conventional melodramatic narrative, as in *Welcome to the Dollhouse*, *Passion Fish* marks its characters off from those of the standard generic types, as a way for indie realism at once to aspire to lifelike representation and mark its difference from studio films. The characters in this film appeal on the basis of their departure from type, both from the generic types familiar from movies, television, and other forms of media, and from social types familiar from the real world, types as general as woman and African-American and New Yorker and as specific as paraplegic and recovering addict and soap opera actress. The use of soap opera in particular and television in general within the narrative world of *Passion Fish* functions effectively, like the Rita Hayworth poster in *Bicycle Thieves*, to mark a distance from one representation to another.[27] The implied value of television, as a profession where May-Alice used to work and as a domestic appliance to help her pass the time after her injury, is established as inauthentic and contrived, as a waste of people's time and as an escape from reality. The film thus implies that its own narrative, by contradistinction, has greater authenticity, and in particular it is the characters who depart from melodramatic type to stand as more vividly lifelike figures.

There is no way a character can be utterly atypical, despite what filmmakers and admiring critics might sometimes claim. Every character is a combination of familiar and surprising materials. The effect of lifelike characterization must come not from total originality—not a possible or even likely goal for storytellers aimed at addressing real-world conditions—but from a combination of predictability and unpredictability. Donald Richie says of Ozu Yasujiro's characters that they seem real because, like real people, they can be complex and illogical.[28] Unpredictability is the opposite of formula, of predetermined outcomes. Just as characters surprise us, so does characterization— the process whereby characters are presented to the audience. For instance, Noriko's wedding, a crucial event in Ozu's *Late Spring* (1949), is never shown, and by withholding the information about her at this moment the film's characterization is creating a significant gap that we cannot fill in ourselves without interpreting beyond what the movie offers us.[29] The characters in *Passion Fish* and many independent films aiming at social realism are, like Ozu's, often waiting to surprise us. The art in their characterization comes from the tension between familiarity and freshness, between what we are made to expect and what we see instead.

A more typical, conventional approach to *Passion Fish*'s basic narrative materials—two women, one paraplegic and the other a recovering drug addict—might set specific goals and force difficult choices as a way of structuring the large-scale narrative. The Hollywood approach is to engage viewers with deadlines and appointments, structures of anticipation that focus the viewer's attention on what's next.[30] These are retardatory or dilatory devices; one does not introduce a bomb set to explode after 60 minutes only to cut ahead 59 minutes and 30 seconds. Roland Barthes' notion of a hermeneutic code, one that introduces questions or enigmas to be sorted out by the progression of a narrative toward its conclusion, implies the delay of the satisfaction of those questions and enigmas.[31] We might think of anticipatory hermeneutic structures as weak or strong. The ticking bomb or four o'clock train or election day toward which everyone is looking forward are most likely strong, but the more languorous and observational narrative design in many indie and art films, including *Passion Fish*, asks us to anticipate "what will happen?" without guiding our thinking too much by posing fixed alternatives (stay or go? wife or lover? city or country?) or deadlines.[32]

A movie like *Passion Fish* could easily structure its narrative with strong anticipatory devices, but it quite rigorously avoids doing so. For instance, near the end of the film—more than two hours into its running time—the producer of the show May-Alice used to act on appears, offering to bring her back to the television screen, an idea she considers with a degree of hostility (fig. 3.10). The choice this poses as the film approaches its conclusion, of whether or not to return to soap acting, would have a dramatically different impact if it were posed, say, halfway through the movie. In one more classical,

FIGURE 3.10 The soap opera producer shows up to offer May-Alice a possibility of returning to acting, but only approaching the film's end.

canonical film, *Meet Me in St. Louis* (1944), the impending departure of the Smith family from St. Louis to New York City is announced at the midpoint, and anticipation of this event and its consequences shapes every scene after that. But *Passion Fish* makes the stakes much less dramatic than those of *Meet Me in St. Louis*. We are never asked to consider the possibility of May-Alice taking any kind of work until this late stage, never asked to wonder whether staying in Louisiana is her best option.

The nurse Chantelle's story is similarly deprived of a strong anticipatory design. Played by Alfre Woodard, Chantelle emerges at the end of a sort of "bad dates" montage of nurse interviews, and we learn nothing of her past in the earliest scenes in which she appears—all we know really is that she is black, taciturn, and not obnoxious like the others. If we knew at first that she would be struggling to stay clean of drugs and that this would be a condition to meet if she intends to reclaim custody of her child, this would make for a much different movie. One significant function of suppressing these anticipatory structures is to ratchet down a certain kind of emotional engagement focused on specific hopes and fears and to direct our attention to other things, especially on the small details of the characters, their interactions with one another, and especially, as in *Lost in Translation*, on the parallelism between them. Each moment seems to bear its own weight more when it is seen less as one domino falling into the next and leading toward the inevitable final falling one, and more as its own object for our attention, like one bead along a string.

This is reinforced by the movie's episodic narration. In *Passion Fish* the narrative is presented as a succession of visits, none announced or planned for in advance, in which friends, acquaintances, or relatives drop by to see May-Alice (at first) or Chantelle (later on). With the exception of the soap producer who is the last to arrive, the purpose of these visits is never to present the characters with a choice or even a plan of action (unless you count a boat ride around the swamps of the area). Rather, each visit opens a window onto the characters, projecting us back into moments of their past. Although the film is strictly linear in its narration, these conversations take us back in time, by referencing past events (e.g., Chantelle's addiction) and by engaging our imagination about what life might have been like for the characters before the story began. These are ways of fleshing out characters and rooting them in a social world with distinct and sometimes shifting identities.

Many of these encounters probe the racial dynamics of the characters' world, effectively making the theme of racial identity more prominent in the film's narrative. For instance, the second visit after May-Alice's charming gay uncle (he is described as "literary," a code word) is a pair of sisters, friends from adolescence. Their names at once give away their provincial gentility: Tia-Marie and Precious Robichaux. As Chantelle serves them soup, they mistake her for domestic help and assume that her people had worked for May-Alice's family. They speak to May-Alice of African-Americans in racist terms, complaining that "ours down here certainly seemed to have caught an attitude." We understand in this brief exchange that May-Alice had seen her life as an escape from a benighted backwater for the more liberal and modern New York City of her adult years, and that she had reason to want to leave her home beyond merely desiring success as an actress or television star. At once we see a picture of her teenage years, her upbringing. This is fleshed out further when Rennie drops by, an acquaintance from those days (played by Sayles regular David Strathairn), who shared a mutual, unsatisfied attraction with May-Alice. His identity as potential but problematic suitor (he is married and has children) advances the promise to May-Alice of overcoming a social barrier of her childhood between rich and poor whites, her people and the "real swamp Cajuns," as she describes Rennie's family. These encounters are to show us that May-Alice's recovery must involve more than physical rehabilitation. She needs to overcome many kinds of difference: old and new, country and city, rich and poor, black and white, modernity and tradition, independence and dependence. These are presented as differences in identity. Later Rennie drops by to get her boat back in shape and offers to take her and Chantelle out to show them the neighborhood. Their dialogue reveals a central theme of the film:

> RENNIE: You never did like it much down here.
> MAY-ALICE: The place is all right. I just had problems with who people expected me to be.

The narrative of the film is the story of the realignment of May-Alice's identities, as this quotation implies. She is moving in the direction of liking it down there, but only by growing into an identity that combines her various roles in a way she finds acceptable and satisfying, and this includes her identities as a rich white woman, and now also as a disabled person.

Chantelle's visitors come later in the film, and they bring the movie's biggest surprises. Luther, a black man in dark glasses who introduces himself as "Bad News," arrives when Chantelle is away, and this narrational choice is strategic. When he encounters May-Alice instead, we share in her surprise (and perhaps her fear) when she sees him. Luther reveals that Chantelle is a recovering drug addict, and this comes more than halfway through the film. By withholding this detail, the film has deprived us of some of the drama it might have achieved earlier on. But it also affects the characterization of Chantelle. We do not type her initially as a druggie, as someone struggling against her demons. Her role initially is defined in relation to May-Alice: caregiver in relation to patient, black in relation to white, northerner in relation to southerner. We are more likely to explore the character's social identities as such in our engagement with the film as

FIGURE 3.11 Only when Chantelle (*right*) meets Dawn (*left*) and they discuss their upbringing, do we learn of Chantelle's upper-middle-class background.

they are revealed to us piecemeal rather than all at once. The effect of the surprise about Chantelle's past is its own kind of dramatic charge, and it forces a reevaluation of her character. We had thought of May-Alice as the one in need of recovery, but it is actually Chantelle just as much who is undergoing rehabilitation. This presents identity not as fixed or binary, but as multi-axial and dimensional, which fits well within a larger discourse of progressive multiculturalism.

A further surprise about Chantelle comes in the next visit, from the soap opera actresses. This is a sequence that works to reveal both main characters. In one moment in the kitchen between Chantelle and one of the women, an actress played by Angela Bassett, we learn that Chantelle came from a wealthy family and that her father is a doctor (fig. 3.11). This forces another revision of our typing. We might have assumed that a black nurse would be socially disadvantaged in various ways, but Chantelle seems more fully lifelike and three-dimensional once we learn that she is not as typical as we might have guessed.

These women's visit also clarifies the significance of May-Alice's trajectory from south to north and back again. The actresses are modern and sophisticated independent women, which is what May-Alice sought to become in moving away from home and achieving her professional success. But her independence was taken from her when she was injured, and to reclaim it she will need to do so through a return to her past, her roots, her people and land, and the things that originally made her who she is. The women notice, for instance, that her accent has changed when she pronounces Arthur "awthuh." What they see is May-Alice no longer covering up so much, no longer passing. We see that the modern, sophisticated, independent woman was a role she had put on because she didn't like the self she was expected to perform in her hometown. Now that she is reverting to old ways, there are new racial and class dimensions creeping into her self-fashioning. It is to underscore this point that Chantelle remarks of the change in accent, "May-Alice is turning back into a cracker."

The biggest surprise of the film comes when May-Alice hears an answering machine message from Chantelle's father discussing plans for a visit with Dinita, Chantelle's daughter. This comes at the 114-minute mark, as the film is approaching its dénouement. It is the final fleshing out of Chantelle's character, filling in her history just as previous visitors have filled in May-Alice's. But this surprise, like that of the soap actresses, reveals as much about May-Alice's character as it does Chantelle's. In particular, this revelation forces May-Alice to reconsider her role in relation to Chantelle. She now sees herself as a support system for her caregiver rather than seeing her caregiver as her support system. In order for Chantelle to proceed in putting her life back together, she needs her job, she needs May-Alice. This is the culmination of the film's role reversal, and it marks its most profound thematic statement as the white woman is now to be seen as the helper to the black woman rather than the other way around. A mainstream Hollywood film might never challenge our original understanding of a character's typing. Characters might change and grow, but in the classical paradigm their traits are small in number and redundantly represented (unless some are suppressed for a big plot twist, as in *The Da Vinci Code*, 2006), and transformations in a character most often require the discovery of a true self à la *Jerry Maguire*.[33] *Passion Fish* works rather differently. The film introduces types only to multiply and subvert them. Chantelle is a black nurse, but also an addict, and also well-to-do (in terms of her family). May-Alice is a rich white paraplegic, but also a drunk, and also a photographer, and also a real friend to her caregiver, no longer merely a white employer of black labor but, as the symbolism of the film's final shot announces, happily in the same boat with a close friend. This is a way of underscoring the outcome of the question the film poses at the end—will May-Alice stay or go?—but it is the culmination of a whole film of encounters in which these women's characters are slowly and often surprisingly revealed. This is a pattern supported by episodic, character-focused narration.

A pattern of unannounced visits supports a certain kind of characterization in which surprise is a key element; surprise in turn allows for a kind of freshness and vitality to the presentation of characters while still engaging in the emblematizing of social identities such as race, region, ability, and gender. But in favoring an episodic approach, *Passion Fish* departs from a mode of narration more standard of narratives that tell similar kinds of stories, especially melodramas.

A melodramatic mode of narration in which our knowledge of events is unrestricted and open might favor a pattern in which characters discuss events before they occur and then reflect on their meaning afterwards. This pattern, which we might call recursive narration, is the standard format of many feminized forms of storytelling (i.e., forms that *Passion Fish* resembles or invokes), such as films known as "women's pictures," daytime television dramas, and reality shows like *Laguna Beach* (MTV, 2004–2006). Recursive narration is a powerful way of establishing and reinforcing character emotions. We know how a character feels in relation to an event and this helps us to formulate our own feelings of sympathy or empathy in response. Discussions in an event's aftermath further reinforce these emotional responses and underline the meanings of a narrative.

Passion Fish avoids both of these conventional structures and by doing so allows for characterizations that are more likely to surprise us; this facilitates reading them as realistic. The non-recursive structure does not necessarily cut off any reference to earlier or later events in the film's dialogue; May-Alice's injury and disability is an obvious example of material that is frequently mentioned. But few scenes are focused on anticipatory or reflective discussion. This is a function partly of the device of the unannounced visit. It is a significant narrative strategy to diminish the significance of plot in the film. It is also

FIGURE 3.12 Chantelle (*left*) and May-Alice (*right*) listening to Rennie while on their boating excursion.

a function of the topics characters discuss in their encounters, such as events in the distant past, like May-Alice's childhood. In scenes between Chantelle and May-Alice, there are occasional moments of recollection and analysis of these visits, as when May-Alice compliments Chantelle for her help making Tia-Marie and Precious leave the impromptu lunch at which she serves the soup in impersonation of a domestic servant, performing a kind of southern blackness that is actually alien to her nature. But seldom do they prepare for an event in a way that enhances our anticipation of it. The exception to this is the boat outing with Rennie, and this is a special moment as it again gives us a window into the character's past, as we see May-Alice reverting to schoolgirl ways, worrying over what a boy might think about her (fig. 3.12). Perhaps Sayles makes this exception here to underline the significance of the scene to come, to mark it off against the others. This would make sense because it is while on their boat trip that we get the scene in which the film's title is invoked, and this is an anticipatory moment. Rennie has caught a fish and, following Cajun custom, he opens it up to see what's in its belly, claiming that this is a way of seeing a person's future. Inside the fish's belly is a pair of passion fish, and he tells each woman to hold one in her hand and think of a person who they hope will give them some loving. Chantelle thinks this is corny and May-Alice finds it embarrassing, since it is obviously Rennie whom she will think of. But the greater significance of the fish as a motif is that there are two of them in that fish's belly, and that they represent the two women of the film. It is ultimately each other from whom May-Alice and Chantelle get the most important love. The subtlety with which this is presented is the opposite of the kind of obvious and overt recursive narration typical of more conventional feminized forms.

The combination of episodic and non-recursive narration, which play into one another, means that each event in the narrative of *Passion Fish* stands on its own more than fitting into a linked chain of inevitable developments. This allows for certain patterns to emerge. Rather than consequential actions, we get more parallelism between May-Alice and Chantelle: eventually we see that each of them is in recovery, each one needs the other, each is wary of entanglements with men, and each is in search of something. And rather than a certain kind of emotional engagement in which the film solicits clear hopes and fears in relation to the characters' outcomes, we have a more distanced, reflective emotional rhetoric which encourages our feeling with the characters but not as a product of specific outcomes like the choice to return to work, which the film saves for the point at which our engagement with the characters is already essentially accomplished.

Like many films admired for their realism, including several by directors discussed above (Ozu and de Sica) and *Lost in Translation*, *Passion Fish* ends without resolving all of its questions. Life goes on, the realist film says, and we capture that by leaving some loose ends. *Passion Fish* is constantly offering us comparisons between the dual protagonists, and one of special significance is that both become involved with men of somewhat questionable suitability. Chantelle has a fling with Sugar, who has children by various women and seems too charming to be authentic although he is authentically charming. May-Alice and Rennie seem to be exploring a relationship that means more than just friendship, though the film never represents a physical or sexual encounter or suggests that one takes place. But the real relationship of the narrative is between the women, and it ends with them together, with May-Alice telling Chantelle that she is going to have to learn to cook. Cooking is a motif that runs throughout the film. Chantelle serves Campbell's soup to Tia-Marie and Precious because she doesn't know how to make anything else, and they perceive this as gauche, which delights May-Alice. Sugar Ledoux, the black cowboy working on seducing Chantelle, feeds her his own cooking, a court bouillon, during one of their first encounters, and this is a signal of his interest in her. At one point, May-Alice tells Chantelle that in Louisiana everyone knows how to cook, clarifying that this is a matter of regional identity that transcends race, class, and gender; reiterating this as the film's last line indicates that both women are claiming an identity connected to the place that May-Alice had once rejected. And yet their friendship, strong as it may be, cannot be a substitute for the love of family and is a happy-sad ending in the manner of Douglas Sirk, since it leaves a part of each person unfulfilled. We don't really know what will happen to May-Alice and Chantelle, and *Passion Fish* does not make it seem as though they might have formed a feminist utopia by film's end. The solution to their problems seems tentative and temporary. This is a progressive way to conclude, to think positively about social change but to acknowledge the reality that any progress is most likely to be partial and that more always waits to be done. By concluding on such a note, the film gives the audience a feeling of resolution to some of the narrative's problems but not all, and withholds the rush of emotional release that more conventional mainstream narratives promise in their often contrived happy endings.

Along with the tendency toward measured emotional rhetoric and restrained gestures, the film's camera style also keeps us at a certain distance, choosing at key moments to keep faces offscreen or in distant framings when showing them might seem emotionally overwrought, a device also used in certain moments of *Lost in Translation* and *Welcome to the Dollhouse*. For instance, in the film's opening sequence in the hospital, we see May-Alice interacting with various personnel but we see only her face, never theirs. This cuts off the possibility of our sympathizing with their reactions to her injury and condition, and works as a distancing device. The surprises of the film's storytelling structure do a similar thing, and this kind of narration is something we can rightly think of as character- rather than plot-centric. It works within the conventions of socially engaged realism that help indie cinema craft its appeal.

Conclusion

In the examples considered above, as in many independent films of the Sundance-Miramax era, character functions as a central appeal. These analyses have been offered as models for understanding the value of character-centered narrative forms that integrate thematic interest in identity with specific storytelling strategies. I argue that this combination functions rhetorically, within the contexts of indie culture, to appeal as a more realistic mode of storytelling than mainstream cinema, and to distinguish independent film artistically, especially in relation to Hollywood blockbusters. The point has not been that the typical multiplex film is devoid of interest in character. This hardly seems like a credible notion. It has, rather, been to identify the textual components of American independent cinema of a certain strain that support being understood in certain ways. The films I have chosen to stand as exemplary of this strain are not necessarily the aesthetically most advanced or the very epitomes of indie realism. They are meant to be broadly representative of a trend in film practice, and if the arguments here succeed it will be by the applicability of my points made about these films to many other instances of indie realism, of films about engaging characters from the more marginal sectors of American film practice in the 1980s, 1990s, and 2000s.

Rhetorics of distinction, however, can function in many contexts, using many narrative strategies. Some indie cinema might depart in certain ways from the straightforward and linear presentation of films like *Walking and Talking*, while still maintaining a realism appeal. Some indie dramas and comedies might push quirky characters at the expense of realism, and as a trend within indie cinema, especially of the later 1990s and 2000s, the quirk of a Wes Anderson, a *Garden State*, *Little Miss Sunshine* (2006), *Juno* (2007), or *(500) Days of Summer* (2009) might offer a number of revisions to the formula described here. The quirky indie might be seen as a hybrid of two strains of film style: the realist strain I have just described, and the styles of formal play to be addressed in the next two chapters.

part III   FORMAL PLAY

chapter 4   PASTICHE AS PLAY

| The Coen Brothers | Being original . . .

is incredibly overrated.—ETHAN COEN[1]

Blood Simple (1984), Joel and Ethan Coen's first feature, was hailed at the 1985 New York Film Festival as an auspicious debut, compared by *Time* magazine's reviewer to *Citizen Kane*.[2] It would become an exemplar of a strain of American indie cinema concerned with exploring formal and generic terrain. But although *Blood Simple* is now quite widely and affectionately admired, not only for launching a unique directing tandem on a celebrated career but also for its contribution to the revival and revision of *film noir*, its initial critical reception was mixed. Some critics praised its visual and narrative daring. The film is among other things a succession of astonishing set pieces: the Coens track a camera across a bar and have it hop over a passed-out drunk; in one climactic scene, they show a knife impaling a hand against a windowsill; in another they have a man, buried alive and assumed dead, rise from his shallow grave. But despite their enthusiasm for its bravura approach, some criticized *Blood Simple* for having style in place of substance, making it a cold, empty exercise in technique. J. Hoberman of the *Village Voice* was merely the pithiest of its critics when he described the film having "the heart of a Bloomingdale's window and the soul of a resumé."[3]

Like all of the Coen brothers' films, *Blood Simple* can be appreciated in two distinct ways. First, it engages the viewer in a conventional narrative of crime, sex, and betrayal, an engrossing murder

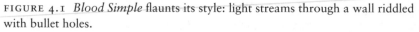

FIGURE 4.1 *Blood Simple* flaunts its style: light streams through a wall riddled with bullet holes.

melodrama with vicious double-crosses and devastating misunderstandings. It proceeds in high style, offering virtuoso camera movements, aggressively high- and low-angle shots, and dazzling lighting effects, as in the sequence when thin beams of white light shine through a wall freshly punctured by bullets (fig. 4.1). To the typical moviegoer seeking entertainment, the film offers many of the pleasures of its genre, and of popular narrative art more generally: suspense, intrigue, surprise, irony, humor, identification, visual pleasure, moral judgment—in sum, the experience of a good story well told.

At the same time, though, *Blood Simple* can be seen as a text self-consciously working with and against various traditions of storytelling, with and against a number of influences. These include horror films, a source for the film's graphic presentation of blood and vomit, its use of sound cues to startle (e.g., a newspaper rattling a screen door), and its breathtaking violence. Joel Coen's first job in film production was on the splatter film *The Evil Dead* (1982), and both brothers count its director, Sam Raimi, as a friend and occasional collaborator. A more significant source for *Blood Simple* is the crime novels of James M. Cain, such as *The Postman Always Rings Twice* and *Double Indemnity*. The Coens have said that in making *Blood Simple* they wanted most of all to tell a James M. Cain kind of story.[4] Like Cain's fiction and its adaptations to cinema, *Blood Simple* tells a dark, violent story about the devastating consequences of forbidden sexual encounters. Its style, like Cain's, favors action over thought. And like Cain's characters, those in *Blood Simple* are ordinary folks whose illicit desires lead them into a spiral of inevitable destruction. A related influence is 1940s and '50s Hollywood dramas about lurid or tawdry crime, films that rely on shadowy black-and-white scenes with hard, low-key lighting, striking camera angles, confessional voice-over narration in the past tense, and motifs such as ceiling fans, curtains, snap-brim hats, and venetian blinds—a category, *film noir*, that would include adaptations of James M. Cain.

All narratives draw some of their material from various sources, but some make especially prominent their debt. This is what is going on with *Blood Simple*. A second, self-conscious, mode of appreciation that recognizes the film's relation to its sources is signaled by several textual and contextual cues. Cain's novels and their most familiar cinematic renderings are rooted in a historical era in which mores were different from those of the 1960s and since. The desire depicted in Cain, in combination with the highly gendered norms of social propriety in the mid-century period, make for a narrative world in which men and women have a more circumscribed environment than they do after the sexual revolution and other social upheavals of the 1960s and '70s, when the Coens and other indie filmmakers are working. The Cain style, whether literary or cinematic, is incompatible not only with shifting norms of gender relations and with the Raimi-influenced horror touches but also with the norms of post-studio-era filmmaking, with its standardization of color cinematography and location shooting, its greater freedom to represent sex, violence, and taboo speech after the passing of the Production Code, and its influence, initially from foreign art cinema, toward narrative indeterminacy and ambiguity. *Blood Simple* is an exaggeration, a distortion of 1940s hard-boiled melodrama insofar as it represents what was once forbidden or impossible in the realms of lustful action and bodily harm. It achieves its effects without much self-reflexive wink-winking, but to a cinema-literate audience the tension between text and context may be noticeable. One bit of indication the film does offer is a song on the soundtrack, which first is played on the jukebox of the bar owned by Marty, Dan Hedaya's character (a stand-in for the character referred to as "the Greek" in *Postman*): "The Same Old Song," by the Four Tops. The importance of "The Same Old Song" is underlined when it plays over the film's closing credits, repeating the chorus, "Now it's the same old song, but with a different meaning since you been gone." There are several layers of reference here: the lovers of the song's narrative are like the husband and wife of the film's narrative, once in love but now separated (in the film by his murder). But we can also see the song conveying that the film is a kind of uncanny return of mid-century hard-boiled murder melodrama, at once familiar and unfamiliar. In reworking this literary and cinematic genre for a new era, *Blood Simple* shares with other post-studio-era American crime films like *Chinatown* (1974), *Body Heat* (1981), and *Pulp Fiction* (1994) a sense of both enthusiastic stylistic revival and longing for an unattainable past, and this ambivalent combination of tones is what has led critics to term these films *neo-noir*, indicating a crucial distance from and critical engagement with a historical style rather than simply membership in a category.[5] "Neo," in effect, says "same song, different meaning." There is thus a friction between *Blood Simple* and its influences, and—to those prepared to recognize it, at least—this generates an interest in its own right. We might say then that *Blood Simple*, like much of the Coen oeuvre, is on one level of meaning about this friction.

The revival of the hard-boiled style in the 1980s decontextualized its meanings and turned it into a play of surface textures, which can be appreciated by literate audiences as a *pastiche*, an affectionate imitation. Richard Dyer defines genre pastiche as "displays of generic form *qua* form"[6] and describes, in relation to spaghetti westerns, how the audience is invited to "savor generic elements as generic elements,"[7] a notion that should be familiar to Coen brothers fans. In her review of *Blood Simple*, Pauline Kael disapprovingly called these references "*film noir* in-jokes."[8] A second mode of viewing, then, depends on familiarity with conventions and sources on which the filmmakers are drawing, and which they play with. This metaphor, play, is central to the mode of appreciation that has arisen around the Coens, along with a number of other culturally literate and self-conscious indie filmmakers, Quentin Tarantino being perhaps the most prominent.[9] Many independent films make a special appeal of their form, whether conceived as generic plot, character, and setting archetypes and iconographies, or narrative conventions such as temporal structures. In particular, the indie approach to foregrounded form is playful and, I argue, game-like. The idea that the Coens play with genre or that *Pulp Fiction* and *Memento* (2000) play with narrative structure suggests that they do this for fun rather than for some more serious purpose, and that the "in-crowd" appreciates play on the level mainly of having fun, though this does not mean it has no more significant functions. (Indeed, I shall argue that play with form functions as a critical practice.) When approaching a film with the expectation of ludic form, the audience gets aesthetic satisfaction from engaging with the game-like qualities of the experience, which may be considered an end in themselves rather than a vehicle for deeper meaning or for greater emotional engagement, though the game-like qualities typically offer other pleasures as well beyond merely offering an experience of play. The point of play, it is often said, is that it need not have a point beyond itself—that play is the purpose of play, and that as such play is not supposed to serve other ends.[10] But of course, play always has other purposes, such as social cohesion. The playful forms of indie cinema also have social functions. Among other things, game-like form functions to bring the indie audience together as a community with shared expectations about cinematic experiences, the better to mark itself off against a cultural mainstream.[11]

Making a game of genre and influences, playing with the audience's expectations about form and meaning, are central appeals of *Blood Simple*, and in their various ways of all of the Coens' films since. This point matches formal play with another key element of indie culture's viewing strategies: authorship as means of focusing textual meanings across many films that constitute an oeuvre. As a culture more focused on "personal" filmmaking than Hollywood and always seeking aesthetic distinction in relation to it, indie cinema relies considerably on *auteur* readings and on the categorization of films by artist, often parallel with or even ahead of genre or star. Indie filmmakers, more than many Hollywood counterparts, are expected to maintain a vision that is prioritized ahead of commercial considerations, and to cultivate a personal style across a body of work which helps to distinguish itself against mainstream film culture. Their emergence in the 1980s, part of an original wave of indies in the Sundance-

Miramax era, established the Coens as influential models, and while their *auteur* identity by the late 2000s might seem less central to indie culture than other directors, their historical role bespeaks their centrality to conceptions of indie culture. The Coens are offered here not only as paradigmatic pasticheurs, but also as exemplars of auteurist practice in indie cinema. The central thematic of their *auteur* identities, I argue, is playfulness. For instance, Jonathan Romney, writing about *The Big Lebowski* in *Sight and Sound*, described the Coen brothers as "the most purely ludic of contemporary American filmmakers."[12]

Consider these brief examples:

- The titles at the beginning of *Fargo* (1996) and *O Brother, Where Art Thou?* (2000) announce those films as a true story and an adaptation of the *Odyssey*, respectively, even though neither of these claims is literally true.
- The video introduction to the DVD collector's edition of *The Big Lebowski* is by Mortimer Young, a fake film scholar who pontificates in a parody of scholarly discourse about the film's restoration.
- Many Coens films use introductory voice-over narrations that seem knowingly silly, such as H.I.'s monologue over the opening sequence of *Raising Arizona* and the Stranger's monologue introducing the Dude in *Lebowski*.
- The endings of several Coens films are frustrating, confusing, or incongruous. Consider the sci-fi sharp left turn and abstraction of *The Man Who Wasn't There* (2001), the abrupt shift in style and mood in *No Country for Old Men* (2007), and the total ambiguity of *Barton Fink* (1991). All of these may be interpreted as playing with the convention of the neat and tidy ending, of satisfying the audience's desire for conventional climax and closure, much in the tradition of European art cinema and its international imitators.

This ludic appeal has been most important in critical appraisals of the Coens and in their canonization as indie and as postmodernist *auteurs*. According to this mode of reception, the Coen brothers' films are movies about movies and narratives about narratives and pop culture about pop culture.[13] They seem sometimes to refer to nothing much outside of themselves and the reference points they flauntingly copy; they do not seem concerned to engage with social issues in any thoughtful way (Joel and Ethan Coen never leave the impression that they think movies have any relevance to the social or political in their appearances in the press). This is not to deny that one might interpret their films thematically, as many have done, but only to assert that a central appeal of their films is precisely their interest in form as form rather than as vehicle for deeper meaning. To those who take these characterizations to be failings, the Coens' films are works of formalist self-gratification, art for art's sake, technically adept but ultimately of little lasting value, a lot of sizzle but not much bacon.[14] To many admirers of their work, however, the Coen brothers are masters of a certain mode of contemporary filmmaking that is at once highly referential but also idiosyncratically individualistic: their work, like Tarantino's, is based at the same time on an advertised debt to an eclectic hodgepodge of sources and on the creation of a universe where people talk and act in a way that exists only in their movies, in Coen Country or Quentinland. As with many of the most acclaimed independent film directors in the post-1970s era, form is given special emphasis and weight in the Coens' movies. Barry Sonnenfeld, who shot the Coens' first few films, confirmed as much when he told an interviewer that theme is "incredibly unimportant to them" and that they are more interested in "structure and style and words."[15] How we make sense of this approach to form is the topic of this chapter.

Intertextuality and Allusion: Understanding Imitative Form

One central aspect of form given emphasis in the Coens' movies is their imitative quality. Their films foreground formal influences such as *film noir*, hard-boiled fiction, screwball comedy, and horror. They are highly derivative. Originality is generally considered an asset of any artwork, and yet the Coens take the opposite approach to creativity, making salient their duplication of existing styles. They do so in a way that, rather than detracting from their aesthetic integrity, focuses an appreciative audience's attention on the relation between target texts and their imitation. What might appear to be a simple failure of originality—one critic upon seeing *Miller's Crossing* wrote that Dashiell Hammett's estate should sue for plagiarism[16]—is actually a point of interest. The Coens have an original way of being unoriginal. This is what people mean when they say that the Coens play with genre: genres are among their influences, and the way these influences are repurposed and inhabited in the Coen brothers' work is a central appeal of their aesthetic. The typical genre film is one of many members in a category, to an extent interchangeable with the other members. The Coen brothers, like a number of their contemporaries in independent cinema, make membership in a category into something out of the ordinary. How this works demands a theoretical appraisal of artistic imitation, and an understanding of how different ways of describing imitation offer differing notions of the artistic merits and demerits of a highly imitative approach to creativity.

Imitation of one artistic work by another, conscious or not, is such a fundamental feature of creative expression that scores of terms are used, some interchangeably or with only the subtlest shadings of different meaning, to describe similarities among texts. The poststructuralist term *intertextuality* is often meant to capture an idea of aesthetic indebtedness. It is tempting to think of the Coens' films as simply intertextual, but intertextuality is often wanting as a critical concept for a number of reasons.

In the original Bakhtinian sense given it by Julia Kristeva, intertextuality names a fundamental feature of textuality, the notion that original or authorial meanings are always reproduced from earlier texts, indeed that all of culture is a kind of imitation of one text by another, all the way down to the present.[17] Michael Riffaterre defines intertextuality as "the perception . . . of the relationship between a work and others that have either preceded or followed it" and understands it to be an essence of literariness.[18] If the point of a concept for artistic imitation is to apply it selectively within critical contexts aiming at understanding specific texts and groups of texts, however, an approach to textuality that seeks universals and essences will probably not suffice as a way of establishing how certain texts make their debts especially prominent.

Another meaning, more frequently employed, refers to a specific kind of referentiality some texts have in greater supply. For instance, it is often said of the films of the French New Wave and Godard in particular that they are especially intertextual, as they often incorporate bits of classic Hollywood iconography and references to various artistic and intellectual sources.[19] *Breathless* (1959), for instance, manages to incorporate, among other things, Monogram Pictures and Humphrey Bogart; paintings by Picasso, Klee, and Renoir; Mozart's clarinet concerto; Faulkner's *Wild Palms*; poetry by Aragon and Apollinaire; and Nietzschean and existentialist philosophy. Its basic situation of an independent American girl in Europe recalls Henry James. That character, Patricia, is also thought to be a kind of continuation of the character played by the actress who portrays her, Jean Seberg, in Otto Preminger's *Bonjour Tristesse* (1958). Godard, like many modernists, advertises his debts to his many inspirations; this is a significant dimension of his aesthetic.

But to lump all of these instances of one text connecting to other texts in one big category called intertextuality lacks precision. When a character imitates another character, that might be an homage. When a line of dialogue from one film repeats in another, or when a character reads from a novel, that would be a quotation. A film may quote visually as well, as when a zoom-in/track-out shot recalls *Vertigo* (1958) or a pattern of striped shadows evokes *film noir*. Or we might call this allusion, a reference from one work to another that often requires a degree of familiarity, of literacy, for it to be caught. Like Godard, the Coen brothers are promiscuously allusive, as in *Raising Arizona* (1987) with its scraps of *Mad Max* (1979) and Chuck Jones, *Barton Fink* with its fictionalized versions of literary and Hollywood personalities like William Faulkner and Clifford Odets, *The Big Lebowski* (1998) with its assortment of 1960s reference points from 'Nam to Fluxus, and *O Brother, Where Art Thou?* with its cornucopia of Southern characters (real and imagined) and stereotypes layered onto palimpsests of Preston Sturges and Homer.

It matters that we call these allusions rather than intertexts because allusions are authorial, intentional meanings that audiences are meant to recognize, while intertexts include these among many other forms of reference, similarity, and occasional relation. Authorial meanings, as Peter J. Rabinowitz argues, are meanings that readers or audiences construct as products of a work's author. Rabinowitz argues that readers of literary works typically seek authorial meanings.[20] Although this may not be equally, generally true of spectators in the cinema, it is more likely to be true of spectators of films for which an authorial agency has been positioned as significant within the discourses through which we arrive at the experience of a movie. Indie cinema, and films by the Coen brothers in particular, fit this description especially well. In the case of allusive works in any medium, authorial, intentional meanings are especially central since an allusion is specifically a reference made by an author that is meant to be recognized as such by a reader. An allusion is a special kind of intertextuality that operates as an exchange of knowledge among producer and consumer, not simply a similarity or reference or echo of one work in another. Although it is passé to take intentions to be a key to the interpretation of a work, it is plainly obvious that artists intend for their works to be as they are, and audiences assume as much routinely, though of course some elements of their works escape artists' intentions or are viewed differently by different audiences. This is not to maintain that nothing in a work is outside of intentions or that all meanings always are found in them and only in them. But in the case of allusions, one essential point of the meanings they convey is that they are produced in an encounter of mutual understanding between reader and writer or filmmaker and audience, and they cannot function absent the prior knowledge, the common culture, that makes them work. Allusions only happen when author and audience *get* each other, which makes them especially important for modes of film-making that are culturally circumscribed, like indie cinema, as compared with those seeking wider, mass appeal. Of course, Hollywood films are also allusive; the distinction here is one of balance. *Raiders of the Lost Ark* (1981) is allusive, but the pleasures and meanings of the film depend much less on its allusions than on its conventional, crowd-pleasing, roller-coaster-ride appeals.

Allusion is a capacious category, but it is still merely one among a great many ways of identifying relations among texts, and it may come in combination with other forms of relation. When an allusive text copies another's form in a derisive, mocking, critical, comical, or even affectionate way, we might call it a parody, travesty, burlesque, send-up, or spoof. When it copies in a way that seems meant to be noticed, but not in a critical or comical fashion, we call that pastiche. (When one text borrows from another in a way that is not meant to be noticed, it might be an instance of plagiarism or fakery, but not allusion.) Allusion and intertextuality might both also cover such relations among texts as are captured in the terms *remake, adaptation, revision, spin-off, sequel,* and *prequel.* Films may relate to one another in unique ways, as *Rumor Has It . . .* (2005) carries on part of the narrative of *The Graduate* (1967) several decades after its ending. A film (or other kind of narrative) may retell a story or a portion of one from a different perspective, in the manner of the play and film *Rosencrantz and Guildenstern are Dead* (1990) or the novel and stage musical *Wicked*. And then there are translations, copies, reproductions, and alternate versions (e.g., shortened or modified to suit certain audiences, as in literary bowdlerizations and sanitized versions of movies and TV shows used on broadcast or basic cable TV), which are allusive in some ways but not others. Genre is a form of intertextuality—every instance of a genre draws as its source material on other instances—but not necessarily of allusion. So often is an author's oeuvre, or a nation's, intertextual by nature.[21] If intertextuality covers all of these possibilities—and why should it not?—then it cannot help us appreciate distinctions among them. We might say that some texts foreground intertextuality, as some certainly do. But we have terms to describe this dynamic use of sources that have more analytical purchase than "intertextuality": reference, quotation, allusion, parody, and pastiche. The films of the Coen brothers contain all of these forms of intertextuality, but they are often distinct from one another. It helps us to be able to distinguish among the strategies of managing source material in the Coens' oeuvre, since this aspect of their filmmaking is so central to their work. In particular, the Coens favor pastiche as a guiding principle of creativity, and their aesthetic of allusive pastiche unifies their work more than any other aspect. Something is at stake in determining their films to be pastiches rather than parodies, travesties, or homages, and our appreciation of their meaning in relation to their target texts hinges on this distinction. All of these different imitative forms have different effects. Appreciating the way the Coens favor pastiche over parody is especially significant in understanding how their films emphasize form.

Parody, Pastiche, Pop Pomo

Despite being distinct textual modes, parody and pastiche have some key features in common. In particular, both a parody and a pastiche are essentially mimetic, closely resembling a text or the prototypical features of an author, genre, or style.[22] Crucially, both parody and pastiche depend on an audience who is in the know, prepared to decode the imitation as such.[23] Neither can achieve the power that comes from its form without summoning specific extratextual knowledge, often supplied through metatextual and paratextual discourses, but often also already part of a culture shared by producers and consumers of films.[24] Although one might find it to be quite a nice song and may derive pleasure from it, Weird Al Yankovic's "Eat It" cannot be appreciated as parody if the listener isn't already familiar with Michael Jackson's earlier hit, "Beat It." Thus "Beat It" is an essential paratext for apprehending its authorial meanings. Parody and pastiche, like allusion and quotation, traffic in existing meanings and build upon them. In a sense, a pastiche or parody is an allusion stretched out to define an entire text. Because they require this prior knowledge, the meanings of such texts have a particular kind of heightened reliance on producers and consumers of cultural products belonging to the same interpretive community—they occupy a realm of shared reference. Like much humor, they set a certain standard for "getting it." If you don't understand the allusion or recognize it as such, you are without access to a basic kind of meaning. The social constraints on appreciating these forms suggest that one central function of allusiveness is communal.[25] We understand our place belonging to the community through the experience of sharing in its specialized knowledge. Parody and pastiche traffic in cultural capital that circulates among readers and writers, artists and audiences, filmmakers and cinemagoers. In Barbara Klinger's formulation, parody is "a mirror held up to viewers in which they see their own capabilities as interpreters."[26] Just because they are in the know does not necessarily make them elites, although it does bestow a certain power. Weird Al's songs are aimed at kids who like pop music, hardly a group invested with great power. But in the case of American independent films and other movies likely to screen in U.S. art houses, at film festivals and campus film society programs, and on boutique indie cable stations such as IFC and Sundance, the demographic group is literate, educated, cultured, and adult. It is a psychographic well recognized by the advertisers in *Filmmaker* magazine and niche movie purveyors like James Schamus, Bob Shaye, Harvey Weinstein, and Bingham Ray. The language of cinema may be universal, as Landmark Cinemas used to tell us before every screening in its art house auditoriums, but the language of allusive cinematic forms such as parody and pastiche are quite specific to the communities that produce and consume them.

It may appear that because their films are often comic, playful, and irreverent, and because their approach to genre source material is so faithfully imitative, that the Coen brothers' films should be considered parodic. There are certainly numerous parodic passages in their films, such as the character of the movie mogul in Barton Fink who is a parody of the Louis B. Mayer or Harry Cohn cigar-chomping Hollywood producer type, or such as the opening voice-over monologue of *The Big Lebowski* by the character called the Stranger, which is a parody of the sort of voice-over introduction one might find in a western film. But I contend that the Coen brothers' oeuvre is best understood not as parody but as pastiche. The mode of appreciation most consistently applied to their films by critics and cinephiles is that of pastiche, whether audiences and writers use that term or not (many do). This is not to argue that all of their films are always best described this way or that this idea is the key to unlocking all meanings in their work. Their most acclaimed films, *Fargo* and *No Country for Old Men*, are also their least imitative of specific, familiar textual forms. But the Coens' identity as *auteurs* depends on a certain kind of imitativeness that pastiche best captures. And the brothers themselves think of their work as more neutral in relation to its sources than mocking or simply paying tribute. Joel Coen has said in an interview, "We've never considered our stuff either homage or spoof. Those are things other people call it, and it's always puzzled me that they do."[27]

Let's consider pastiche in two senses—one as a description of a text, a formal designation. The other is a way of making sense of a text, an interpretive approach. It may seem uncontroversial to call films like *Miller's Crossing* and *O Brother* pastiches, yet not everyone sees them that way. Audiences innocent of their literary and cinematic sources may not approach *Miller's Crossing* as a pastiche, just as audiences unfamiliar with *O Brother*'s influences might think it's just a zany romp and not wonder about its degree of originality. In order for the interpretive community to appreciate the film as pastiche, it needs to have both a familiarity with the forms being imitated, and also with pastiche as a formal strategy of self-conscious imitation. It has to apply this knowledge as its interpretive frame.

This is true also of parody, but there is a significant difference between a parody and a pastiche, and it is a matter of one of the trickiest of qualities to capture in description and analysis: tone. Parody is by its nature ironic and often comical, but it would be incorrect to assume that a pastiche lacks humor whereas a parody is funny. *The Hudsucker Proxy* (1994), for example, is a comical pastiche of Capra, Hawks, and Sturges. *The Big Lebowski* is a comical pastiche, among other things, of Raymond Chandler and films adapted from his novels. Rather, parody derives its humor from having a polemical quality of criticism, of satiric mockery, even if it is of a gentle sort.[28] Parody is like repeating someone's ill-considered words back to them with unwelcome added emphasis, much as Jon Stewart might do with an absurd statement by a politician or cable news blowhard. Pastiche involves a different sort of repetition and imitation. It isn't interested in subjecting its source material to ridicule, no matter how gentle, and is not finding fault with its points of inspiration. But neither is it simply paying homage or tribute.

A pastiche is also a critical form, but critical here has a different sense. I propose that we think of pastiches such as the Coens' films as professional analogues of the participatory fan productions (fictions, songs, videos) that scholars such as Henry Jenkins have studied.[29] These may be parodic, as in the numerous gently mocking *Star Wars* videos like *George Lucas in Love* (1999), but I am thinking more of those that traffic in novel combinations of existing images and sounds such as mash-ups and songvids that use commercial media texts as the raw materials of transformative works that are at once deeply imitative and imaginatively creative. For instance, Danger Mouse's mash-up *The Grey Album*, combining recordings by the Beatles (the White Album, officially titled *The Beatles*) and Jay-Z (*The Black Album*) into a single new work, is not a parodic work of mockery or ridicule, however affectionate, but a pastiche that re-creates those existing original elements in such a way that you are invited to notice their re-creation and their novel recontextualization. Luminosity's video *Vogue/300* sets the imagery of the film 300 to Madonna's "Vogue," homoeroticizing a movie about masculine heroism and courage, but not in a tone of fun or in the spirit of a putdown.[30] The point of participatory culture's imitative forms is often deeply critical, but not necessarily as parody is critical, by which I mean mocking, ridiculing, poking fun, or roasting. Pastiche is critical in the sense of exercising judgment, of selecting and emphasizing, and of having an analytical perspective.

The Coens' pastiches do a critical job of selecting, collecting, foregrounding, curating, preserving, archiving, interpreting, and reimagining the media that have been significant in their lives and in the lives of the community that shares their specific cultural literacy. By their choice of objects of their pastiche, the Coens' oeuvre functions as a kind of imaginative, creative literary and film scholarship, of history and criticism of twentieth-century popular culture, and in particular a history and criticism of literary and film genres from the popular traditions of the 1930s, '40s, and '50s, including screwball comedies and detective or "tough-guy" stories. The Coens certainly have a countercultural sensibility, bringing irreverent and subversive comedy and splatter and profanity to the screen in ways that pay no heed to canons of bourgeois good taste. But they have no interest in subverting the sources of their imitation, sources they clearly adore.

Many critics, popular and scholarly alike, identify both pastiche and the cinema of Joel and Ethan Coen with postmodernism. Following Fredric Jameson, a sort of consensus emerged that the culture of postmodernist theory's heyday in the 1980s and '90s was characterized by a nostalgic, fragmentary, and uncritical revival of old forms and iconographies, and that this was symptomatic of the depthlessness, the emptiness endemic to the postmodern condition. Parody, a mode favored by radicals for its potential to challenge dominant discourses in their very language, was seen to have been replaced by pastiche, a mode whose similarity to parody was seen to belie its politically opposite valence as uncritical, toothless. Although Jameson's *Postmodernism* ranges widely over many cultural forms, from architecture to literature, his discussions of postmodernist imitativeness and pastiche center on film examples: in particular *Chinatown*, *Blade Runner* (1982), and *Body Heat*.[31] He was not alone in recognizing the extent to which American cinema in the 1970s and '80s was invested in revivals of old Hollywood forms. From a different critical perspective, unencumbered by Jameson's Marxist political philosophy and poststructuralist jargon, Noël Carroll in 1981 made a much more exhaustively detailed and persuasive case for a similar idea, which he called allusionism. Carroll's discussion extends only to the very early 1980s and focuses on the films and directors we would now call Hollywood Renaissance: Altman, Coppola, Schrader, Spielberg, Scorsese, Lucas, et al.[32] The Coens are the best case of this development in U.S. cinema extending, as a tradition of sorts, into the generation of the 1980s indies, providing a line of continuity from earlier traditions and movements to the independent cinema of the 1980s and '90s and beyond. It is unsurprising that the most prevalent scholarly approach to interpreting the Coens' pictures is through the rubric of postmodern culture, since they seem to fit so well into Jameson's schema and since their films are obviously part of a larger trend in American filmmaking of what David Bordwell, borrowing from Harold Bloom, has termed "belatedness," a sense of coming after a great tradition—in this case the classical Hollywood cinema of the studio era—that affects filmmakers of the contemporary era stretching back to the 1960s.[33] Whether one accepts or rejects postmodernism as a way of understanding history and culture, a cultural fixation on retrospection is simply a fact of American representations in myriad forms since the coming of age of the baby boom generation.

Like many critics, I consider postmodernism to be a significant category to consider in relation to the Coens, and more generally to indie films that, like theirs, foreground form. In particular, what interests me is how discourses of postmodernism trickle down from the level of scholarly, Marxist cultural theory, which seeks to connect *late capitalism*, a sweeping term that refers to the entirety of postindustrial politics and economics in the West in particular but also on a global scale, with virtually anything about that period's culture, broadly construed. According to this scheme, specific instances of cultural production are identified rather deterministically as symptoms of a specific conjunction of politics and economics after the 1960s (periodizing it is of course one of postmodernity's many impossible dimensions). I would prefer to stay out of any debate about the merits of this approach, and instead to think of postmodernism as a discourse in the background against which indie cinema and culture come into circulation in the 1980s and '90s, and which is pulled forward as an explanatory concept when critics—and in part through their influence, audiences—find it useful to do so. I would like to think of it in much simpler terms than Jameson's, not as a global explanatory framework to apply to anything that occurs under late capitalism, but as a heuristic that some people use in making sense of specific texts in their local contexts. This isn't to say that I find postmodernism to be a useful interpretive heuristic, since I am skeptical of its claims as a generalization about the culture of late capitalism. But since the idea was *au courant* when the Coens' reputation was established, it came to be an influence on the context of their reception just as existentialism was an influence on the context of Bergman's (no matter his avowed personal dislike for existentialism—the idea was in the air). Postmodernism may begin as a top-down theory that looks for instances of culture to illustrate its claims, but it is appropriated in a more bottom-up fashion, opportunistically (when it works) to explain the appeal of specific texts, genres, styles, or oeuvres. This trickle-down postmodernism—call it pop pomo—at some point became as much a descriptive shorthand employed even by reviewers for the mainstream media to describe anything self-reflexive, formally playful, inventive, or invested too much in its surface appearance. For instance, in surveying their career to date on the release of *O Brother* in 2000, Michiko Kakutani of the *New York Times* referred to the Coens as "chilly post-modern auteurs."[34] Another appreciation of their work in the *Times* in 2000, by Franz Lidz, called them "the premier post-modernists of pop movies."[35] This is an excellent case of an academic humanities notion becoming popularized, no doubt through the agency of liberal arts undergrads going off to write cultural criticism in the mainstream press. My interest in postmodernism as a template for understanding the Coens puts much more stake in pop pomo than in Jameson's theory, and it contests his contention that pastiche is blank or empty parody. Richard Dyer has convincingly put this notion to rest, arguing forcefully that pastiche is a legitimate and indeed rich and worthy form that is itself no less critical than parody. (In a modest aside, Dyer refers to his book, *Pastiche*, as an effort to "rescue pastiche from postmodernism," a task he certainly accomplishes.)[36] In particular, Dyer suggests that pastiche functions as a kind of creative historiography and, rather than being "empty" of content, makes a point about the gaps between past and present works and worlds. Moreover, in the hands of a popular critic rather than an academic theorist, pomo potentially becomes a term of praise, a way of calling something fresh or inventive, a way of signaling appreciation for something novel and sophisticated and *now*. Depending on shifting patterns of usage, pop pomo may be descriptive rather than analytical, and celebratory rather than critical. In the world of pop pomo, pastiche isn't failed parody; rather, pastiche is doing its own thing and offers its own rewards.

Pop pomo is one key to understanding how viewers make sense of indie cinema's more formally playful textual modes. The Coens stand for one kind of formal play in particular: play with expectations about genre conventions in a way that may be interpreted not just as subversion or experimentation, but as commentary of a subtle sort that requires recognition as pastiche. That is, pop pomo authorizes an appreciation of pastiche, a context for understanding its imitativeness, its prominent surface qualities. It considers the arrangement of "surface" in uncanny or otherwise pleasantly surprising fashion to be as desirable an aesthetic virtue as formal unity or thematic richness. In earlier eras, pastiche might have been seen as a term of opprobrium, or as a trivial or trifling minor form. By being perceived as pomo, though, a highly "surface-y" text is invested with significance. The Coens thus authorize two interpretive frames that in combination lend themselves to generating cultural cachet—they have both a pop-pomo style and an individualized, authorial presence. Indeed, their authorial mark is a product of textual values that can be approached through a pop-pomo frame quite fruitfully. Thus does their work lend itself to a cultlike appreciation.

There are two broad categories of culture within which the Coen brothers' films work their allusive pastiche aesthetic: melodrama, in the sense that term had during the studio era of Hollywood, referring to narratives of crime and passion; and comedy, especially of the screwball variety.[37] In both of these genres, the Coens exploit similar aesthetics, especially using sharply drawn character types who speak in a heightened patois typical of their role. In the remaining pages of this chapter, I will turn first to a number of examples of the Coens' comedic work; then I will consider their melodrama in relation to one film in particular, *Miller's Crossing* (1991), which adopts the language and iconography of mid-century crime narrative. I emphasize early films (such as *Raising Arizona* and *Miller's Crossing*) in this discussion partly because these works are especially allusive, but also because they were instrumental in establishing the Coens' reputation as pasticheurs, setting expectations to be applied across the decades of their work.

Comic Pastiche

The Coens announced with the precredit sequence of their second film that they were not the kind of filmmakers to stick to a single style or genre. *Raising Arizona* begins with an extended voice-over sequence narrated by Nicholas Cage's character, H.I., a recently released ex-convict. Like the film generally, everything in this introductory sequence is heightened well beyond realism. This includes the mise-en-scène, a stylized combination of comic deadpan performance, flamboyant costumes, grooming and makeup, vivid color, high-key lighting, and western landscape. It includes wide-angle cine-matography with aggressive foregrounds (a signature style of Barry Sonnenfeld's camerawork) and comically high and low angles. And it includes the script, an unreliable aw-shucks monologue in H.I.'s drawling voice adopting and heightening the speech and thought patterns of an ignorant and naive but lovable reformed crook. Pastiche often works by heightening, exaggerating, amplifying, distorting, and stylizing, all of which function to draw attention to imitation. Minor characters speak in an especially stylized regional style of accent and intonation, mispronouncing and overemphasizing words and offering up colloquial and slang expressions for our amusement, as when a parole board member tells H.I., whom the board is reluctantly releasing from prison after twenty months served for armed robbery, "These doors are gonna swing wide!" When describing the early days of his marriage to "Ed" (Holly Hunter, as Edwina), the police photographer who always takes his mug shot when he gets busted, H.I. narrates over a wide-angle shot of aluminum folding chairs in front of a trailer, a cactus and a satellite dish in the distance, and H.I. attired like a suburban dad in shorts and flip-flops, fiddling with a garden hose: "These were the happy days, the salad days as they say, and Ed felt that having a critter was the next logical step." The tune accompanying this portion of the opening is a banjo rendition of the *Ode to Joy* from Pete Seeger's "Goofing Off Suite." The combination of accent, diction, accompaniment, and subject matter makes the character seem at once sweet and idiotic, puts distance between us and him (what petty criminal says "salad days" and who calls a child a critter?), and gives the film's world a quality of unrealism. Körte and Seesslen find the voice-over to be parodic, poking fun at the sincerity of the typical film's introductory narration. Accents and diction are a source of humor throughout the film. For instance, the bombastic antagonist, Nathan Arizona, yells into a telephone, "if a frog had wings it wouldn't bump its ass a-hopping!" Indeed, heightened quirks of speech pervade the Coens' work in comedy and drama alike, and although they may be going for authenticity in some cases, their effect is more typically one of distancing the spectator from the character, who is being presented quite self-consciously as a type. This isn't to say that we don't feel affection for these types, however. H.I. is presented as hapless and sympathetic even as he is a recidivist criminal. We feel for him when he locks his keys in the car when holding up a convenience store and must submit to the overbearing prison counseling sessions of a macho Jewish shrink. As he continually appears before Ed to have his mug shot taken, we begin to pity the endearing criminal who always gets caught, mainly because of the lightness of the film's tone, which is about as distant as one can imagine from the noirish murk and eerieness of *Blood Simple*. It is, by contrast, a live action cartoon and the influence of animation is made clear in the opening sequence. The third time before Ed, H.I. is instructed to bare his tattoo for the camera—a tattoo of Mr. Horsepower, the cartoon woodpecker.

So, much of the film's style is cartoonish, from the dialogue to the staging to the camera angles, and its narrative is as well. Ulrich Kriest describes *Raising Arizona* as "a turbulent, high-speed cartoon, laced with surreal effects, which quotes liberally from all sorts of popular genres, mixes them together and stands back in amazement to observe the result."[38] As in *Blood Simple*, the Coens announce up front that they are not interested in any kind of cinematic realism or naturalism, which is a prompt to read for pastiche. The story is about the theft of a baby, one of the Arizona quintuplets born to the wife of Nathan Arizona, a small businessman who appears in obnoxious local television commercials for his furniture store. As the film progresses, it layers on further outlandish, cartoonish subplots and characters, including a mangy, leather-clad motorcycle thug (fig. 4.2) who seems to have stepped out of a *Mad Max* movie, and a series of chases, crashes, and explosions. Carter Burwell's scoring with whistling, guitar, banjo, and plaintive, yodeling vocals, which includes excerpts of Seeger's "Goofing Off Suite," introduces a folk culture element. It might have seemed to audiences and critics upon its release that *Raising Arizona* was quoting in a sort of profligate, senseless fashion, a product of film school ecstasy of influence. Influential critics picked up on the prominence of its imitativeness, but were not yet prepared to apply the interpretive frame of pastiche as a positive term, a term of praise and appreciation.

For example, Vincent Canby's review in the *New York Times* enumerated various allusions: "In addition to this utterly pointless reference to the 'Road Warrior' films, 'Raising Arizona' also 'quotes' from 'Carrie,' 'Badlands' and, I suspect, from other movies I didn't immediately recognize."[39] Canby continued, "When Jean-Luc Godard and François Truffaut did this sort of thing 25 years ago, it served as an affirmation of their regard for works too long unrecognized. It

FIGURE 4.2 Raising Arizona's allusionistic, cartoonish mise-en-scène: a motor-cycle thug, like many of the film's characters, is a thinly drawn homage.

announced pride in what then seemed to be an arcane heritage. Today it seems mostly a film-school affectation, which is a major problem with 'Raising Arizona.' Like 'Blood Simple,' it's full of technical expertise but has no life of its own." Roger Ebert had similar complaints about the film's in-quotation-marks style, describing it as a film in which "everybody talks as if they were reading out of an old novel about a bunch of would-be colorful characters. They usually end up sounding silly."[40] Ebert also called the dialogue "arch and artificial."

The reputation of the Coens as masters of tone and style could not have been established had these reactions come to typify a prevailing wisdom or critical consensus on their work. It was probably significant that their next two films were both back on noirish ground, and that the subsequent comedy, *The Hudsucker Proxy* was widely received as their weakest work to date. And yet from the perspective of the early 2010s, the strength of the Coens' comedies looks to rival that of their dramas. *The Big Lebowski* and *O Brother* are highly regarded and *Raising Arizona* has become a modern classic.

Perhaps the most significant testament to its enduring value is that a whole generation of television comedies has mimicked its live-action-cartoon style, coming to be known as single-camera sitcoms. The combination of fantastical, colorful imagery, using editing to sell a joke, ironic voice-over narration, and amusing, exaggerated scoring is now a standard cluster of conventions in shows such as *My Name Is Earl*, which claims it as inspiration.[41]

Raising Arizona betrays other influences in its heightened, in-quotation-marks style. Kriest identifies prison and gangster films, domestic and screwball comedies, apocalypse movies, and spaghetti westerns in addition to cartoons, and refers to this style as postmodern.[42] Carolyn R. Russell also cites screwball influences and notes that the use of matter-of-fact descriptive titles over the shots introducing the Arizona family spoofs the crime docudrama genre.[43] James Mottram rejects screwball comedies as an influence (I would agree that sophisticated romantic comedies like *The Philadelphia Story* [1940] seem distant from *Raising Arizona*'s aesthetic even though the Coens do like sparring couples speaking fast-paced banter). Mottram points to yet other influences: *Vanishing Point* (a desert highway film, 1971), *Bonnie and Clyde* (1967), the Keystone Kops, and Buster Keaton.[44] He writes that, "The colorful landscape of *Raising Arizona* acts as a washing machine, churning up film references to see what will come out of the wash."[45] And he quotes Pauline Kael's review: "At times it has a Preston Sturges spirit crossed with the cartoon abandon of the early Gene Wilder and Mel Brooks comedies. It's the appropriation of a movie." Finally, Mottram finds that the film's cinematography "marries Bertolucci and Chuck Jones," noting that the Coens and Barry Sonnenfeld screened *The Conformist* (1970) before shooting the film, as well as *The Third Man* (1949). Russell is no less enthralled by the film's allusionism. She admires the film's visual style for its very unreality. While the film is nominally set in Tempe, she writes, "its filmspace delineates an imaginary geography which combines the architectural style of a theme park with the contours of a Warner Brothers [sic] cartoon. It is pure synthetic post-modern fabulism, a projected world where each image is metaphoric and highly allusive." Whereas Roger Ebert found the heightened and artificial dialogue to be an aesthetic liability, Russell makes the opposite conclusions. In *Raising Arizona*, the Coen brothers use the spoken word to convey the importance of artifice in their system of representation. The film's characters "composed themselves from language appropriated from various sources. Their clichéd speech reveals the pop cultural foundations of their existence."[46] Thus the film is a classic "postmodern bricolage" whose "fervid absurdisms incorporate and transcend the conventions of many disparate film forms."[47] (Wikipedia adds yet additional allusions: for instance, bathroom graffiti in the film reading "P.O.E." is a reference to *Dr. Strangelove* [1964], in which those letters stand for both "peace on earth" and "purity of essence.")[48]

The pop-pomo interpretive strategy sets the expectations for further excursions into Coen comedy territory. The use of allusionism and pastiche—a clear sense of debt to sources and an unreal quality to the way reality is represented on screen—establishes that their comedy should be taken a certain way: as a carnivalesque mishmash of styles and characters, images and references. And these very qualities are themselves sources not only of aesthetic interest but of humor. If comedy, among other things, is the product of incongruity, then a pastiche approach such as the Coens' can itself be a source of amusement. In the case of *Raising Arizona* the incongruity might include the combination of live-action and cartoon influences, the collision of western and science fiction imagery, and as in many of their films, the contradiction of stupid or hickish characters speaking too smartly (e.g., John Goodman in *O Brother* uses the term "tout court"). The rampant allusionism and quotation create expectations for future films in a humorous vein. Their subsequent comedies have fulfilled this promise, often pursuing the hodgepodge approach to managing influences. (This is in contrast to the approach more typical of the dramas, to stick to a more central source as in *Miller's Crossing*, which is pretty well restricted to riffing on Dashiell Hammett and Hollywood gangster films.) In order for the brothers' reputation to grow and for their alternative vision to remain distinct from the mainstream Hollywood approach to managing influences, the postmodernist interpretive schema had to replace the more staid and conservative frame applied by critics like Ebert and Canby.

In some way, every Coen brothers film until *Fargo* has some deep connection to the mid-century era in American popular culture; each of these films bears a relation of influence to texts, genres, characters, settings, and archetypes of this time. The *Hudsucker Proxy* maintained the interest all of the previous Coens films had in the studio era of Hollywood. In this case, however, the influences are more specifically cinematic and more legitimately screwball, and in particular the films of Preston Sturges, Howard Hawks, and especially Frank Capra. *Hudsucker* is among the Coens films most clearly inspired by a film-maker, the Capra of optimistic ordinary Joe heroes who ascend, in fairy-tale fashion, to ranks of power they could never have imagined, only to discover grim realities about power and ambition. Todd Mc-Carthy in *Variety* makes clear the debt owed not only to Capra but to each Hollywood screwball director who inspired the film: " 'Hud-sucker' plays like a Frank Capra film with a Preston Sturges hero and dialogue direction by Howard Hawks." And like many critics of his generation, McCarthy faulted the Coens for taking the allusive approach to their work: " 'The Hudsucker Proxy' is no doubt one of the most inspired and technically stunning pastiches of old Hollywood pictures ever to come out of the New Hollywood. But a pastiche it remains, as nearly everything in the Coen brothers' latest and biggest film seems like a wizardly but artificial synthesis, leaving a hole in the middle where some emotion and humanity should be."[49] The elements of pastiche are clear to those looking for them. Tim Robbins plays a screwball everyman, while Jennifer Jason Leigh is the fast-talking Hawksian woman, like Rosalind Russell in *His Girl Friday* (1940) crossed with the Jean Arthur character in *Mr. Smith Goes to Washington* (1939), whose feelings about the naive hero change as she overcomes her cynicism. Meanwhile, her accent channels Katherine Hepburn (fig. 4.3).

Janet Maslin in the *Times* made clear that what is a failure to the Coens' detractors is an achievement in the eyes of an admirer like herself: "To appreciate the Coens, it is necessary to delight in their films' stylized, surface charms."[50] Even fence-sitters like Ebert, who wrote his review as a dialogue between the angel and devil on either of his shoulders pushing him one way and the other in his evaluation of the Coens' pastiche, could not help but be impressed by the homage to studio-era aesthetics. The film was made on a relatively lavish budget for 1994 of $40 million and produced by Joel Silver in one of those many ill-fated encounters between the indies and the studios. This enabled the Coens to re-create art deco décor and architecture on a monumental scale, pushing the cartoonish exaggeration of *Raising Arizona* into period urban interiors, with high ceilings and board-room conference tables like racetracks, skyscraper doorways several stories high, a hectic mailroom with labyrinthine hydraulic tubes and

FIGURE 4.3 Jennifer Jason Leigh as screwball heroine in the mold of Jean Arthur or Rosalind Russell in *The Hudsucker Proxy*.

letters cascading into overflowing bins, and a clocktower works of
mammoth gears overlooking the city and presented to the accompaniment of comically grandiose voices-of-angles choral scoring. Interiors
are appointed with elegant symmetry and cool corporate blues and
grays. A filing cabinet soars above the office floor so that a secretary
has to climb a ladder (fig. 4.4). In the accounting office, identical rows
of blue-gray metal desks recede into an almost infinite distance with
almost identical gray-suited middle-aged men seated at them. When
Norville (Robbins) enters Mr. Mussberger's office to deliver a letter,
he has to cross a huge expanse of carpet before getting to the man's
desk (fig. 4.5).

Even the film's subtle and less elaborate moments are played for
exaggeration. When Norville and Amy (Leigh) kiss, the swell of or-
chestral scoring mocks them in its excessive emotion, and the shadowy shapes of skyscrapers in the background seem too romantic for
the moment. The film's basic plot has similar qualities of excess: a

FIGURES 4.4 AND 4.5 Mise-en-scène exaggerated for comical effect in
The Hudsucker Proxy.

rube from the sticks is supposed to sink a company that needs to de-
flate its stock price, and they follow his idea for a big hoop toy that
the board hopes will fail, only to see it turn into a craze: the hula
hoop. As in *Raising Arizona*, exaggeration and stylization draw attention to imitative form.

The introduction of the newspaper office comes in a scene that
epitomizes the tough-talking newspaper editor, played by John Ma-
honey, yelling at a breakneck pace at his reporters to get the story on
the guy who no one knows anything about, barking questions like
"What makes the Idea Man tick?" and "Has he got a girl? Has he
got parents?" The editor's office is cramped, crowded, and dark in
comparison to the Hudsucker sets, with more compact desks and
chairs and venetian blinds filtering the light. Leigh's Amy Archer is
a pastiche of mid-century masculinized career girls like *His Girl Friday*'s Hildy, storming out of rooms and slapping men who offend her.
This is as much a hardscrabble exaggeration of the news office as the
corporate interiors are a stylization of the excess and drama of the

modernist American office. The stylization of the film's re-creation of period is of a piece with its dialogue, overwritten to match the visuals. Armed with the reading strategies now familiar from previous encounters with the Coens' films, critics and admirers could take the pastiche of styles and historical re-creation to be a virtue, to invite a pleasurable reconstruction of influences, a gratifying "getting it."

There are moments of extra wink-winking, self-conscious passages in which the narrative is literally set at a remove from the audience. One of these is the first meeting of Amy and Norville in the coffee shop, narrated by a pair of cabbies at a counter who observe the scene that plays out between our two main characters. One whistles as Amy walks in the door, narrating: "Enter the dame" while the other replies, "There's one in every story." They continue their play-by-play: "She's looking for her mark." She sees Norville. "She finds him. She sits down and orders . . ." And later in the same scene: "She's losin' him, Lou." "Maybe she's wise." "She don't look wise." Another is the mock-newsreel segment called "Tidbits of Time" that tells the story of the rise of the hula hoop. Mock-newsreels are themselves such standards of Hollywood filmmaking, from *Citizen Kane* (1941) on, that this segment might be considered a pastiche of a pastiche, with flashbulbs firing and Norville surrounded by microphones, and a scientist in a white coat explaining the hula hoop in a German accent. Another comical German accent comes in the segment of a psychoanalyst discussing Norville as a case of severe mental illness presented through a pseudoscientific lecture to the Hudsucker board illustrated by amateur film footage of Norville. In the climactic scene as Norville's plunge from the forty-fourth story is halted, frozen in time, Waring Hudsucker appears as an angel with a halo and a white ukulele, an exaggeration of Clarence from *It's a Wonderful Life* (1946). And the dialogue even in ordinary scenes can be ironic at the expense of plausibility, as when Amy says of the hula hoop, "finally there would be a . . . a thing-a-ma-jig that would bring everyone together . . . even if it kept them apart spatially . . . you know, for kids." All of these devices function to emphasize the surface, to push the audience toward pastiche as a reading strategy, and to play the game of form.

Like many of the Coens' films, whether comic or melodramatic, *The Hudsucker Proxy* opens with a monologue in a voice-over spoken in a distinct idiolect, in this case that of a wise African-American old-timer speaking omnisciently about Norville Barnes (considering a jump of dozens of stories to his death), and in more general, pontificating terms about the human desire to seize time. He speaks in a slangy idiom. To describe the coming of a new year, he speaks of "Old Daddy Earth fixing to start one more trip around the sun," and in contemplating the character's suicide he asks, "Is Norville really going to jelly up the sidewalk?" As in *Raising Arizona* and *The Big Lebowski*, this device distances the audience and indicates the humorous tone of the film. It reminds us not to take the Coens seriously in the sense that their stories are not meant as documents of real life. To the pop-pomo spectator, these voice-overs come off as pastiches of introductory narrations, voice-overs implicitly about voice-overs. And they only get more inane as the Coens' career progresses, especially in the case of the Stranger, the cowboy character played by Sam Elliott, who introduces *The Big Lebowski*. Openings of films set expectations for the formal patterning of the whole work, and in the case of the Coen brothers' comedies, the tone established by the voice-over introduction functions to put the audience on notice that exaggeration and stylization will rule the day. Dialogue throughout *The Hudsucker Proxy* works in a similar way to the introductory monologue, heightened, stylized, and idiolectic. The elevator operator, for instance, is an obnoxious chatterbox with a Brooklyn accent, telling awful jokes and then explaining them: "it's a pun, it's a knee-slapper, it's a play on . . ." The script also gets laughs from the repetition of inane lines, like Norville's explanation of his sketch of a hula hoop, a plain circle on a piece of brown paper, which he describes only with the line, "you know, for kids!"

The key to the Coens' reputation as pastiche artists would seem to be a recognition that no deeper thematic significance is necessary to appreciate their imitations. With *The Big Lebowski*, the comic pastiche reaches its most elaborate and outrageous heights. Each character is his or her own little unlikely pastiche of clashing types, and each speaks in his or her own idiolect: the Dude (Jeff Bridges), a SoCal hippie who is thrust into the role of private eye; Walter (John Goodman), an easily enraged Vietnam vet who is also an Orthodox Jew; Maude Lebowski (Julianne Moore), the feminist/Fluxus artist who is also an heiress with an upper-crust society accent. The nihilists who threaten the Dude are a parody of the German synthesizer band Kraftwerk, and their accents and diction are likewise absurd, threatening the Dude's "Johnson" and pronouncing the "w" in Lebowski like a "v." Jesus Quintana, John Turturro's flamboyant purple-clad bowler, is a study of Latino machismo with a feminine undercurrent and a criminal past. The Stranger who introduces the film in voice-over and reappears at the midpoint and conclusion is a western character, drawling against the accompaniment of "Tumblin' Tumbleweeds." The protagonist's nickname, "the Dude," is also a product of the world of the western. All of these different identities are incongruously brought together through the culture of bowling.

In addition to these incongruous character-texts, the film has its most central cinematic and literary allusions. To Raymond Chandler's *The Big Sleep* and the 1946 film adapted from it, *Lebowski* owes not only its title but also its scenario of a detective working for a man who is concerned for a young, irresponsible, female member of the household and its structure of episodic encounters with colorful characters. And to Busby Berkeley it owes its dream/fantasy sequence, "Gutterballs," with chorines in bowling-pin headdresses,

FIGURE 4.6 A Busby Berkeley pastiche dream sequence in *The Big Lebowski*.

kaleidoscopic flowers of girls, and a through-the-legs shot astride a bowling lane (fig. 4.6).

The Dude's dialogue in *Lebowski* gives us an epitome of the Coens' style in the way the character appropriates other people's words. The Dude repurposes George H. W. Bush's remark that "this aggression will not stand" (a reference to Iraq's invasion of Kuwait) in complaining to the big Lebowski about his rug. He uses Maude Lebowski's phrase "in the parlance of our times" in qualifying his reference to the big Lebowski's spouse, Bunny Lebowski, as a "trophy wife." Central plot devices in the film, a faked kidnapping and a briefcase full of cash, are borrowed from the Coens' previous film, *Fargo*. Like the Dude, the Coens see what they like and just use it, and this might be the best explanation for the form of *The Big Lebowski* we could want. Like the Dude, the Coens often prefer imitation to originality, and this paradoxically is their style. The Coens are fans of culture, and their filmmaking is a professional extension of their fandom. Pastiche is a way of appreciating the things one likes or finds interesting. In this sense it does have a critical function, though not critical in the way parody is critical, by putting down.

Lebowski is the Coen brothers film that has the strongest affinity with amateur fan cultures of recycling and appropriation. In this film, their play is that of wide-eyed enthusiasts who want to participate in their culture, to experience it as creators and not just as consumers, and to encourage others to share their passions. From this perspective, it is not surprising that an elaborate cult following has attached itself to *Lebowski*, a community of admirers devoted precisely to the repetition and re-creation of the object of its affection. The gatherings such as Lebowskifest, the T-shirts and bumper stickers, the book *I'm a Lebowski, You're a Lebowski*, the culture of *Lebowski* fandom, is dedicated to nothing more than the consecration of lines of dialog and images from the film as culturally significant.[51] The biggest kick the *Lebowski* fan gets would seem to be from finding novel ways of repeating moments from the film to an audience that will recognize them. The Coen brothers aesthetic could not be better epitomized than it is by this mode of communal, fetishizing appreciation.

Miller's Crossing

The Coen brothers' comedies generally function according to principles of wildly clashing styles, hodgepodge aesthetics bringing together disparate elements, and exaggeration and stylization of familiar historical forms. The tone of their melodramas is quite different in many ways. These films are renowned for their extreme violence, their sense of inevitable destruction and mayhem. In terms of their approach to pastiche, the Coens' melodramas tend much more toward appropriating a more circumscribed set of influences. *Blood Simple* takes on *noir* and James M. Cain. *The Man Who Wasn't There* is generally seen as an evocation of Hitchcock, especially in its choice of an everyman hero and the setting of Santa Rosa, California, where *Shadow of a Doubt* takes place. *Barton Fink* is highly evocative, but formally unconventional, veering as it progresses toward its obscure conclusion into more arty and esoteric territory. By the end it seems more like a parody of an art film than a pastiche of a Hollywood genre. *Fargo* and *No Country for Old Men* are melodramas in the old-fashioned sense and imitate familiar genres and conventions least

FIGURES 4.7 AND 4.8 Both the title shot and the final shot in *Miller's Crossing* emphasize the iconic gangster's fedora.

of all, though both are of course in the tradition of American crime stories about foolish men whose bad decisions wreak incredible havoc and destruction on themselves and those around them.[52]

Miller's Crossing is the Coen brothers melodrama most indebted to familiar forms, most pastiche-like, though its pastiche is more focused on a small number of devices in contrast to the brothers' comedies, which are more wide-ranging. The acknowledged central source of *Miller's Crossing* is literary: the novels of Dashiell Hammett. Ethan Coen told an interviewer, "*Miller's Crossing* is pretty much just a shameless rip-off of Dashiell Hammett, mostly his novel *The Glass Key*, but to a lesser extent *Red Harvest*. More than anything else, it was an enthusiasm for Hammett's writing that was the genesis of that movie. It's Hammett—in a word, that's what it is."[53] Catherine Russell observes of the film that in addition to Hammett, the Coens took inspiration from classic gangster films including *Little Caesar* (1931), *The Public Enemy* (1931), and *The Godfather* cycle (1972, 1974, 1990). She makes clear as well that the film works within the

allusive pastiche aesthetics that also characterizes their comedies. "*Miller's Crossing* relies, as do all Coen films, upon a shared frame of reference between filmmakers and audience; this intersubjectivity allows for a complex and witty deployment of generic conventions. There is a sharp sense of ironic glee in the Coens' strategic manipulations, which work well because they are rooted in clear affection for and appreciation of the classic modality."[54] In support of her points she quotes Terrence Rafferty's review in the *New Yorker* that the film "is not so much a gangster movie as an extended, elaborate allusion to one."[55] James Naremore seizes on *Miller's Crossing* as "one of cinema's purest examples of what Jameson means by pastiche," drawing on Hammett without directly quoting or adapting him, and also lifting mise-en-scène from *The Maltese Falcon* (1941) and the 1942 adaptation of *The Glass Key* directed by Stuart Heisler.[56]

One device in *Miller's Crossing* functions especially prominently within this aesthetic: the male characters' hats (figs. 4.7 and 4.8). Naremore asserts that the film is "about" hats more than anything else, and in particular their glamour. To some critics, the film's emphasis on hats is so excessive that nothing can account for it beyond the filmmakers' fetishistic interest in them as such. Denby calls them "symbol[s] . . . without referent[s]."[57] In this context Naremore faults the Coens for being mere pasticheurs: "Such attention to fetishistic detail is appropriate to the genre, but *Miller's Crossing* differs strikingly from any of its predecessors in its refusal to engage seriously with American political or social history . . . it is incapable of creating a sense of tragedy. Moreover, in contrast to even the most conservative forms of comic parody, it does not even make us laugh at the things it imitates."[58] This is as clear an extension of Jamesonian critique to the Coen brothers as one might find, and while I concur that the film is "about" its hats among other surface details, the point that the film cannot be praised unless it engages seriously with history fails to notice that the film engages with nothing *but* history—with the cultural history of images and words and customs that have been collected in the genres of murder melodrama, *film noir*, gangster movies, and related modes of representation.

Hats in *Miller's Crossing* serve as an overdetermined metaphor of violent masculinity and its power, and they achieve their effects through the associations viewers are expected to have with men's hats, in particular from representations in media, especially old movies like *The Maltese Falcon* and newer movies set in historical periods like *The Godfather* (1972) and *The Untouchables* (1987).[59] While characters in American studio-era films wear hats in many genres, from musicals and screwball comedies to prestige dramas and detective films, an emphasis on male characters' haberdashery recalls gangster films in particular, and in particular their representations of masculine tragic heroes. The 1990s retro cycle of pre-1960s-set American gangster films, of which *Miller's Crossing* is one central example, makes men's hats one central icon of tough-guy male identity, typically reducing them "to an unambiguous symbol of male authority, gender conformity, and masculine self-possession."[60]

Few spectators of indie films in the 1990s were old enough to remember a time when men ordinarily wore the style of hats depicted in the film, or when a man would not think to go out without a hat, would feel naked without it as the film's protagonist Tom Regan (Gabriel Byrne) clearly does in the early scenes of *Miller's Crossing*. The audience for *Miller's Crossing* at the time of its release would have had only mediated experience of men in hats. Indeed, few sartorial icons of the twentieth century can be so evocative of lost time. Unlike other items of men's apparel, the hat was obligatory for much of the century, but then quickly went out of fashion in the late 1950s and early 1960s.[61] Why this happened has been subject to great speculation and debate, but it was certainly part of the loosening of social rigidity and the spread of casual and often working-class dress to all echelons of society, which was part of a wider social transformation that included the emergence of teenagers with consumer power and a culture of their own. Like the sexual revolution and the civil rights movement, changes in dress transformed everyday life. To depict a world in which hats are not just worn but emphasized is to call forth associations with a great before, a historical period markedly different from our own, distant and yet familiar through the filter of photography and cinematography. The Coens use hats to convey a theme, but more significantly within the context of their oeuvre and my discussion of it here, they use hats to refer and evoke, to curate the styles of the past as a critical project, styles which the literate audience for indie cinema is expected to recognize and appreciate.

All of the male characters in *Miller's Crossing* wear hats, but they do not all wear the same kind. They also do not wear them in every scene; some characters go hatless at times, which may be motivated by etiquette (men would doff their hats as specific occasions would demand, for instance in a restaurant or club) or dramatic logic (Tom loses his hat in a poker game and has to retrieve it; a man—the same man—who is about to be killed has his hat tossed away by his assailant). The presence or absence of the hat and the choice of style are significant motifs that express character traits and convey plot information. And the way the film emphasizes hats, for instance by having the dialogue refer to them explicitly or by having them pulled down over a character's eyes, makes clear that this motif is to be noticed and appreciated.

Rather than merely dressing all of the men in the same snap-brim fedora, the film varies style according to character and situation. Tom is the flawed hero playing his boss, his boss's rival, his boss's girl, and his boss's enemies all against each other. He wears the classic fedora, often pulled down past his eyes. We know this is a significant motif as soon as we see it in the credit sequence under the words "Miller's Crossing." Tom is matched in his hat style by his counterpart Eddie

Dane (J. E. Freeman), the taciturn tough guy who serves as right hand to Johnnie Caspar (Jon Polito), an Italian rival to Tom's Irish boss, Leo (Albert Finney), and himself a pastiche of ethnic gangster characters. (When he is in a hat, Caspar wears a homburg, which is like a fedora but with an upturned brim, a style often called the "Godfather," which is associated with Italian organized crime and its cinematic representations.) Eddie Dane is violent, sarcastic, stoical, and hypermasculine, and he would be a cliché of gangster-tough manliness if not for his homosexuality. The fact that Tom and Dane wear the same style of hat establishes them as parallel characters: both are henchman to a more powerful, more diminutive, older boss. Both are presumably expected to serve as both counsel and muscle.

Early in the film, a private eye character named Rug Daniels is found murdered by a boy in a cap. A cap is a softer, more casual hat, more likely than a hat with a brim all around to be worn by children and the working class. It is thus significant that later, this style of hat will reappear on the head of Bernie Birnbaum (John Turturro), the "shmatte kid" (*shmatte* is Yiddish for "rag" and this nickname reinforces Bernie's Jewish ethnicity) who is a weaselly, chiseling bookie who tries to peddle influence with more powerful men through the agency of his lover, Eddie Mink (Steve Buscemi), and his sister, Verna (Marcia Gay Harden), who is in bed with Leo. Bernie also appears in a bowler, a more old-fashioned style than a fedora that viewers might associate with dandies and Englishmen but certainly not manly gangsters. The film begins with Johnnie Caspar seeking Leo's permission to kill Bernie, but Leo resists him because of Verna. In the film's first climactic scene at Miller's Crossing, Tom Regan in a fedora is entrusted with murdering a hatless Bernie, but Bernie weeps and pleads for his life and Tom, in a moment of injudicious mercy, spares Bernie's life. Thus the use of haberdashery styles—fedora, homburg, bowler, cap, hatlessness—represents character traits, especially traits of manliness and toughness that are essential in defining the gangster characters who stand at the center of the film in terms both of the narrative situation and the Coens' larger ambitions of critical pastiche.

But the sheer preponderance of hat images and references cannot be explained entirely by characterization. The emphasis on hats is virtually constant and emphatically signaled as important. When Caspar is offended, he accuses interlocutors of showing him "the high hat." When Verna and Tom are about to have sex, she removes his

hat and it falls on the seat of a chair as a synecdoche for their un-
dressing to get in bed. Later Tom narrates a dream he has of chasing
his hat across a forest (an image foreshadowed in the opening credit
sequence), and here is where he articulates the film's aphoristic theme:
"there's nothing more foolish than a man chasin' his hat." When Tom
is about to kill Bernie at Miller's Crossing, he has his hat brim pulled
low over his eyes. But when Tom is about to be killed in that very
spot, his hat is tossed away by Eddie Dane. When Johnnie Caspar has
been killed by Bernie Birnbaum but not shown onscreen, we find out
that this has happened when we see Johnnie's homburg on a flight
of stairs, the headless hat shown as a sign of the character's demise.
(This bit of artful narration may be evocative of 1930s crime films:
Esther Sonnet and Peter Stanfield note that in the 1931 gangster picture *City Streets*, "an unattended hat is a metonym for the death of
its owner.")[62] The removal of a hat may signal an impending death,
and death is omnipresent in the world of the film. But having your hat
on is no guarantee you will live; Eddie Dane is killed by his own boss
while wearing his.

The final shot of the film pushes in on Tom, standing by a tree in
Miller's Crossing, his hat again pulled down low. Eventually it finds
his eyes peering out from underneath, a look that mixes anxiety and
perseverance. Tom has been many other characters' punching bag,
but he survives and keeps his hat as a kind of armor to protect himself and establish his toughness even though, as we know by the end,
he is actually quite soft on the inside: fearful, merciful, and avoiding
having to commit violence himself. Thus the hat is an ironic icon,
promising tough masculinity but also hiding the compassionate and
humane side of the gangster hero who according to genre mythology
is supposed to be strong to the core.

And yet even as I offer this interpretation, one that I think is
rather obvious, I also feel strongly that it cannot explain the power of
the hats in a film so suffused with their images. It might be tempting
to view the hats as figures of excess, of meaning that cannot be contained within a textual system that points to a rupture in signification.
We might feel we are being asked to pay more attention to hats than
they really warrant, and the attention thus can be seen as escaping the
meaning a thematic interpretation can offer. But "excess" arguments
often fail to account for the power of extratextual references to be
assimilated within larger frameworks of interpretation and meaning-

making.[63] An "excess" position on the hats in *Miller's Crossing* might avail itself of a psychoanalytic perspective (e.g., it stands for unconscious sexual desire) or a poststructuralist Marxist one (e.g., it stands for the insoluble contradictions of capitalism). But these modes of interpretation still locate meaning at the textual level. I propose that in addition to interpretive opportunities at the level of plot and character, hats in *Miller's Crossing* offer an invitation for play with historical iconography and cinematic style, especially available to literate audiences whose frame of reference is shared with the filmmakers.

Like the literary and filmic and musical allusions so many of their films make, like the mischievous titles introducing *Fargo* and *O, Brother*, like the refusal of *Barton Fink* and *No Country* to tell their stories straightforwardly, the suffusion of hat images in *Miller's Crossing* functions to direct the audience's interest outward from the text to its context, to appreciate the relation between the movie and its inspirations, models (whether positive or negative), and countertexts like gangster films and Hammett novels. As Harold Bloom argues of the works of great literature, the Coens' films arise from a negotiation of influences, and they dramatize this process and its implications, making their cultural and historical sources as much a thematic preoccupation as anything else they have made movies about.[64] The point in *Miller's Crossing* is not just to struggle against any particular film or novel. The point is also to play with the language of Hollywood's representations of the prohibition-era gangster (and cop, politician, moll, etc.), with its diction and prosody, its sartorial style, its ethical codes, its gender and ethnic types, and its social customs. This play functions to assess the historical distance from then to now, to compare the present against the past and better understand where we are and begin to see the implications of our specific location in history as measured against another era. Thus there is a sociological and historical value to a film set in the past that is so invested in reviving its images and sounds—not the value of being an accurate representation of past reality, of fetishizing historicity, since the Coens obviously are not interested in that, but the value of consecrating an idea of the past as it has been represented culturally. To genre artists like the Coens, the function of play with sources is to curate popular culture's representations of a time, its personalities, its imagery and argots.

It is an affectionate tribute, but also an effort at preservation and critical exaggeration. One essential component of Coen genre play is exaggeration and supplementation, as *Blood Simple* peppers horror-film iconography on a *film noir* situation. One locus of exaggeration in *Miller's Crossing* is a sequence in which Leo is ambushed in his home by Johnnie Caspar's thugs. He manages to elude them craftily, hopping out a bedroom window and down to the ground below while the house burns. From the ground he sees a goon with a gun in the bedroom above and Leo kills him with an incredible fusillade of machine-gun fire. The death above against the backdrop of flames is enacted as a "Tommy Gun ballet" of extended duration to the accompaniment of "Danny Boy" from Leo's Victrola. The manic gunfire and the baroque death dance exceed in visceral impact anything one might find in classical-era gangster cinema (part of its art was in indirection, evading the Production Code by artfully staging deaths in shadow or offscreen). Devices like these insist on distance between past and present, the better to recognize the past as having its own distinct period and style. Appreciating a film like *Miller's Crossing* requires a recognition of a distance between then and now. The Coens are not interested in re-creating an old style as it was; pastiche only works when the audience recognizes that the form being copied is a copy, that it has formal similarity without being identical. (It is for this reason that the film is not an adaptation of Hammett, since an adaptation works differently from a pastiche.) Pastiche can never copy everything; when it does so, it ceases to be pastiche.

So with the film's dialogue: no Hammett novel or Hollywood crime film of the 1930s or '40s has the exact diction and rhythm of *Miller's Crossing*, and yet the use of slang and cadences of speech are highly evocative. In many of their films, the Coens achieve a kind of linguistic pastiche, adopting a style of talk without lifting lines directly. The signature greeting of *Miller's Crossing*, "What's the Rumpus?" appears in Hammett, but *Miller's Crossing* makes it into a slogan. Caspar's repetition of the phrase, "I'm sick of the high hat!" establishes that he speaks in an idiomatic idiolect without necessarily evoking any gangster in particular. Slang words like "dangle" (for "leave") and "twist" (for "woman") are spoken in a way that encourages the audience to appreciate their distinctive periodicity and genericity. Part of this sense might come simply from the reputation of the Coens as genre pasticheurs, which creates a kind of feedback loop of meaning: they don't even need to exaggerate to make their historical settings into pastiche because the audience expects them to be so and applies their interpretive frame. But the audience did not get its idea of the Coens' aesthetic from nowhere; it was the product of a body of work in which history lives in the present, in the museum of past styles that is Joel and Ethan Coen's oeuvre.

Conclusion

This chapter began with the idea that the Coen brothers' films can be appreciated on two levels: the conventional one that pleases the average moviegoer with standard narrative appeals, and the allusive one of imitative form—of pastiche. This distinction implies that one need not appreciate the Coens' imitativeness to enjoy their films, which helps explain how their work has managed to carve out more than just a small niche in the blockbuster era of American cinema. Palmer describes this double-faced quality in *Blood Simple* as "commercial/independent."[65] Thus *Lebowski* works as zany comedy and *Miller's Crossing* has the appeal of a gripping, tightly plotted thriller. The Coen brothers' work has been appreciated through the rubric of maverick, outsider, indie cinema even as many of their films have been released by major distributors.

This double-level quality puts their work squarely within the pop-pomo mode of cultural appropriation, in the good company of *The Simpsons* and *The Matrix* (1999) and many other instances of culture one would not likely call independent or indie. At the same time, however, the Coens have maintained an outsider identity in American filmmaking by insisting so much on their distinctive, stylized, imitative approach. They manage to be crowd-pleasing and alternative at the same time, and in this they are emblematic of much of the elite American culture of their era. The divorce of independent cinema and Hollywood has always been exaggerated—often even imaginary—and in the Sundance-Miramax era the connections between these modes of filmmaking are everywhere from economics to aesthetics. Still, the concept of indie persists in the face of this, and the formal play of the Coens' films persists as one paradigm of indie film practice. By offering their audience something more on that second level of pastiche, by refusing to compromise their rigorous referentiality, by pushing the surface to such prominence over so many films, Joel and Ethan Coen have maintained the identity they owned up to when receiving the

Academy Award for *No Country for Old Men*: playing in their corner of the sandbox, a space apart from the rest of the mainstream Hollywood playground.[66]

Playing with form, making it a game for the audience to participate in rather than merely a conduit for narrative as in less ludic modes of cinema, offers a distinct appeal within the culture of moviegoing. In the case of the films of Joel and Ethan Coen, this is principally play with genre and with inspiring literary and cinematic sources, with conventions of plot, character, setting, and theme, with iconography and language. And although this kind of play offers its own rewards, it also functions as creative historiography, repurposing the images and ideas of the past in a new context. Another kind of play in American independent cinema is on the level of narrative structures. This complementary game of form is the subject of the next chapter.

chapter 5 GAMES OF NARRATIVE FORM | Pulp Fiction and Beyond | [Tarantino]

represents the final triumph of postmodernism, which is to empty the artwork of all content.—James Wood[1]

If the American independent cinema of the Sundance-Miramax era has produced a masterpiece, it is *Pulp Fiction* (1994). Tarantino's opus topped many critics' best of the 1990s lists and was crowned by *Entertainment Weekly* in 2008 as the #1 classic of the past twenty-five years.[2] *Pulp Fiction* has been celebrated for many of its qualities (and damned in some quarters for the very same ones). Like the Coen brothers' films, *Pulp Ficiton* is densely referential, packed with allusions and homages to everything from *Bande à Parte* (1964) and *Deliverance* (1972) to *Happy Days* (ABC, 1974–1984) and *Kung Fu* (ABC, 1972–1975). Tarantino is much more catholic than the Coens in his taste, with a predilection for ephemera and trash like no other in the pantheon of American directors. In the opening scene of *Reservoir Dogs* (1992), his feature film debut, Tarantino established as one of his signatures the lively idle chatter of hoodlums about popular culture. That scene's ostensible subject is the meaning of "Like a Virgin," and its principle speaker is the character played by the director, Mr. Brown, who asserts that the song "is a metaphor for big dicks." This scene announced not only a profane, humorous personal style but also a mode of reception for Tarantino and the many films that would follow his lead: they were to be taken not just as thrill-rides of macho bravado, violence, and smart banter but also as *meta*, as pop culture about pop culture, appealing surface textures that satisfy their audience as such. *Pulp Fiction* is about hamburgers (like the Big Kahuna burger Jules tastes before killing a man, and the Royale with cheese that Vincent ate in Europe). It is about the 1950s Hollywood icons who populate Jack Rabbit Slim's, a retro diner where the characters dance the twist. It is about the glowing briefcase borrowed from *Kiss Me Deadly* (1955) and the Mexican standoff borrowed from *Reservoir Dogs* and Hong Kong action films like *City of Fire* (1987), which it casually copies. The film is a series of riffs. An analysis of Tarantino's allusive aesthetics would support the same kind of approach to his films, as a central body of work within the corpus of American independent cinema, as I have taken to the Coens: they have a critical historiographic function, training the audience's eye on the relics of our cultural past that Tarantino considers worth preserving. Many of the same points could be made about *Pulp Fiction*'s multiple sources and their relationship to the meanings of the film and the oeuvre of its director. But this chapter will focus on a different aspect of his films, and more generally of American independent cinema, that puts an emphasis on form, and in particular—as in the previous chapter—on ludic or game-like form, form that offers its own rewards, its own pleasures.

One of *Pulp Fiction*'s most distinctive features is its unconventional, out-of-order storytelling. While hardly the first film ever to offer its narrative in a jumbled sequence, when *Pulp Fiction* appeared in 1994 it appealed to a young audience that had not been very often exposed to such experimental form in feature films. On the level of narrative ordering, *Pulp Fiction* offers up a smattering of surprises. The first scene is also the last. One of the main characters, Vincent Vega (John Travolta), is shot dead in the middle of the movie, only to be "revived" in subsequent passages. At the film's ending he is alive, but the audience knows he will soon die. The film's narrative is actually several episodes involving different characters, all of whom are only loosely connected to one another, and who are each introduced by their own chapter titles such as "The Gold Watch" and "The Bonnie Situation." And these episodes are presented out of chronological order, though without the conventional motivation of character flashbacks cued by storytelling or memory. The events of the opening scene with Pumpkin (Tim Roth) and Honey Bunny (Amanda Plummer) in the diner occur after the second scene with Vincent and Jules (Samuel L. Jackson) driving, but when the diner situation recurs and

FIGURE 5.1 Butch and Vincent meet early in *Pulp Fiction*, a moment that perhaps can be fully appreciated only on a second viewing.

continues in the film's last scene, it is now earlier than many of the scenes it succeeds, such as those of Vincent and Mia's (Uma Thurman) date and the entire "Gold Watch" segment. A moment in which characters from the first segment and the second one are all at once present—as when Butch (Bruce Willis) is getting instructions from Marsellus Wallace (Ving Rhames) about throwing his boxing match just as Vincent and Jules appear to deliver Marsellus's mysteriously glowing briefcase—can be appreciated only in retrospect, at the end of the film upon reflection or repeated viewing, for bringing together characters from the various strands of the film's multilayered narrative (fig. 5.1). (Like many viewers, I suspect, I caught the significance of this scene only when watching the film a second time.) An essential part of the experience of the film is rearranging its segments to form a coherent linear story, and perhaps more importantly, appreciating the novelty and excitement of being presented a cinematic narrative in such an unorthodox, puzzle-like format.

The metaphor most often employed in critical discourse to account for the formal distinctiveness of Tarantino is *play*. In Tarantino, form is figured as a game for the director and audience to engage in for fun, rather than (or in addition to) as a vehicle for thematic meaning.

In his survey of independent cinema, Emmanuel Levy asserts that Tarantino plays with the audience's expectations.[3] The appeal of Tarantino, according to Levy, is not so much the stories he tells as the way he tells them, and especially the ways these practices of storytelling diverge from mainstream Hollywood practice.[4] Dana Polan, in his monograph on the film, argues that those who like *Pulp Fiction* admire the way it "renders cinematic experience as pure play."[5] Polan links the film's ludicity to its puzzle-like form, demanding that the spectator arrange the pieces in the correct fashion.[6] Describing the film's divergent tones from sequence to sequence, mixing comedy and violence, he writes that "the film seems deliberately to play with the audience and keeps it on its toes."[7] But unlike modernist game-like forms such as the puzzle films of the 1960s by Alain Resnais, Polan argues that *Pulp Fiction* has no deeper meanings to be pursued beneath its ludic surface. "The breaking down of narrative in *Pulp Fiction* becomes a game, a light puzzle to be engaged in playfully, rather than a discourse on, say, perspectives of knowledge."[8] Many of the indie films that have come after *Pulp Fiction* and follow in its tradition of disordered and challenging narration have been explained using this same metaphor, as when Steven Soderbergh describes his approach in making *The Limey* (1999), a film with a much more disorienting temporal ordering than *Pulp Fiction*, as taking an opportunity to "play with narrative."[9] Soderbergh's identity as an indie *auteur* is in part a product of his preoccupation with time and the ways it can be shaped and reshaped by techniques of cinematic storytelling.[10] In comparing Soderbergh's studio films like *Erin Brockovich* (2000) and his indie films like *The Girlfriend Experience* (2009), one significant difference is that the studio films are far less playful, and thus more classical, in their temporality, though some of his crime films like *Out of Sight* (1998) and *Ocean's Twelve* (2004) do use flashbacks to generate suspense.

While he does not adopt the play metaphor specifically in reference to *Pulp Fiction*, Geoff King does accept that its aesthetic is one of surfaces rather than depths, of form as its own appeal rather than as a vehicle for deeper meaning. The effect of *Pulp Fiction* and films in its vein, he writes, is "a celebration of the mastery of cinematic flair and technique that exists as much for its own enjoyment as to be subordinated to any other motivating structure."[11] King does refer to play and game-like form in addressing the appeals of indie films in the

Pulp Fiction tradition, such as Hal Hartley's *Flirt* (1995) and Spike Jonze's *Adaptation* (2002), which he describes as "a narrative game in which the viewer is encouraged to take pleasure in the style and verve with which it eventually flips its own structure inside out."[12] Filmmakers are also sometimes fond of this metaphor; as we saw in the first chapter, Todd Haynes sees himself playing with the audience's expectations.

Accounting for Tarantino's style and the style of the indie films under his influence by using the play metaphor does not deny that there are other dimensions to this aesthetic. But play is a salient reading strategy within the culture of independent cinema, motivating filmmakers to adopt unconventional forms and motivating audiences to see such forms not only as pleasing diversions, as clever puzzles and brainteasers, but also as a means of commentary on conventional cinema—as part of the rhetoric of independent cinema's opposition, its identity as an alternative. Soderbergh, distinguishing his more formally playful indie efforts like *The Limey* and *Full Frontal* (2002) from his more mainstream crowd-pleasers, describes play with narrative as standing between the screen and the audience and waving his arms.[13] Some films, he says, do not suit such formal obtrusiveness, and in his oeuvre these less obtrusive films are precisely the more marketable, profitable studio outings, the ones that pay the way of the offbeat indies. As Soderbergh's bifurcated career illustrates, prominence of form can be one mark of indieness.

The Indie Game-Text: The Age of *Pulp Fiction*

Many American independent films of the era of Sundance and Miramax have narrative structures that are in some way similar to *Pulp Fiction*—many of these are to some extent products of Tarantino's influence, though some predate his emergence in the early 1990s. Often unconventional narrative form which can be motivated as play is also supposed to be a rejection of mainstream conventions of storytelling, according to which form is not supposed to be seen as an appeal in its own right but rather as a transparent vehicle for plot and character. Tarantino himself rigorously avoids linearity. *Jackie Brown* (1997) is probably his most conventional narrative, but in its climactic caper scene it retells the same segment of story three times, from three different characters' perspectives, each time filling in narrative information not given in the others. This is a moment of heightened self-consciousness, making the work of storytelling prominent in a way that it is not in the rest of the movie. *Kill Bill Vol I* (2003) and *Vol II*. (2004) are his most out-of-order, spreading events covering years of his characters' lives over four hours of screen time, with many jumps back and forth. And his contribution to the double-bill *Grindhouse*, *Death Proof* (2007), is an episodic concatenation of two quite different stories, with one carry-over character but totally independent situations. It too has a sequence of radical temporal discontinuity, a crash sequence at the climax of the first part with multiple overlapping shots showing the anticipation and impact from many perspectives.

Many indie films have a number of narratives presented as a series of discrete segments, such as Todd Haynes's *Poison* (1991) and Todd Solondz's *Storytelling* (2001). Richard Linklater's *Slacker* (1991) and *Waking Life* (2001) represent numerous characters each, with only tenuous, often incidental connections from one to the next. Hal Hartley's *Flirt* presents the same narrative three times, in three different settings and with different ensembles of actors.[14] Jim Jarmusch's films are often segmented by episode and in some instances also present their events out of linear order. *Mystery Train* (1989) and *Night on Earth* (1991) both represent parallel, concurrent events, with segments presented in series which occupy the same periods of time, so that the clock turns back at the beginning of segment B to where it was at the beginning of segment A. *Coffee and Cigarettes* (2003), not a conventional dramatic narrative, presents eleven chapter-titled segments that are thematically connected but shot over more than a dozen years and featuring an assortment of performers. *Broken Flowers* (2005) does follow a single character along the pursuit of a clearly defined goal, but it is episodic in the extreme, presenting a series of visits a main character makes to old lovers to discover the identity of a hitherto unknown child. Each segment is connected to the others not so much by causality as by parallelism and visual motifs such as the color pink that recur throughout. As André Bazin observed of *Bicycle Thieves* (1947), sequences in *Broken Flowers* proceed according to a logic of "then" rather than "therefore," which is an essential characteristic of episodic rather than causal narration.[15]

Doug Liman's *Go* (1999) presents a series of events that converge on a single moment in a supermarket, some which happened before the central moment, and some which occur after it. It has an overlapping temporal structure of large-scale segments about different characters, some of which are concurrent. Similarly, the narrative strands of Alejandro Gonzalez Iñarritù's 21 *Grams* (2003) converge on a fatal auto collision, in which one character kills another, after which the dead man's heart is transplanted into the body of a third character. Of course, these events are told in scrambled order, so that we meet the transplant recipient before the scene of the deadly accident. Likewise, Atom Egoyan's *The Sweet Hereafter* (1997) employs an anti-chronological unfolding in which events before and after a central catastrophic event, in this case a school bus crash, are represented in ambiguous sequence of before and after scenes. Charles Ramirez Berg calls this a "hub-and-spoke" structure.[16]

Soderbergh's films often scramble their chronology, so that *Out of Sight*, which has numerous movements back and forth in time, presents an encounter between two characters (Jack Foley and Karen Sisco: George Clooney and Jennifer Lopez, respectively) that includes drinks in a hotel bar and sex a little bit later in a hotel bed in alternating shots, with sound of the present overlapping shots of the future, flaunting its flash-forward moments without motivating them in character psychology. Like many of his playful moves, this sequence is also Soderbergh's homage to formally challenging filmmaking of the 1960s and '70s, in this case Nicholas Roeg's *Don't Look Now* (1974), which has a similar sequence alternating the coital and postcoital moments of the film's main characters, played by Julie Christie and Donald Sutherland. *The Limey* goes into much more challenging territory in its use of flash-forwards, peppering them throughout the film. Many of its shots are impossible to place as flashback or flash-forward upon first viewing (as one critic remarked of its temporal ordering, it offers both flash*backs* and flash*waybacks*),[17] especially throughout its expository sequences early in the film when one most expects coherent, straightforward narration. *The Limey* also presents single conversations in multiple locations, impossibly transporting characters from one setting to another in the middle of an exchange, so that one dialogue scene actually covers several spaces and times of day, evening and afternoon, patio and car. Like Soderbergh's earlier time-scrambling, the form of *The Limey* can be appreciated not only as play with narrative structure but also as allusion and tribute. On the DVD commentary track, the director says he had in mind to make *Get Carter* (1971) as if directed by Alain Resnais.

Christopher Nolan's *Memento* (2000), taking a page at once from Harold Pinter and *Seinfeld* (NBC, 1990–1998), famously tells its story backwards and forwards at once, alternating color scenes that move from effect to cause with black-and-white scenes that push forward and eventually converge with the backwards events to explain the mysteries at the root of the film. *Memento* is about a character who cannot form new memories, so the lack of conventional expository storytelling offers an analogue for his psychological perspective at the same time that it appeals as play, as storytelling that makes its own meta appeal and implicit critiques of conventional linearity in narration. Greg Marcks's 11:14 (2003) poaches elements of form from *Pulp Fiction*, *Go*, and *Memento*, telling a hub-and-spoke story about multiple, convergent situations presented in a series of sequences each taking us back five minutes earlier than the previous one. Like *Pulp Fiction*, 11:14 tells many stories with surprising connections among characters; like *Go* it returns several times to the same scene, each time offering us a new way of seeing it with our newly learned information; and like *Memento* it begins at the end and works backwards from effects to causes, reversing the logic of conventional story structure.

More Games: Subjective Play and Expanded Canvases

In addition to and overlapping with these and other time-scrambling films, there are indie films that offer events that are of ambiguous or impossible ontological status within their fictional worlds, somewhere between representation of objective reality and representation of fiction within fiction or subjective character fantasy. These cannot so easily be located within the sphere of Tarantino's influence, though they are just as playful—if not more playful in their own ways—than his work. These movies often borrow elements of fantasy and science fiction without fitting neatly into any genre category. Films based on the screenplays of Charlie Kaufman offer a number of examples. In *Being John Malkovich* (1999), characters discover a portal into the mind of an actor, showing us scenes through the eyes of a character who is supposed to be occupying John Malkovich's mind,

FIGURE 5.2 An indoor rainstorm represents overlapping space and time in *Eternal Sunshine of the Spotless Mind*, a film that plays with objective and subjective representation.

while in *Adaptation* the movie eventually seems to become the script being written by the main character, who is supposed to be a version of Charlie Kaufman himself. *Eternal Sunshine of the Spotless Mind* (2004) represents scenes of characters' memories that merge more than one space or time, so that characters experience a rainstorm indoors (fig. 5.2). *Eternal Sunshine* merges the ambiguity of objectivity and subjectivity with temporal play, joining them inventively through the device of the erasure of characters' memories. Thus characters who seem to be meeting for the first time in the film's expository scenes actually have a long history together, which we do not figure out until later on in the film. As with *Pulp Fiction*, we might only appreciate the full effect of this temporality on repeated viewing.

 Synecdoche, New York (2008) plays not only with character subjectivity, suggesting that its main character imagines himself to have a variety of disgusting physical ailments, but with the ambiguity between reality and its representation in narrative art. The grand theatrical work that is the life project of the protagonist, Caden (Philip Seymour Hoffman), requires the re-creation of a whole city's domestic reality inside an enormous warehouse, and the line between the sources of the art and the art itself becomes blurry as real people and the characters based on them interact and influence one another. Numerous reviewers referred to this aspect of the film as a "mindfuck."[18]

Indies offer experiments with subjective narration such as *The Nines* (2007), an unassuming quasi-science-fiction film whose sequences might be understood to be occurring in the minds of characters, some of whom may be a character's fantasy within a fantasy, and which suggests in the end that the whole film's narrative might be subjective. Like *Broken Flowers*, *The Nines* orders its sequences around the repetition of motifs, such as the term "the nines," which refers to different things in different segments. It has a nested structure: the characters in one segment are suggested to be the fictional creations of characters in another, and the same cast plays different roles in each segment, suggesting continuity of identities across different roles. *Primer* (2004), an ultra-low-budget indie that also veers into sci-fi territory, presents a mind-bending time-travel narrative in which time is represented as reversible in such a way that characters from the past interact with their "doubles" in the present. Straightening out the temporal order of this film requires considerably more cognitive power than is demanded by the likes of *Pulp Fiction*, and has been a pursuit of obsessive fans who publish their elaborate visual mapping of the film's temporal scheme online.[19]

Just as flashbacks and flash-forwards are often motivated in part by the inheritance of *film noir*, the genres of fantasy and science fiction inform the playful ambiguities of films like *Primer*, *The Nines*, and *Donnie Darko* (2001), a contemporary cult classic about a disaffected suburban teenage boy in the 1980s who communicates with a demonic, human-size rabbit and has strange special powers to manipulate time. *Donnie Darko* hints at various subjective effects without answering some of the most basic questions it poses, and makes vague whether some of its narrative events are really supposed to occur in the world of the fiction. Some might interpret much of the film to be a hypothetical flash-forward, or a counterfactual fantasy.

In typical movies and TV, it was long a convention that temporal manipulation in the form of flashbacks and flash-forwards are introduced as subjective narration, as memory or dream or fantasy.

FIGURE 5.3 Wilson staring ahead, one of many shots in *The Limey* that are hard to place temporally, and make following the narrative game-like.

So even when the more explicit cues typical of canonical storytelling like a camera pushing in or a musical motif are absent, spectators are likely to infer that temporal reorderings are motivated by character narration. In *The Limey*, for instance, one is tempted to read the avant-garde temporal form as an expression of the main character's psychology. Many times the film cuts to an image of the main character, Wilson (Terence Stamp), sitting on an airplane staring ahead, and it is tempting to see the whole film as the thoughts he has while flying (fig. 5.3). Audiences bring an expectation that temporal disorder will often have a source in subjective narration, thus although the two need not necessarily be connected, many spectators may infer such connections even when they are not made explicit.

Art cinema of the 1960s was notable for frustrating the audience's expectations of straightforward character-motivated temporal reordering. Films like *Persona* (1966) seem subjective, but as Susan Sontag noted of Bergman's narration in this experimental modernist limit-case, one cannot really construct a coherent and straightforward summary of the plot.[20] Subjectivity is a strategy audiences can apply to understanding a confusing plot by attributing the things most difficult to understand to representations of complex or troubled character psychology. But in the game-forms of indie cinema, the ambiguity between objective and subjective narration is not necessarily best read this way; it can be just as useful to the audience with an appreciation for the playful approach to narration to read ambiguity as play rather than as deep thematic meaning or as exploration of the human condition. It can also be read as allusion or homage, and as adopting styles of narration from other media such as literature.[21]

Some Hollywood *auteurs* with indie origins like Darren Aronofsky and Bryan Singer have established reputations with films that navigate ambiguously between objective and subjective realms. Aronofsky's π (also *Pi*, 1998) moves ambiguously between objective and subjective realms to represent the madness of its main character, Max, an obsessive mathematician who hallucinates. The gimmick of *The Usual Suspects* (1995) is the game it plays with subjective narration, revealing in its stunt of an ending that all of Verbal Kint's, i.e., Keyser Söze's (Kevin Spacey), stories, dramatized onscreen throughout the film, have been subjective in a different sense than the viewer had assumed—not just narrated by Verbal, but invented by him out of whole cloth. The pre-indie generations of American directors include the likes of Woody Allen, who in *Melinda and Melinda* (2004) offers a pair of versions of a fictionalization of a story one character tells that is supposed to be true within the narrative world of the film, one version comic and the other tragic. In structure this resembles the cross-Atlantic indie *Sliding Doors* (1998), with its bifurcated outcomes following an initiating event. But Allen has long experimented with self-reflexivity and audacious narrative conceits, as in the mock-documentary *Zelig* (1983) and the *Sherlock Jr.* (1924)-esque *Purple Rose of Cairo* (1984), in which characters move between an objective reality that the film represents as working-class New Jersey during the Depression and the fictional world of a Hollywood adventure drama that the main character goes to see at her neighborhood theater.

And then there are the sprawling, Altmanesque indie films about ensembles of interconnected characters, John Sayles's *City of Hope* (1991) and *Sunshine State* (2002), P. T. Anderson's *Boogie Nights* (1997) and *Magnolia* (1999), *Thirteen Conversations About One*

Thing (2002), and *Crash* (2004). As with Altman's *Nashville* (1976) and *Short Cuts* (1993), the pleasures of these ensemble films accrue from the discovery of connections among characters—connections that the narration has strategically withheld from the viewer until a Eureka! moment of pleasant surprise, like what in reality TV is called a "reveal." In *Short Cuts* the interconnection of characters is elaborate and systematic: any two characters from among the dramatis personae of more than two dozen are likely to have some connection within the enormous metropolis of Los Angeles. Doreen (Lily Tomlin) is the waitress who serves Stuart (Fred Ward), who goes fishing and brings back a catch to cook for dinner with Ralph (Matthew Modine), a doctor looking after the child of Howard (Bruce Davison), who is a local television personality and next door neighbor of Tess (Annie Ross), who performs in a nightclub for Bill (Robert Downey, Jr.), and so on. The connections keep multiplying and complexifying as the film progresses, enmeshing everyone in an elaborate web, so that Bill's friend Jerry (Chris Penn) cleans Tess's pool, and Doreen is the one responsible for running over Howard's son, and Doreen's husband Earl (Tom Waits) turns up at Tess's performance too. And this description, convoluted as it seems, accounts for only a fraction of the film's more than twenty "main" characters. Unlike the daisy-chain structure of *Slacker* or *Twenty Bucks* (1993), the latter of which follows a bill passed from character to character, the ensemble of *Short Cuts* is presented in the style of a television drama, cutting from scene to scene in parallel time. Unlike TV drama, however, the audience's interest in the characters stems from unfamiliarity and surprising connections rather than familiarity and conventional suspense. It also stems from the novelty of the form, its rarity and originality and its difference from canonical story formats.

Pulp Fiction, Go, 21 Grams, 11:14, as well as more Woody Allen films like *Hannah and Her Sisters* (1986) and *Crimes and Misdemeanors* (1989), fit this category to varying extents as well, each one unfolding a series of stories about different characters who turn out to have unexpected connections to one another which the narrative has withheld, or who develop new ones over the course of the narrative, as in *Hannah*, when the neurotic Mickey (Woody Allen) winds up married to his ex-wife Hannah's younger sister, Leigh (Dianne Wiest). One such Altmanesque indie film is Don Roos's *Happy Endings* (2005), in which a central part of the experience of watching is making connections among characters and anticipating their correspondences. Sometimes these are tenuous happenstances, as when one main character (Lisa Kudrow's Mamie) happens to be the abortion clinic counselor of another main character (Maggie Gyllenhaal's Jude). These two are also connected via parallelism, as Mamie and Jude are both impregnated by a different gay young man, and Mamie ends up marrying Frank (Tom Arnold), the father of Jude's gay lover, whom she had earlier seduced. For most of the film, however, these two female characters appear in different scenes, with different other characters, without having a direct connection to one another.

Much of the pleasure of such a narrative is in recognizing connections, whether direct or indirect and implicit or explicit, or in appreciating their richness when the film gets around to making them evident to the viewer. Often such connections are offered as thematic parallelisms that the audience has to "get." The coincidences and correspondences and parallelisms are on offer but require an active participation. *Traffic* (2000), *Syriana* (2005), and *Babel* (2006) all work this way, by telling stories about characters who have ties to one another that may be concrete, as in a personal relationship, or abstract, as in a thematic correspondence or similarity, but which must be actively pieced together while watching. In Soderbergh's *Traffic*, we are introduced to a number of characters who have some involvement in the drug trade. *Syriana*, like *Traffic* written by Paul Gaghan and also directed by him, works a similar way but substitutes the oil business and makes the connections less obvious, upping the ante in spectatorial attentiveness. Whether the characters ever meet or are even aware of each other's existence, their connections are the point of the spread-out, mosaic-like structure combining segments featuring so many different kinds of people. *The Hours* (2002) offers many of the same pleasures and challenges of films like *Traffic* and *Syriana*, but with a clearer, more rigorous structure of nested characters who are parallel to one another and who have no direct connection but whose experiences are in many ways parallel: Virginia Woolf (Nicole Kidman), a reader (Julianne Moore) of Woolf's novel *Mrs. Dalloway*, and a woman (Meryl Streep) who shares the book's main character's name, Clarissa, and many of her and Woolf's characteristics.

Rather than attempt to create my own taxonomy of playful narrative structures aiming to cover all possible texts slotted into discrete categories like separate file folders,[22] I propose that we see a number of overlapping storytelling trends in evidence here; many items will belong in more than one folder. The novel spatiotemporal design, the expanded canvas, and the subjectively playful narrative are three categories I have offered above to make sense of a diverse body of works in the field of indie cinema, and some films are instances of more than one of these. *Pulp Fiction* and *Happy Endings* belong to the first and second; *The Nines* and *The Limey*, depending on your interpretation, might fit both the first and third. I am more concerned to understand indie culture's interpretive approaches to such narrative structures than to mark them off from one another, and while there is substantial diversity in the styles and effects of playful form, there is also some unity in its meanings.

Naming an Indie Trend

Many terms have been coined to capture the characteristics of formally playful films, several of which are shared by some mainstream Hollywood films like *Minority Report* (2002), which flaunts its counterfactual flash-forwards, and *A Beautiful Mind* (2001), with its subjective narration which the narrative has suppressed for most of the film, as well as foreign imports like the German cult classic *Run Lola Run* (1998), the Hong Kong *Sliding Doors*-style trifurcated narrative *Too Many Ways To Be No. 1* (1997), and the backwards-told art-core French film *Irreversible* (2002). Films like these in the *Pulp Fiction* tradition have been described, depending on their particular formal configurations, as nonlinear films, puzzle films, hyperlink films, forking-paths narratives, mindbenders or mind-game films, multiple-draft films, multistrand narratives, database narratives, modular narratives, fractured narratives, and network narratives.[23] In his taxonomy of such films, Charles Ramirez Berg catalogs twelve types, such as the parallel plot, the daisy chain, and the aforementioned hub-and-spoke.[24] Such films, as well as TV shows that share many of their qualities, are also often said to be characterized by narrative complexity, though of course there are many ways for a narrative to be complex that have nothing to do with temporal structures, expressionistic mind-trips, or game-like form.[25] While not all of the examples I have canvassed are as playful, as meta, as *Pulp Fiction*—some are much more invested in profound thematic meanings (e.g., *Babel*, *Crash*)—I propose that we think of all of the various terms converging on play as a viewing strategy they potentially solicit (alongside others, such as conventional narrative engagement and thematic interpretation), and which some solicit as a more central activity than others. Since there are nonlinear, complex, and playful narratives in many forms, genres, media, and national and historical contexts, I certainly cannot claim that they are essentially indie. But such texts certainly do often present their narrative forms as distinctive and nontraditional, often as implicit challenges to ordinary storytelling. Bordwell cogently argues that forking-paths and network films tend to have "one foot in classical tradition,"[26] but I argue that their other foot dangling into distinctively playful currents is significant for the indie film's alternative cultural appeal. Hollywood screenwriters most typically tell stories with a beginning, middle, and end, and in that order. Mainstream screenplay advice manuals assume linear structure and advise caution in the use of flashbacks.[27] While temporal fragmentation in mainstream cinema is hardly unusual, ideals of mainstream narrative structure place high value on wide accessibility and conventional pleasures. This sort of default setting for mass-market movies makes game-like narrative forms an appeal some indie films can offer as a means of distinction in relation to mainstream cinema, when held up against the expectations audiences have of the output of the Hollywood studios. As J. J. Murphy writes, Tarantino's extensive use of flashbacks in *Reservoir Dogs* flies in the face of Hollywood screenwriting orthodoxy and is motivated by the director's desire to subvert the audience's calcified habits of viewing, the safe, set expectations encouraged by canonical storytelling.[28] This motivation is one indies often share with some international festival and art house cinema, which like American independent films pursues the agenda of cultural distinction. Although narrative complexity is hardly the exclusive turf of American independent cinema, since the 1980s independent cinema has distinguished itself, among many other appeals, as the alternative to Hollywood mainstream cinema for formal approaches that foreground playful narrative structure. Hollywood is seen as the home of safe forms, which are more transparent as vehicles for conventional content (plots, stars, etc.)—forms with tried-and-true emotional payoffs. Experimental form is comparatively risky, and indie films that take risks are often rewarded with critical admiration and cultural cachet.

There are many ways of motivating unconventional form, and play is only one of them. As David Bordwell argues in his survey of experimental narrative in contemporary American cinema, the influence of *film noir* is often one source of flashbacks, a debt Tarantino acknowledges by referring to Kubrick's *The Killing* (1956) in discussing his use of temporal fragmentation in *Reservoir Dogs*. Many of the titles I have surveyed so far have noirish elements, from the hard-boiled crime narrative of *The Usual Suspects* to the doomed protagonist of *Memento*. Paranoia and self-doubt, two *film noir* afflictions, pervade *The Limey* and *The Nines*. Another influence some writers and directors acknowledge is literary form. Tarantino asserts that the structure of *Reservoir Dogs* is novelistic, noting that literary narration is freer than cinematic narration to jump around in time.[29] Many of the most temporally disjunctive films in American cinema have literary sources, including *Point Blank* (1967) and *Petulia* (1968). Both of these are films of the 1960s, and homage to art cinema of this period is another way of motivating unconventional form. Soderbergh and Tarantino often reference Godard. *The Limey* is an excellent example of all of these trends, combining noirish narrative situations with homages to art cinema and the 1960s more generally. And yet a sense of play persists, a sense that the formal ingenuity of Soderbergh's storytelling cannot fully be accounted for by noting influences and antecedents. Play also seems to be an end in itself, a pursuit the filmmakers take on to satisfying an urge to experiment with the forms of cinematic expression. We must avoid the tendency to see motivations as singular or exclusive. We can understand the form of *The Limey* in a number of ways, and the function of experimental narration as ludic is not mitigated by other functions.

The fact that the terms above have all been coined and widely discussed in recent years signals that they name a significant trend in storytelling. They all suggest that for films fitting into this trend, formal play is a salient feature, one that audiences and critics can fasten onto and appreciate in its own right.

Game Processes: Viewing Strategies in Action

As a viewing strategy, regarding form as a game encourages a number of familiar processes which can be applied to the experience of a film that presents challenges of narrative organization. "Ludic form" suggests cognitive processes of play that this strain of indie films encourages, and that the experience of viewing ludic forms has something in common with the experience of games or puzzles. Films solicit these processes, which rise to a level of significance that may be unusual in the experience of more straightforwardly narrated films. These processes are all variations on one central function of narrative comprehension: *finding coherence*.[30] Spectators generally make sense of narratives as they do the everyday environment, by seeking coherence among the multiple stimuli, the myriad bits of information they constantly take in.[31] In narrative comprehension, coherence-making allows filmmakers to rely on the spectator's inferential filling-in of important narrative information such as characters' motivations and unrepresented actions. Complex game narratives, as with films with experimental formal qualities generally, can make the coherence task more complicated and challenging, and presumably part of their pleasure and their spectatorial appeal is the active puzzling they afford.

One way of finding coherence is by tracking parallelisms among disparate strands of narrative. Many complex films offer large ensembles of characters, and to make the whole film work as a coherent whole, the viewer needs a context within which the events of the various segments are meaningfully intertwined. It helps that these films tend to be set in a single location, like the typical television drama: *Nashville* and *Short Cuts*, *Boogie Nights* and *Magnolia*, *Thirteen Conversations About One Thing*, *Happy Endings*, not to mention *Love Actually* (2003) and *Crash*, are concentrated in a single city. The presence of all of the characters in a given geographical space encourages the audience to see connections among them, which the films eventually make explicit. This sort of helping hand which narration offers the spectator ensures that storytelling is not excessively confusing or ambiguous.

Films that spread characters out spatially need to make salient the connections among them even more, and demand more coherence-making on the part of the spectator, as is true of *The Hours*, *Babel*, *Traffic*, and *Syriana*, which make more onerous cognitive demands than a film like *Love Actually*.

Typically, films like *Pulp Fiction* with multiple discrete storylines intertwine characters, as Tarantino does through the "hub" character of Marsellus Wallace, around whom radiate the other characters:

Butch, Mia, the Wolf (Harvey Keitel), and Jules and Vincent. The connections among all of these characters are only revealed as the film goes along, rather than in a concentrated opening expository passage. And yet the different segments have parallel aspects of criminal situations teetering out of control and long periods of atmosphere-setting talk that does little to advance the action.

More importantly, as the various strands of the plot unravel, the challenge of the film's form pays off when characters make connections with one another. The film sets up questions or enigmas; we might see these as jigsaw puzzle pieces missing from a bigger picture, and as the story unfolds we seek the pieces that will fit. Sometimes the missing pieces appear to us as surprises—we didn't realize what was missing until it turns up. On a local level, when Captain Koons (Christopher Walken) tells his lengthy story about salvaging his buddy's watch in Vietnam, we don't know what the significance will be, but Tarantino rewards our attention when salvaging the watch again becomes Butch's reason for returning to his apartment. But there are puzzles on more of a global level, such as the outcome of the scene in which Vincent and Jules shoot the kids who had offended Marsellus after Jules eats the Big Kahuna burger and the significance of the opening diner scene. The puzzle of the film's narrative is to make the parts fit together, and these plot connections allow us to accomplish this goal. Sometimes the film presents pieces to the puzzle which fill in spots we might not even have noticed as a gap. When Butch returns to his apartment and finds the gun on the kitchen counter, we realize that Vincent is there, at which point Vincent is abruptly murdered by Butch. This makes a connection between disparate strands of the film's narrative, answering the question of what they might have to do with one another, but it also comes as a huge surprise the first time one watches it, as we had not suspected that Vincent was in the apartment and were never led to expect him to be killed. When Wolf orders Jules and Vincent to disrobe before he hoses the blood off of them, we realize how Jules and Vincent have wound up wearing surfer dude attire—the opposite in cool terms from their dark suits and ties—in an earlier scene. And in the final scene, it is partly because we have seen Vincent gunned down that we can more easily place the diner scene chronologically in a linear progression of events. We now see that the diner scene comes before the whole Butch story, but after the "Vincent Vega and Marsellus Wallace's Wife" segment. There is pleasure in making sense of this kind of information, in being able to sort out the parts and make them cohere.

This is one of the pleasures of the temporally disjunctive narrative—not-fully-intelligible fragments eventually form a whole, confusion gives way to sense. Consider the charge audiences get as the final scene of *Pulp Fiction* plays out when they recognize, oh, now we're back in that diner, the one about to be held up. Tarantino is careful to signal this with Pumpkin's unusual diction, calling a waitress "Garçon!" (In the opening scene, he is corrected, drawing extra attention to this bit of dialog.) Likewise much of the interest in *Memento* is recognizing the patterning of color and black-and-white sequences, the progression in convergent opposite directions toward an ending in which they will essentially fit together. Films that save a surprise for the ending, like *The Usual Suspects* (as well as less "indie" examples such as *Fight Club* and *The Sixth Sense,* both released in 1999), depend on a breathtaking effect in the moment that the narrative conceit is finally unveiled after such a long, suspenseful withholding. In 21 *Grams,* the recognition that Jack's (Benicio Del Toro) accident killed Cristina's (Naomi Watts) husband, whose heart was transplanted to Paul's (Sean Penn) chest, brings the satisfaction of clarity and a somewhat frustrating half-hour or so of inscrutability.

The Limey offers numerous examples of this kind of fitting-together process. Many of the pieces in this narrative are flash-forwards that recur, as in the scene in which the character Terry Valentine (Peter Fonda) is introduced in an MTV-style montage set to the Hollies's "King Midas in Reverse" (fig. 5.4). A flurry of images of the character flash quickly by, none of them anchored in any accessible narrative context. Terry gestures, smiles, looks afraid, acts ambiguously, appears to speak but without direct sound to convey his words. Only as the film progresses toward its climax and especially on repeated viewing does the spectator place these fragmentary first glimpses of Terry Valentine when they are repeated as moments in the narrative present and given their fuller context. Similarly, an enigmatic voice-over before the opening credits of the film, the first thing the audience hears, is an insistent, repeated demand, "Tell me about Jenny!" Only in the climactic confrontation of Terry Valentine and the protagonist Wilson does this narrative enigma gain meaning, as Wilson pounces on Terry and demands that he tell him what happened to his daughter, whose death Wilson has come to America to understand and avenge.

FIGURE 5.4 A shot from the "King Midas in Reverse" montage introducing Terry Valentine in *The Limey* is one of several fragmentary flash-forwards to scenes much later in the story.

One term that seems especially apt for understanding this process (without necessarily being a satisfying term to describe all such narratives) is *hyperlink film*, which suggests a relationship of affinity between emergent media technologies and narrative form.[32] Whether or not this connection is genuine, the metaphor of the link sheds some light on the experience of certain kinds of complex narrative. On the World Wide Web, a link functions as the path from one page to another, as a virtual structure joining the pages and indicating a relationship between them. It also functions as the convention writers for the Web adopt for supporting ideas with sources, essentially for offering more information to the reader who desires it. The objects being linked together in a complex narrative like *Pulp Fiction* or *Syriana* are typically characters. The links are like lines connecting nodes in a visualization of characters and their relationships. The unfolding of a hyperlink film's plot is the establishment of links from character to character, and occasionally the film seems metaphorically to click on one of these, taking us from one character to another.

Alisa Quart, who coined the term "hyperlink film," also observes that films like *Happy Endings* can toggle from their beginning to their ending and back again (like *Pulp Fiction*, *Happy Endings* moves from effect to cause by presenting a scene from the end at the beginning).[33] The links may be among various components of narrative. Hyperlink thus suggests an architecture of narrative information that decentralizes the linear progression of causal logic and offers in its place alternative notions of connectivity. The activity of engaging with such a text, despite the fact that stories still necessarily unfold in linear time on the level of *fabula*,[34] is of discovering and following the links, which may be from effect to cause or vice versa, from one character to another to another. The spectator explores this architecture as one might the pages of a Web site, jumping from here to there, gaining bits of knowledge which lead to other bits, but organized as a network of points rather than a linear array. And this is also a coherence-making activity, discovering an architecture of links that fill in a complete picture with meaning and unity.

In *Happy Endings*, for instance, the narrative begins with the backstory that Mamie was impregnated as a teenager by her gay stepbrother. Much later on in the film, another character, Jude, is likely impregnated by the gay son of the man to whom she is engaged. The replication of the initial situation creates a thematic parallel between these otherwise unconnected characters, and we have a pleasure of recognition as in any theme-and-variations pattern. (Later, when Mamie becomes the boy's stepmother, a series of thematic connections is completed.)

Some films emphasize pattern as a primary focus; for instance, consider Jim Jarmusch's *Mystery Train*. Like many playful indies, this is a prominently segmented text, with three distinct narratives introduced by titles. The first segment, "Far from Yokohama," introduces many motifs which we do not recognize as significant until the subsequent segments. "Far from Yokohama" begins on a train bound for Memphis on which two young Japanese hipsters, Jun and Mitzuko, argue about whether Carl Perkins or Elvis Presley is more deserving of their admiration. After arriving, they spend an afternoon walking around some of the more decrepit neighborhoods of Memphis, passing an abandoned theater, a bar called Shades with a sign in italic capital letters, a diner open late into the night across the street from a hotel where they check in. They visit Sun Studios and totally fail to understand their tour guide because of linguistic differences. In their hotel room they listen to the radio as a gravel-voiced DJ (Tom Waits) gives the time ("it's 2:17 . . .") and announces Elvis Presley singing "Blue Moon." In the morning after dressing and packing their suitcase, they are startled by the sound of a gunshot. Two subsequent segments, each with its own foreigner characters, an Italian woman and a British man respectively, revisit similar locations, events, and themes of cultural dislocation. All of the three include the hotel and environs, the DJ, and the gunshot. Although the three stories have scant causal connections to unite them, they have coincident settings and time frames, and the film is on some level about coincidence of events in time and place, about the disconnection of the people who all experience the same places and events. Jarmusch works in series instead of parallel as a way of emphasizing the similarities, the parallelisms, among the three narrative strands. This makes the narrative fit the hyperlink conception by providing links from storyline to storyline through the prominence of motifs like the hotel's dingy lobby and front desk (which appear in all three sections), the DJ and Elvis song, and the gunshot.[35]

The genre-label "hyperlink films" is premised on this feature of play, this feeling of mastery over the confusing or seemingly random array of characters and situations presented by the narrative. The hyperlinks in Altmanesque network narratives often take the form of surprising character connections, coincidental relationships that integrate the dramatis personae in a convoluted web of explicit connections and implicit parallelisms. *Magnolia* is an excellent example, a film in which more than a dozen characters are related to one another by blood and marriage, by occupying similar roles (such as parent/child, caregiver, drug abuser, unfaithful romantic partner, and game show contestant), and by living through the same biblical plague of frogs. The network of mutual interconnection produces a sort of intoxicating complexity of relationships that we marvel at ourselves for mastering, even only partially on the first pass. This is hardly novel; it is a staple of sprawling realist novels like those of Dickens and Tolstoy, of ensemble films like *Grand Hotel* (1932) and *Rules of the Game* (1939), and of television dramas from *As the World Turns* (CBS, 1956–) to *The Wire* (HBO, 2002–2008). More middle-of-the-road comedies like *Valentine's Day* (2010) depend on similar effects, though indie films might push the complexity and surprise factors farther than would be typical of texts aiming more for mass appeal.

Functions of Play: Critical Dimensions

Just as pastiche can have a critical function, play with narrative forms such as plot structures, character interconnection, and ambiguous registers of narration can be seen not merely as a surface feature that satisfies its audience as such but also as conveying a deeper significance. Contrary to the claim that a postmodern emphasis on form necessarily entails emptiness of all content—total vacuity, as this chapter's epigraph asserts—we can find rationales for formal prominence that function critically, that make play worthwhile in a larger sense and give it a purpose beyond itself.

Films like *Pulp Fiction* train audiences to see narrative form *qua* form rather than as limiting it to being a vehicle for the conventional pleasures of entertainment or for thematic meaning. Complexity of the sort independent films often offer directs attention to the mechanics of storytelling. Appreciating the jumbled time frame of an experimental narrative makes one more aware of the linearity and straightforwardness of the typical, canonical story format. The sprawling, convoluted character ensembles of Altmanesque narratives potentially make one more aware of the focus of ordinary films on a single protagonist or perhaps a pair of buddies or lovers. The seamless shifting between "reality" and other unusual levels of narration in films like *Eternal Sunshine of the Spotless Mind* potentially makes one aware of the convention of a mode of realism in mainstream movies. And at the same time that such experimental forms train us to appreciate conventional form, they also present their own deviation from norms of narration as an appeal alongside those more typical of popular cinema such as emotional engagement and visual pleasure.

This makes formal experimentation on the level of narrative structures into an indie appeal. As I have argued, independent films are not unique in this, but it functions within the contexts of indie film institutions and discourses as a mark of difference from the ordinary and mainstream. Independent films are perceived to be freer than Hollywood studio releases to play, to innovate formally, to explore new (or old) modes of storytelling that self-consciously deviate from expected norms.[36] In much film scholarship this kind of deviation has often been understood as an implicit political or ideological challenge, a kind of resistance to Hollywood on multiple fronts. For instance, the "Brechtian" techniques of the political modernist cinema of the 1960s and '70s, especially self-reflexivity as in the opening shot of *Tout va bien* (1972) in which Godard shows the check that financed the film, have often been thought a challenge to the "classic realist" text and its putative transparency, its masking of the marks of "enunciation."[37] By resisting the convention of transparency, films with novel narrative forms were offered up as oppositional texts. The spirit of independent cinema is rarely oppositional in this way, but the dynamic of its formal logic is analogous. By playing with narrative form, independent cinema positions itself relationally to Hollywood and offers its own approach as a kind of antidote. But unlike the politically charged approach to formal difference, which insists on the difference from Hollywood being a matter of resisting dominant meanings and countering their messages with those of a leftist resistance, the formally playful indie film is more likely to offer its deviations from Hollywood as a construction of a more refined artistic sensibility, which translates for the indie audience as the appeal to consumer preference. Formal play functions as a mark of taste for a cultural elite. This echoes Pierre Bourdieu's theorizing of bourgeois aesthetics as focused on an appreciation of form as opposed to substance or function.[38]

Narratives with such complex structures must make their deviation salient, must mark the difference as different. This is done both textually and contextually. The more audacious experiments like *Pulp Fiction* beg to be noticed for their formal play, and critical and promotional discourse clues spectators into the significance of this feature. The cultural circulation of such texts also provides an indication of the significance of form for the audience for independent cinema. Through both of these levels of appeal, textual and contextual, the narratively complex film demands its own mode of viewer engagement. Jason Mittell has written about the concurrent rise of such narrative complexity in American television of the 1990s and 2000s, in shows as varied as *The Simpsons, Seinfeld, Arrested Development, 24, Lost,* and *Veronica Mars.* Borrowing from Neil Harris's study of P. T. Barnum, via Tom Gunning's influential work on early cinema,

Mittell identifies an "operational aesthetic" in the television versions of narrative complexity. Such texts direct their audience's attention to the level of storytelling as much as that of story, and demand to be appreciated for the mode of presentation as much as the content.[39] For instance, a real-time narrative like 24's, which extends in each season over a full day of fictional time, calls attention to its own narrative structure as a prominent textual appeal. Independent cinema is full of examples of texts that make prominent similar appeals, such as Mike Figgis's *Timecode* (2000), with its own novel real-time gimmick of four quadrants of the screen, each with its own camera shot in sync with the others. *Slacker* is a movie that introduces a new character every few minutes even as it leaves the old ones behind. *Night on Earth* presents five different segments, all of them occurring at the exact same time, in cities around the world, from New York to Helsinki. *Memento* was publicized—and is remembered—as the backwards movie. One rarely hears of a mainstream Hollywood film described in terms of its narrative structure, à la "a man pursues a series of well-defined goals across a linear succession of scenes." Texts that exploit an operational aesthetic are different because they make their form so prominent. Just as it is the "quality" prime-time television series that most often appeal to their audience as complex (a "quality" audience, i.e., adult and upscale, to match the content), so the indie game texts wear their complexity as a badge of aesthetic sophistication.

P. T. Barnum's aesthetic in his museum exhibits and practical jokes encouraged the audience to fixate on not just the "what" (the mermaid, for instance, who was actually parts of a fish and a monkey joined together and displayed for a credulous audience) but also on the "how" (the methods Barnum used to effect his hoaxes). As Harris writes, an essential part of the experience of Barnum's attractions was the process of figuring out whether they were legitimate and how their mechanics were orchestrated. The audience engaged with Barnum as problem-solvers and information-collectors.[40] Likewise, in the early cinema of the late 1890s and early 1900s, spectators were encouraged to take interest not just in the actions and events captured on film, but on the technology of the cinematic apparatus and its possibilities—for instance, its ability to reverse time or speed it up or slow it down or even just to represent the moving image as a document of real space and time, replete with revealing details. Gunning argues that with the rise to dominance of classical narrative cinema, films were much less likely to call attention to their formal qualities and to their technological base.[41]

Along with the 1970s era of film theorists, Gunning seems to accept the realist transparency of classical narrative cinema as a given. Independent cinema arises in a context that some have described as "post-classicism," an era in American cinema of the return to dominance of commercial entertainment after the Hollywood Renaissance era of auteurism and experimentation. Some critics have charged the postclassical blockbuster era cinema with accepting degrees of narrative incoherence and spectacle unheard of during the studio era.[42] But others like David Bordwell and Kristin Thompson have countered that this is an exaggeration, insisting that the coherence of the classical system has hardly been cast aside by the new generation of Hollywood filmmakers.[43] Whichever side one takes in this debate, all should agree that the standard Hollywood studio film of the period under consideration here is marked by many different narrative appeals than the indie films whose forms, as described above, are playful. Although contemporary Hollywood cinema may be much less straightforward than the studio era film in many respects (it is generally faster cut, films are often longer and have more scenes, and some have quite convoluted plots), Hollywood has certainly not abandoned linear storytelling, character-motivated causality, and narrative closure. Many of the same kinds of transparency as were standard in the studio era are still observed: for instance, performers still avoid looking into the camera, and fictional movies rarely acknowledge their status as fictions. Standard schemes of lighting and framing persist, as does (with some modifications) the continuity editing system. Some of Hollywood's narrative and stylistic norms have been amped up or intensified, as Bordwell argues,[44] but the system in place since the 1910s has hardly been cast aside. (These conventions apply to independent films as well, of course, and indies can also oppose each other in their formal appeals.) All of this means that in the Sundance-Miramax era, independent filmmakers have a background of a dominant industry and its norms against which they may experiment and innovate. Only by understanding that there are stable mainstream film narrative norms, those of the classical (and postclassical) cinema, can the operational aesthetic of formally playful indie films come into focus.

If films such as *Pulp Fiction* and *Memento* work according to an operational aesthetic, this assumes that the explanation for their forms is that they are self-consciously deviating from a norm or convention of canonical narrative. But the explanation for the form of any artwork worth considering is rarely singular or simple, as we have seen. In the case of playful narratives in indie cinema, there are often multiple functions one can ascribe to their formal qualities. For example, *Memento*'s narrative form functions as a means of representing the main character's peculiar psychological disability. Leonard has no ability to make new memories, and so our experience of a narrative that moves backwards rather than forwards (in much of the film) replicates to an extent the experience of not knowing what came before. *The Nines*'s narrative form in which different levels of reality bleed into one another ambiguously functions as a means of representing the experience of a storyteller (John August himself explains it this way, referring to his time as a television showrunner)[45] who is so close to the characters, so immersed in their fictional world, that he begins to have trouble telling reality from fiction. Tarantino has said that the achronological structures of his film are novelistic, replicating the experience in a novel of easily moving back and forth in time, and has also said that he chooses his narrative structures merely because he finds them to be more "resonant."[46] (Historically, new ways of representing time in film, from Eisenstein to present day, have been explained by a literary analogy that seeks for cinema the same freedom that novels have to shift locales and temporalities.)[47] The temporal games of *The Limey* are attributed to the influence on Steven Soderbergh of New Wave films of the 1960s from France, Britain, and the United States. There are thus multiple modes of explanation at work within the contexts and paratexts of independent cinema that aim to account for game-like form, most of which have nothing to do with being distinct from the mainstream of Hollywood entertainment. Some explanations are thematic, some relate to revealing and developing character, and some are explained as allusion or reference. The postmodern criticism that a text is either meaningful or empty, parody or pastiche, significant or merely playful, misses the ability of texts to multiply motivate their appeals.

If filmmakers are often reluctant to explain formal play simply as experimentation, does that mean it is incorrect to understand it as such? Like many elements of an artwork, formal design has multiple functions, and our understanding of playful narrative structures requires that we accept the overdetermination of formal motivation. Overdetermination in this context means that the reasons why a film has the form it does are multiple, overlapping, sometimes even contradictory. There may be many reasons why a film plays with narrative structure. The motivation of narrative devices is the way we explain their presence and how they function. In Kristin Thompson's theory of motivation, borrowed from the Russian formalist literary theorists, a device in a film may be motivated compositionally (by the necessities of storytelling, as when a gun is introduced early in a narrative to set up its use later on), transtextually (as a standard element of a film in a given genre), realistically (as consistent with reality as we understand it outside of the film), or artistically (as the expression of the author).[48] My use of formal play suggests that artistic motivation is behind the narrative games of films like *Pulp Fiction*. But I reject the notion that a device must be ascribed to a single motivation. In independent cinema, formal play can be motivated compositionally (*Memento* needs to be told achronologically to simulate character psychology), transtextually (11:14 adopts the convention of independent films of being formally playful), realistically (John August's ambiguous narrative levels are supposed to represent the authentic psychology of a storyteller who has gotten in too deep), or artistically (as pure play, as the hand of the author—as in Tarantino or Soderbergh, who have made scrambled narrative form elements of their personal style). Artistic motivation, the kind most interesting to the formalists, offers up not only the possibilities of making form an appeal in its own right and of pushing the prominence of the author as the originator of meaning—a significant role in Off-Hollywood cinema in which auteurism is a strong selling point—but also of defamiliarization. This central formalist concept is one way of understanding the purpose of art as such. It may not apply equally well to all genres, but is an especially worthwhile concept for understanding the kinds of representation, like playful, game-like indie films, that reward a special attention to form. When artworks defamiliarize, they show us things we know too well but in a different way, nudging us out of habits of viewing so that we may look upon both art and life with fresh eyes. A film like *Pulp Fiction* defamiliarizes not only Quarter Pounders, allowing us to see them as Europeans do (from the perspective of a metric culture), but also the format of canonical stories. This is artistic motivation, but it does not invalidate the compositional or realistic or generic motivation that the film might also appeal to.

Both the puzzle-piece-fitting, coherence-making viewing strategy and the metatextual, form-*qua*-form viewing strategy are distinctive appeals of the kind of indie cinema that makes form a game. They are hardly contradictory, as the activity of puzzling, when made prominent as an "operational" textual appeal, can encourage spectators to appreciate form in its own right. Ultimately for indie film culture, foregrounding form promotes the distinction of one kind of storytelling in relation to others. This demands a cognizance of storytelling which can only mean that the audience for playful narratives has a critical understanding of story structures and the various possibilities inherent in them. One function of the formally playful strain of indie cinema might thus be the training of audiences to better appreciate the dimensions of cinema as a narrative art—and to appreciate their own appreciation.

Cult Indies

Many of the films that I have considered above, as well as in the previous chapter, are examples of another category in addition to puzzle films or complex narratives or game-texts. Films as different as *Pulp Fiction* and *Kill Bill*, *The Usual Suspects*, *Primer*, *The Big Lebowski*, and *Donnie Darko* are central examples of the cult cinema of the 1990s and 2000s.[49] Cult films are those that inspire intense and exclusive fandoms. Their faithful ritualize the cinematic experience through the repetition of their favorite films and scenes. Once they did this at repertory house cinemas and on late show broadcast television programming, and later (as new technologies permitted) on cable and satellite TV channels, video cassette, DVD, and the Internet.[50] "Cult" suggests a kind of religious mode of engagement, as Matt Hills argues, and the language used to describe these films and their fans makes clear this aspect of their reception: we speak of devoted fans who worship their favorite films and filmmakers.[51] Fans call Tarantino a god among directors. Cultists follow rituals of repeated viewing, of quotation and performance and masquerade, as *Star Trek* fans do when dressing as their favorite characters. The term *cult* itself connotes religious observance and the social organization of members whose affiliation is marked by common belief.

There are crucial links between cult cinema and indie cinema. Both function as alternatives to norms of mainstream film experience. For both cult and indie, subcultural capital circulates among members of a community of insiders who see virtue in obscurity and difference. Subcultural capital, in Sarah Thornton's formulation, is a form of cultural inside knowledge that subcultures use to distinguish themselves from other subcultures and from the mainstream, and which members of a subculture use to assert status within the group.[52] The formal play of some indie films inclines cultists to adopt them as favored fetish objects, to watch multiple times and elevate as objects of special admiration.

Like independent cinema, the category of cult films may be impossible to capture using the tools of rigorous definition. If it has an essence, it is to be found in qualities of reception rather than in forms of textuality. The films included among typical lists of cult hits are heterogeneous, and the reasons for appreciating them are as well. Cult usually means underappreciated—only cultists would like this kind of cult film, such as *Showgirls* (1995). *Showgirls* also demands a special mode of engagement: reading against the grain for "so bad it's good" qualities that the filmmakers likely did not intend. And yet the typical cult film is probably read straight rather than ironically. *Donnie Darko*'s admirers appreciate the film by reading it authorially. But like *Showgirls*, *Donnie Darko* was a commercial flop that was rescued by its cultists. In defending his choice of *Donnie* as the first entry in a series of essays on "The New Cult Canon," Scott Tobias of *The Onion A.V. Club* marshals the evidence of the film's "second-tier distributor" (Newmarket), "feeble box office" (less than half a million dollars in theaters), its rise after the spread of positive word-of-mouth, its screening as a midnight movie, its success on DVD, and only finally, the fact that the film inspires obsessive fans.[53] The rise of a film to cult status often requires just this sort of narrative, a rise from obscurity or ignominy to recognition, a critical rescue operation that arises out of an organic collective of cultists who see aesthetic virtue where others saw little worth noticing.[54] This very dichotomy between the general public's take on the film and the cultists' is at the heart of any cult phenomenon because cultists get a charge from the perceived differentiation of their tastes from those of outsiders. Like

Rocky Horror Picture Show (1975) audiences, the cultists who rescue films like *Showgirls* and *Donnie Darko* get some of the pleasure they find in these texts from the practice of salvaging mainstream detritus, from recognizing value in texts that the majority of critics or viewers did not care about enough or that the cultists believe the mainstream would not "get." In other words, like allusionistic pastiche, cult viewing demands the cultivation of in-group identity. It cannot exist without knowledge and competence shared among members. Their subcultural capital is the prerequisite for the recognition of a cult text's virtue. Knowledge and competence leads to membership in the taste community that forms around the film or other media object at the center of the cult. Thus despite heterogeneity of textual forms and cult approaches, at the center of any cult media phenomenon is a social organization of knowledge.[55]

Why have many of the new cult classics come from the independent sector of the film industry, and why are so many of them films with playful or experimental form? First of all, there is no recipe for cult success, and many of the latest generation of cult films have come from abroad and from studio filmmaking (like *Showgirls*, as well as from huge commercial successes like *Lord of the Rings* [2001, 2002, 2003], *The Matrix* [1999], and *Fight Club*, which might not fit the midnight-movie template of cult films,[56] but which would seem to fit a general description of cult reception). But some of the qualities that make 1990s and 2000s cult films appealing to cultists are the same ones that give them their indieness. The low-budget origins of many indie films motivate a narrative of rescue from obscurity and of unlikely success. Part of the cult of *Donnie Darko* is the story of its production, that Richard Kelly had shopped his script around a long time, that no one wanted to let him direct it, that only with the enthusiasm and intervention of Drew Barrymore was its production made possible, and even then only on a $4.5 million budget.[57] *Primer*, like *El Mariachi* (1992) before it, is a cult film partly because of the admiration of its fans for its four-figure production budget, a reported $7,000, which limited the director to a single take per scene and required extensive pre-production planning to ensure that the film could be made as wanted.[58] Doing more with less appeals to indie audiences, and cultists can find their admiration for such films to be a form of mainstream-snubbing, averring by their fandom that one does not need the resources of commercial entertainment cinema to create aesthetically worthy films. Every new indie *auteur* has an origins story to fill out his (or her) biographical legend, and often these are modest: Tarantino's days as a high school dropout working in a video store, Robert Rodriguez's efforts to make an exploitation film for the Spanish-language straight-to-video market, Richard Linklater's days working on a Gulf of Mexico oil rig and reading Dostoyevsky. Jim Jarmusch was given leftover film by Wim Wenders to make his first film, and the director of *Primer*, Shane Carruth, like so many indie first-timers before him, depended on the largesse of family and friends. Carruth restricted himself to a minuscule crew of multitaskers, himself producing, directing, writing, acting, scoring, and editing the film. Origins narratives like these reward the cult audience for recognizing the value in the modest efforts that operate outside of the established production system.

Another reason indie films might be more likely to attain cult status is that the cult audiences tend to construct themselves as countercultural, going against the tide of mainstream tastes, defying the values of mainstream culture such as belief in the virtue of consumer capitalism and conventional middle-class morality. This has been the case since the early days of midnight movies like *El Topo* (1970) and *Eraserhead* (1977), which dramatized their countercultural values in obvious ways.[59] But the location of the midnight movie in an art house or repertory cinema, and the scheduling of the midnight movie at a time when the mainstream audience (parents and old people, "squares") would be unlikely to attend were also essential to the countercultural values that attached to their social positioning.[60] Indie cinema, as the Other of mainstream Hollywood cinema, is the contemporary heir to countercultural movie scenes of the sixties and beyond. Indies have inherited the art house to become its primary form of programming. And they have inherited the midnight movies' cultural function of offering alternatives to the forms and meanings of the films shown at the regular times of day. Filmmaking seen as subversive, as nontraditional, or even as offbeat or quirky, functions within the context of indie cinema and cult cinema, and as opposed to the conventions of the mainstream. It makes sense, then, that cult films that will serve this countercultural function would be likely to emerge in the context of a movement of filmmaking whose identity is precisely that of an alternative.

The forms of indie cult films are also important to consider, even if cult cinema cannot be reduced to certain kinds of formal features. The puzzle film, the complex narrative, the hyperlink film, the network narrative, and the mind-game movie are all more likely to be made within the contexts of indie film production because these are unorthodox, experimental forms. This isn't to say that the Hollywood studios or the mainstream audience (whoever that is) shun these forms necessarily, only that they have an affinity with indie cinema. The most significant overlap between cult cinema and all of these playful forms is *repeat viewing*—repeat viewing is an essential quality of both the cinema of playful form and of cult cinema.[61] Hollywood is still less likely than indiewood to make films that are difficult to figure out on first viewing. The classical system of narration is first of all a means of appealing to a mass audience to maximize revenue for the film industry. One may assume, however, that narration that confuses the audience significantly, and especially at the end of a film rather than the beginning, is not a quality that a mass audience will often find appealing. Only outside of the studio system is it possible for directors to innovate in the area of confusing the audience. Thus the emergence out of the indie sector of films that professional critics confess they do not fully understand or that they feel they must rewatch in order to appreciate, like *Primer* and *Donnie Darko* and *The Nines* and *Synecoche, New York*. But films that audiences cannot understand, especially on one viewing, are exactly the kind of films that give cult audiences an opportunity to fasten onto them as objects of fascination.[62] This has been true at least since *2001: A Space Odyssey* (1968) set a standard for a new kind of cerebral, art-cinema science fiction that would in some significant sense be inscrutable. Inscrutability was perhaps more possible in the era of the Hollywood Renaissance, when the movie business was in the doldrums, the mass audience had deserted the cinema for television and other amusements, and a countercultural, educated youth audience was seen as a desirable substitute. Within the context of indie film production and reception, a fairly inscrutable film like *Primer* is possible because the niche audience seeking distinction from mainstream cinema likes the idea of a challenge. Repeat viewings of these challenging films then may be necessary to master their convoluted and complex plots (if this is possible at all), and the aesthetic appreciation that follows from repeat viewing adds value as well. One ordinarily watches a movie a second time because of one's admiration for it. Barbara Klinger found that repeat viewers, especially of "puzzle films," often give the rationale of aesthetic appreciation to explain their choice to watch the same film again.[63] By making films that reward repeat viewing, indie filmmakers also indicate the mode of appreciation their films warrant as especially aesthetic, underlining the indie cinema's alternative status in relation to Hollywood being constructed as more artistic, more aesthetically worthwhile.

The cult mode of reception relishes replaying the game of form. Not all game-text indies are cult films and not all cult films figure form as a game, but the significant overlap between these categories is a product of convergent viewing strategies. In the tradition of *Pulp Fiction*, filmmakers and indie audiences have found disruptions to ordinary storytelling to be a virtue and have seized on the idea of play, of storytelling as puzzling or gaming, as a way of understanding their aesthetic project. This way of appreciating stories is an epitome of alternative, underground, or independent culture, trafficking in specialized knowledge and strategies of meaning.

Conclusion

With its antecedents in literary modernism, *film noir*, art cinema, and cult movies, the formally playful indie film offers a sensibility of sophistication and exclusion. Ludic form need not necessarily operate in this mode of distinction, but in the configuration of play as a means of differentiation from dominant norms of storytelling and style, indie films assert a crucial difference. Of all of the means of marking indie cinema off from Hollywood studio films, it is those films that call upon the audience to differentiate itself from the mainstream audience that mark the independent movement as functioning in the way legitimate culture has historically, as a form of aesthetic classification that stands as well for social classification. But this is not the whole story, and form does not determine function; formal play need not necessarily be in the service of distinction. The box office success of *Pulp Fiction*, *Memento*, and *Being John Malkovich* attest to the appeal of formally inventive movies beyond the festival and art house circuits.

To return again to Tarantino and *Pulp Fiction*, we can see that the complaint of that film's emptiness, of its emphasis on surface rather than depth, misreads the appeals that the film and many others like it offer to the audience reading for play rather than (or in addition to) thematic significance. The position that play empties work of content demands an illogical either/or stance, denying the possibility that works can have both surface appeals and deeper thematic ones. But it also denies the validity of filmmakers' and audiences' interest in play as a variety of formal exploration and experimentation, one of the central preoccupations of modernists as well as postmodernists. In a sense there is not that much new about indie cinema's ludic forms, except that they arise in their own specific context within the configuration of independent filmmaking in the era of the blockbuster and conglomerates, and that they emerge as a trend at a particular time, a product of a generation of like-minded artists. As did past masters of legitimate culture from Joyce and Stravinsky to Godard and Pinter, the playful indie director makes prominent an interest in the architecture of cultural works, and signals to the audience the validity of its interest in the very same architecture, also encouraging it. To the extent that form *is* content and that the two are always blended and inseparable, the argument that formal play empties the artwork of content is a nonstarter. But even granting that an emphasis on form might bring with it a de-emphasis on other textual qualities (though it would not necessarily), we can find a number of explanations for the appeal of this emphasis, a number of positive functions that such a textual configuration might well perform. These include promoting the cohesion of an audience as a community—perhaps one as well defined as a cult but more often a looser one of shared knowledge and competence. They also include the appreciation of conventions of narrative and aesthetics more generally, a kind of unofficial education in the canonical formats of popular storytelling and in the potential for deviation from them. Of course, play can also be its own reward. The pleasure of the game is the fun one has discovering its dimensions, and playing again and again.

part IV   AGAINST HOLLYWOOD

chapter 6 INDIE OPPOSITION

| Happiness vs. Juno |—Juno MacGuff: You're, like, the coolest person I've ever met, and you don't even have to try, you know . . .

—Paulie Bleeker: I try really hard, actually.

The strategies of considering characters as emblems of their social identities and of seeing form as a game each correspond to a tendency in independent film toward realism and formalism, respectively. Our final strategy, to read as anti-Hollywood, has to a significant extent been a current running throughout the preceding analyses, functioning to define the festivals, art houses, and other institutions of indie cinema and to motivate realist or formalist aesthetics as reactions against conventions of the mainstream commercial cinema. Realism and formalism are tendencies that might sometimes overlap with classicism, the dominant aesthetic of Hollywood since the late 1910s, but each can also constitute itself as an alternative to classical Hollywood, as they have done historically in alternative cinema movements from the European avant-gardes of the 1920s to the American experimental cinema represented in P. Adams Sitney's *Visionary Film* to the international art and festival cinemas that have persisted since the years after World War II to provide waves of original, adventurous filmmaking which are typically experienced outside of mainstream film exhibition. Insofar as each of these trends goes against the Hollywood grain, each can be viewed as an implicit (or explicit) assault on the conventions of the studio film, the mainstream movie, and the institutions through which it is experienced—or at least as an effort to provide a needed counterbalance and response to it.

One might wonder whether anti-Hollywood viewing would take as its objects films that thematize their opposition to the mainstream, that cast a negative light on the workings of mass media or on the machinations of studio executives, or that deviate from norms of conventional film storytelling in especially self-conscious fashion. Geoff King considers the possibility that American independent cinema might constitute an "alternative narrative mode" alongside classical and art cinema, and finds instead that indie is more like a hybrid of existing modes, and that differences between indie and Hollywood narratives are "relative and variable."[1] Films that self-consciously flaunt an oppositional aesthetics are somewhat rare in American independent cinema. More often, however, the themes of indie films are in some sense critical of mainstream *society*, which can figure as the stand-in for the dominant media industry whose audience is that social mainstream. *Happiness*, like many indie dramas, peels back the façade of complacent suburban life to reveal the anguish beneath the appealing surface. Films representing minority and subaltern identities, such as the New Black and New Queer cinemas which emerged in the 1980s and 1990s, implicitly critique the emphasis of mainstream films on normative identities. The quirkiness of many indie comedies (or dramedies) like *Rushmore* (1998), *Ghost World* (2001), *Garden State* (2004), *Napoleon Dynamite* (2004), *Me and You and Everyone We Know* (2005), *Little Miss Sunshine* (2006), and *Juno* (2007), their tone of arch cleverness and offbeat style, is perfect for representing the nonconformists and free spirits who populate such films.

But beyond the efforts of independent films to figure an anti-Hollywood message textually lie the contexts of independent film production and consumption, which help to demarcate the field of independent cinema as one of opposition. It is only when seeing indie cinema through a frame of oppositionality, through an interpretive lens which casts certain textual features as marks of distinction, that the function of independent cinema as an alternative comes into focus. Thus the oppositions of the indie film are not necessarily and not solely to be found in texts. As chapter 2 described, paratexts and contexts of independent cinema have a significant role in mobilizing and applying this frame.

The Authentic Autonomous Alternative

The distinction between studio and indie filmmaking in American cinema is often rightly criticized as a superficial simplification, but its persistence as way of conceptualizing the field of American feature films suggests an abiding relevance. If not representing a division of true opposites, the categories of mainstream and alternative suggest ideals and identities toward which filmmakers aspire, and which the communities of media audiences can use to organize their experience of movies. In particular, for the community of film enthusiasts who have an investment in independent cinema as a concept and category, this distinction comes with an unambiguous pair of moral valences. Independence is a virtue, and the mainstream is commercialized, over-hyped, sensational, and associated with undesirable conceptions of the cinema audience as an undifferentiated mass, or as an exploit-able niche with inferior taste (e.g., children, girls and women). But although these moral conceptions of mainstream and alternative film culture apply to ideals of each side of a divide, individual films, oeuvres, or genres must be approached on their own terms. The old au-teurist interpretive strategy of finding art in the commercial formats of Hollywood persists. At the same time, some indie films may be found undeserving of the virtue that comes with being "independent" and regarded as shams—as unworthy of such status. Likewise the con-demnation of those who would use indie more as a marketing concept than as a true expression of separation and opposition in relation to Hollywood rests on the assumption that some films do legitimately deserve the honor of being named independent.

One indie tastemaker, *Salon* magazine's critic Andrew O'Hehir, declared, "The term 'independent film' has hovered on the edge of meaninglessness for many years, in fact, and 2006 might be the year it finally fell off the cliff."[2] The cliff in this case is the incorporation of the discourse of independence by the major media industries and their mini-majors' dominance of the market for Oscar-worthy, upscale, ar-tistically ambitious films (in that year, these included *An Inconvenient Truth*, *Little Miss Sunshine*, *The Queen*, and *Pan's Labyrinth*). Like O'Hehir and many cinephile critics, Manohla Dargis of the *New York Times* approaches these concepts skeptically. "Independence in the movies is a cri de coeur and an occasionally profitable branding ploy, but mostly it's a seductive lie."[3] The key here is her qualifier "mostly": the inauthentic indie is the lie, but beyond that sham one might find the real McCoy, which a sensitive critic like her presumably is apt to spot. (Her piece continues by offering examples of a number of recent independent films more worthy of the name that the *Times* reader would be unlikely to have seen or heard of.)

One indication of independent cinema's positive moral valence is the frequency with which puns on American political independence are invoked, such as *The Declaration of Independent Filmmaking* (a how-to book) and "Rejoice! It's Independents' Day" (a newspaper headline).[4] We know the ideals suggested by this rhetorical figure: liberty and equality, justice, and revolutionary change. It implies a quasi-patriotic obligation to defend and celebrate Off-Hollywood cinema. Independence carries connotations of individual self-reliance and freedom from constraint, and independent filmmakers are assumed to be adventurous and uncompromising. Perhaps one reason for the adoption of indie as a substitute for independent was that the community of independent filmmakers and audiences was made uncomfortable by such high and noble expectations, and preferred to think of the distinction between different kinds of filmmaking as stylistic rather than ethical. The substitution of indie for independent also makes clear an awareness of the branding of independent cinema, which is to say the investment of the term with symbolic and emotional associations that go well beyond denotative meanings, and which are not necessarily laden down by all of the associations of "independent."

In struggles to find the real (good) independent films and unveil the impostor independent films, we see a clear instance of a discourse of authenticity. The medium most often considered in terms of investment in authenticity is popular music, especially rock, and many of the same features of the discourse of rock music authenticity are to be found when we consider independent cinema. Philip Auslander considers authenticity in rock music as a value to be found in musical texts, but also as a product of contexts, applied by listeners who experience texts through a frame of "prior musical and extra-musical knowledge and beliefs."[5] Two aspects of the audience's judgment are especially important in informing the discursive construction of authenticity in rock. One pertains to the sincerity and commitment of the artist.[6] In indie cinema, just as in rock music, one does not often find a discourse of authenticity attached to movies that do not origi-

nate from artists (in cinema, typically *auteur* directors) with a high degree of credibility, a perception of artistic integrity, and unwillingness
to compromise for commercial gain. Efforts to formulate the values of
independent cinema often revert to the personal, expressive functions
of individual authorship. James Mottram's celebratory book about
independent cinema introduces its focus as a "romantic idea of the
maverick," a term often used to flatter indie directors and assert for
them a lineage from Welles, Cassavetes, Fuller, and the 1970s Hollywood Renaissance and its enduring, productive figures like Scorsese.[7]
Sharon Waxman prefers "rebel," but the idea is much the same when
she writes, "the rebels did not submit peacefully to the studio process,
and the formula-ready Hollywood system did not necessarily mesh
well with the single-minded egotism of artists whose goals were not
the same as their financiers.'"[8] Geoff Andrew celebrates the countercurrent of personal filmmaking in American cinema by asserting that
even if some authentically indie directors work under the majors or
mini-majors, their work "betoken[s] a forceful individuality, an artistic sensibility which cannot be contained by the resolutely commercial
constraints favored by Hollywood."[9] He adds, defending his choices
of filmmakers who may not fit a strict economic definition of independent such as Scorsese and Altman, "basically, you just feel it in your
bones whether someone is a maverick."[10]

A second aspect is the exercise of comparative judgment between
the authentic and its Other, the inauthentic: "the concept of authenticity has . . . always been exclusionary."[11] In the case of rock, Auslander
notes that the Other is typically pop, but insists that the configurations of authentic/inauthentic shift according to subgenre or historical
context, so that, for instance, music made with synthesizers may be
deemed inauthentic in one period or subgenre but not another.[12] Of
course the Other of indie cinema is Hollywood. As Chuck Kleinhans
argues, independent cinema is a relational category, always defining
itself in opposition to mainstream studio filmmaking.[13] As Stephen
Duncombe writes of DIY zines, the self-conception of alternative culture is a product of negation, of a resistance to dominant media and
its ideologies.[14]

Auslander further distinguishes between a concept of authenticity
as essentialist, viewing it as an inherent property of texts (as the culture of rock music and independent cinema alike use it), and as a discursive effect. Authenticity in rock, he writes, "is a matter of cultur-

ally determined convention, not an expression of essence. It is also a result of practice: the music industry specifically sets out to endow its products with the necessary signs of authenticity."[15] In independent cinema, a process of authentication (or de-authentication) functions within sites of both production and consumption, as a way of guaranteeing the authenticity of texts through positioning in the market for culture. This occurs on multiple levels: textual (forms and meanings of films) and paratextual (promotional discourses such as trailers and ads, as well as critical discourse) and contextual (institutions of cinema and culture).

In indie cinema as in indie rock, indie fashion, and indie video games, the ideal of authenticity is most often figured as autonomy, as the power artists retain to control their creative process and distance from big, powerful corporations. In any commercial medium, the principal threat to autonomy comes from economic constraints and demands. Independent feature filmmaking is almost always to some degree a venture in entrepreneurial capitalism: money is raised in hopes that a film will earn revenue from distribution to a paying audience. Autonomy means that the creative or artistic process is not excessively influenced by commercial demands, but since making the film is in the first place the creation of a consumer product, a cultural artifact intended to be sold in the market, the extent of influence is a matter for interpretation and discursive positioning. It results from a process of authentication.

The ideal of independent cinema is as an authentic, autonomous alternative.[16] Authentic, insofar as a film is recognized to be the sincere production of an artist or group of artists. Autonomous, to the extent that the artist or group of artists is free to pursue their personal agenda and not constrained by business demands. And alternative, as the authenticity and autonomy of the film and its production is regarded as a contrast to the dominant process for making movies, which is the Hollywood studio way. Thus in order to read as anti-Hollywood, the indie audience needs more than just stylistic or thematic differences. It needs knowledge of other kinds of difference as well, such as evidence of authenticity and autonomy that comes from outside of the experience of the film text *per se*.

The authentication and de-authentication of independent cinema in the Sundance-Miramax era often requires an appraisal not only of qualities of a film and the legitimacy of its creators' authority but also of the role of the mini-major distributors, of their efforts to market and promote a film and to shape the discourse surrounding its release in the popular press. Just as the community of indie cinema produces authenticity, it also can withhold it or strip it away from a film that had previously been granted it. To read an indie film as anti-Hollywood, to practice this form of oppositional spectatorship, it often helps to be conscious of how film distribution works. This would be far less complicated in a world in which there were no so-called independent films distributed by companies owned by major media conglomerates—companies like Fox Searchlight which sometimes avail themselves of the money and resources of a major studio, and which are sometimes constrained by corporate imperatives to avoid trouble. It was in recognition of this factor that one defender of a strict conception of indie authenticity dubbed the mini-majors "dependies," thus stripping from them and the movies they release any claim on authenticity.[17]

In what follows, then, I chart the processes of authentication and de-authentication in two indie films by considering two levels of anti-Hollywood discourse for each: the textual, and the paratextual and contextual. *Happiness*, Todd Solondz's 1998 follow-up to *Welcome to the Dollhouse* (1996), will serve as an example of authentication. *Juno*, the "crossover" indie hit of 2007, will demonstrate de-authentication. In both cases, however, the oppositional viewing strategy operates to reproduce the communal values of indie culture.

Authenticating *Happiness*

Independent cinema's authenticity as an alternative to Hollywood is sustained by the notion of the filmmaker as a creative artist working unhampered by corporate influence. This ideal of autonomy is crystallized in moments of confrontation between business logic and art logic, suits and talent. One such instance was the release of Todd Solondz's *Happiness*, a kind of depraved, suburban version of *Hannah and Her Sisters*. The film was produced by independents Ted Hope of Good Machine and Christine Vachon of Killer Films under a distribution agreement with October Films, which was then the specialty division of Universal Pictures. *Happiness* was screened during the Directors Fortnight at the 1998 Cannes Film Festival and won

FIGURES 6.1 AND 6.2 *Happiness* offers dark, unpleasant subject matter, such as a character masturbating while telephoning unsuspecting women, and a child psychiatrist who fantasizes about killing people in a park.

the international critics prize. It attracted considerable buzz, a term the media industries use to describe positive publicity that cannot be bought directly as advertising or promotion and which cannot be captured in dollar value. It would go on to win acclaim at several more prestigious festivals, including Toronto and New York, and win many more honors, including best director at the Independent Spirit Awards. But when Universal's CEO, Ron Meyer, screened the film a few months before its scheduled fall release, he was offended by a masturbation scene. According to Peter Biskind, Meyer immediately ordered October to dump *Happiness* from its slate.[18] Thus was the once-independent October, like Miramax in the case of the (at least) equally controversial *Kids* (1995), revealed to be beholden to its corporate parent, which prevented it from distributing a film on a dark theme by an artist with strong indie credibility. A consideration of how the rhetoric of autonomy and control informed responses to the film reveals much of how indie values are constructed.

In many ways, *Happiness* is the quintessential American independent film. It tackles disturbing subject matter, including pederasty, which mainstream cinema would never represent in such morally ambiguous terms. It has a number of discomforting scenes in which a pathetic lonely man, Allen (Philip Seymour Hoffman), calls strangers on the telephone and masturbates while he talks to them (fig. 6.1). Most notoriously, the film invites sympathy for an adult—Dr. Maplewood (Dylan Baker), a psychotherapist and seemingly upstanding husband and father—plotting to sodomize a child (fig. 6.2). In all of his films, Solondz expresses a countercultural sensibility in exposing the underbelly of complacent suburban life, opposing mainstream values through narrative and thematic configurations. *Happiness* has an aesthetic to match its low budget (nearly $3 million),[19] forswearing fancy set design, expensive stars, and high-gloss technique in favor of a more plain, direct form of realism. Vachon proclaimed that *Happiness*, "like all groundbreaking films, is provocative and cutting edge."[20]

Happiness is just the sort of film that inspires reviewers to praise its honesty and daring, its uncompromising consideration of contemporary living. David Edelstein, then of *Slate* magazine, admired the way it went around "smashing taboos on all sides" and called it "the dark side of *There's Something About Mary*," implying that the film stands as the indie alternative to Hollywood's safer excursion onto similar terrain. Edelstein also worked into his review a dig against Universal's actions in dropping the film. At the time Universal was owned by the Canadian distiller Seagram's, run by the Bronfman family, and so Edelstein wrote, "That the booze-peddling Bronfmans wanted nothing to do with a film that functions as the opposite of an intoxicant is the kind of irony with which *Happiness* teems."[21] The connections are all there: indies are the antidote to the commercial dope of the Hollywood mainstream. *Happiness* is not only different from a mass-market film, but opposed to it.

What makes this logic especially persuasive is the very controversy that supposedly threatened the film's release. That the film was too hot for the studio to touch confirms that it is worthy of authentic indie status. As some popular reviews noted, the film was released without an MPAA rating, meaning that many theaters would not book it and many publications would not advertise it. Thus, this would be a film that could not very easily appeal to a mainstream audience. Many reviews also noted that the film was dropped from distribution and that this was the product of the filmmaker's refusal to compromise by cutting to earn an R rating.[22] As is so often the case, the audience for alternative culture is potentially reassured rather than threatened by subject matter tagged as morally inappropriate by the dominant social structure, in this case by a publicly traded company ostensibly fearful of offending its shareholders. And the marketing of a controversial art house film can under the right circumstances practically take care of itself. As *Variety*'s Todd McCarthy wrote in his Cannes review, "Controversy and critical support will create want-see among discerning and adventurous specialty audiences."[23] Indeed when Good Machine created a domestic distributor to release *Happiness* in the United States, it had no need to use the film's controversial content or its distribution shuffle to woo audiences. Tastemakers like the *Village Voice*'s J. Hoberman knew of all this from following the Hollywood trade press (and the *Voice* itself had already reported it as well, as Hoberman mentions) and happily referenced the studio's rejection in reviews as implicit evidence of the film's uncompromising take on its themes.[24] Bob Berney, the head of Good Machine's distribution arm, told *Variety*, "We pushed the black comedy aspect of the film, knowing reviewers would clue people into the disturbing subject matter."[25]

At the time of its release, *Happiness* was seen as a cautionary tale. Critics took it to be evidence that Hollywood and indie cinema are fundamentally incompatible. One observer wrote, "working outside the studio system is no longer a guarantee against interference and censorship. Since the majors dominate the distribution system, they also—in effect—control the independent sector."[26] Frightening as the prospect of total Hollywood control might have seemed to champions of alternative culture, however, the details of *Happiness*'s release would seem to support a completely contradictory conclusion: that there exist channels outside of the domain of the major studios to distribute works of daring and originality. A partner in October Films, John Schmidt, told *Variety*, "Rather than say to Todd [Solondz], you have to cut your film, which was contractually our right, we sat down with Todd and our partners at Good Machine and decided it would be a terrific situation."[27] That is, the filmmakers were able to circumvent the system and retain control. The film's problematic content was not edited out to satisfy prudish corporate demands. At the same time, however, the independent producers, whose credibility among the alternative cinema community is unimpeachable, were able to claim that the film's lack of box office success was Universal's fault. They claimed that Good Machine, as a novice distributor, was unable to give the film "a proper marketing push."[28] This reveals how the indie scene attempts to have it both ways: it seeks autonomy but also profit, authenticity but also a marketing push, art without the taint of commerce but enough commerce to make the art pay. At the heart of independent filmmaking is thus a contradiction between the nature of feature filmmaking as what one observer calls an "undercapitalized business venture" undertaken by passionate entrepreneurs, and the desire of the indie community to be aloof from anything that seems too much to be driven by the values of business culture.[29]

To some the lesson of *Happiness* was that "movies that might attract controversy and consumer protests will be shunned like the late-capitalist heretics they are."[30] E. Deidre Pribram argues that incidents such as this one are a threat to "independent film's foundational distinction from Hollywood, risking the independent arena's dissolution through the enforced absorption of Hollywood standards."[31] But *Happiness* was hardly shunned. Although it did not earn as much at the box office as its producers and distributor might have liked, it attracted impressive New York audiences upon its release, owing partly to the controversy.[32] In its first week it averaged $34,000 per screen in its release to six theaters, an impressive tally.[33] (*Happiness* grossed $2.5 million in its domestic theatrical release, compared with the $4.4 million *Welcome to the Dollhouse*.)[34] A week after its New York premiere it debuted in Los Angeles, and a week after that it opened in fifteen more cities, a typical "aggressive specialized rollout" for a film being marketed on the basis of controversy, critical praise, and prestige.[35] After four weeks in release it was playing in eighty-three U.S. cities and still increasing its weekly gross.[36]

Indeed, the film was not even really shunned by Universal. Although it refused to allow October to release the film, Universal advanced a loan to the new distributor "under the table," and stood to profit if the film made money.[37] The vanguardist critic could thus call Hollywood on its hypocrisy: the studio didn't want to create negative publicity for its shareholders but still wanted to gain from the movie if it became a hit.[38] But this fact also complicates the issue of autonomy at the heart of this episode. Solondz had autonomy precisely because he stood up to Universal. The fact that his film was distributed with the help of the studios' dirty money is an inconvenient detail for those for whom authenticity is guaranteed by the mutual rejection of visionary indie artists and philistine Hollywood executives.

Whatever the ultimate success or failure of *Happiness* in economic terms, the film was undoubtedly a cultural success. It was well received by tastemakers and critics, helping to further establish an indie *auteur* reputation and to develop the discourse of indie authenticity by positioning the virtuous artist in conflict with the dangerous studio system.

De-Authenticating *Juno*

Reading as anti-Hollywood means more than finding opposition in the forms and meanings of movies. It also functions as a way of managing the contexts of film-viewing and appreciation and of participating in film and media culture. The values of indie cinema are re-iterated and reproduced not only in response to films like *Happiness* that affirm them textually and contextually. They are also exercised through the negation of unworthy films, or of films whose popularity threatens the exclusivity of indie identity. Bourdieu writes that "taste classifies, and it classifies the classifier."[39] In classifying a film with too much marketing behind it—one pursuing and attaining too much commercial success, with too much mass appeal and mainstream media attention—as inauthentically indie, the culture of indie cinema reasserts the hierarchy of autonomous expressive creativity over commercialism. It makes clear that its own identity is characterized by opposition to corporate and mainstream values.

Juno, a comedy about a 16-year-old girl who becomes pregnant the first time she has sex and gives her baby up for adoption, was subject to de-authentication by some tastemakers, part of a regular cycle of delegitimating alternative culture (or what seems to be alternative culture) that becomes too popular to function as subcultural. After an initial wave of positive publicity, including numerous rave reviews written after film festival screenings and the release of trailers to screen before fall releases, the film found itself the object of a "backlash," which took the form not only of a disavowal of the film's aesthetic integrity, but even more so of its *bona fides* as an independent cultural artifact. As in the case of indie rock acts who sign to major labels only to be judged sellouts, films positioned as indie that indie culture judges to be too commercialized may fall victim to the category police, the tastemakers who would withhold authenticity.

Juno was produced on a modest budget of $7.5 million by Mandate Pictures (a production company owned by Lionsgate), with financing from Fox Searchlight, the specialty division of 20th Century Fox, which by 2007 had established a reputation for skillfully marketing offbeat comedies including *Sideways* (2004), *Napoleon Dynamite*, *Garden State*, and *Little Miss Sunshine*, and a track record of earning substantial revenues from them.[40] *Juno* earned enormous profits on a $143.5 million domestic gross.[41] As of late 2008 it had earned $87.7 million in foreign box office as well, to bring its worldwide theatrical total to more than $232 million.[42] This puts the film in the rare category of "indie blockbuster," where it keeps the company of *sex, lies, and videotape* (1989), *Pulp Fiction* (1994), *The Blair Witch Project* (1999), *My Big Fat Greek Wedding* (2002), and *Little*

Miss Sunshine.[43] *Juno* has in common with these other films an enormous return on investment, earning back its budget many times over. It was in part the appeal of this potential profitability on modest investment that made the specialty division a fixture of contemporary Hollywood. (Of course, we must figure in the costs of distributing and promoting the film before judging its financial success. *Variety* reported in March 2008 that the average prints and advertising cost of a "specialty" film in 2007 had risen 44 percent over the previous year to $25.7 million.)[44]

Like *Happiness* and many new indie classics, the "rollout" of *Juno* was engineered to capitalize on buzz. Specialty films positioned this way are screened at multiple festivals to make them available to critics well before their release date. *Juno* was previewed at the Telluride Film Festival, which was followed soon by an official "premiere" at the Toronto International Film Festival, where it was greeted unusually warmly.[45] Although not unanimously positive, the first notices from both film bloggers and reviewers for the mainstream media (and mainstream media bloggers for that matter) included a number of breathless raves. A review on the Cinematical blog by Scott Weinberg sounded typically enthusiastic: "*Juno* might be the smartest 'teen' movie since the also-brilliant *Election*." Weinberg predicted it would become "the next *Napoleon Dynamite*."[46] Roger Ebert gushed over *Juno* from Toronto; a few months later he chose it as his year's favorite.[47] The Web site Slashfilm proclaimed *Juno* the best film of the year so far, and reported that the usually cool critics in the Toronto premiere audience laughed, applauded, and gave the longest standing ovation in the festival's history. It called *Juno* that year's *Little Miss Sunshine*. It compared the film favorably with Wes Anderson's *Rushmore*, and contrasted it against the year's other high-profile unplanned pregnancy picture, *Knocked Up* (2007).[48]

Already in its first encounter with a viewing public, *Juno* was positioned discursively in relation to other films with which it was perceived to have affinities. This is evident in the reference points critics raised, especially *Election* (1999), *Napoleon Dynamite*, *Little Miss Sunshine*, and *Knocked Up*. By aligning *Juno* with previous offbeat indie comedies and in contrast to Hollywood studio films, critics were reproducing indieness in *Juno*.

These critics might have been primed to offer such comparisons by the distributor's production notes, circulated at the Toronto festival. After listing credits, these notes begin by describing the offbeat qualities of the film's "distinctively unique" main character, a "whip-smart Minnesota teen living by her own rules."[49] The notes include extensive biographical details about the film's novice screenwriter, Diablo Cody, and comparison to other films to establish an indie pedigree. Jennifer Garner, who plays the adoptive mother Vanessa, says she was impressed by how the *Juno* screenplay reminded her of *Napoleon Dynamite*, and frequent mention is made of director Jason Reitman's first film, the indie satire *Thank You for Smoking* (2005), and the star Ellen Page's previous role in the indie drama *Hard Candy* (2005).

A number of critics noted the potential of the film to attract large audiences and to be a crowd-pleaser. Todd McCarthy's *Variety* review identified *Juno* as "rather adventurously skedded for release on Dec. 14 and should score well as an alternative holiday choice to year-end blockbusters and serious awards contenders."[50] (Its release was later changed to generate more buzz by platforming first in Los Angeles and New York on December 5 before slowly expanding to more screens after a period of weeks.) Stephanie Zacharek in *Salon* predicted that *Juno* would be "the movie all your friends will be seeing, and urging you to see." Unlike some critics, Zacharek seemed primed to fault the film for its prospective popularity, wary of anything reaching mass appeal, and to sniff out Fox Searchlight's strategy. (As the ironic hipster T-shirt reads, "nothing is any good if other people like it.") Zacharek described *Juno* as "a wall-to-wall carpet of oh-so-clever one-liners," and dubbed it "an indie crowd pleaser that's much more enjoyable—in other words, not nearly as horrifying—as *Little Miss Sunshine*."[51] A cynical or skeptical critic like Zacharek could see that *Juno* was made to be "indie." The frequent comparison to *Little Miss Sunshine* is telling, since that was another film de-authenticated by the indie community when its popularity pushed it beyond the art house theater and audience and into the mainstream, as Fox Searchlight had plotted.

The characters, situations, and soundtrack of *Juno* offer a clear instance of a film performing its own indieness, its own alternative sensibility. Part of this is a product of its quirk, a quality of oddness or eccentricity which comes across (or is intended to) as charming or hip because of its very oddness or eccentricity. Quirk is a natural tone for indie cinema because it is by definition not normal or conventional.[52]

FIGURE 6.3 Her hamburger phone and bedroom décor establish Juno's taste.

Juno is quirky in numerous ways, such as its main character's uncommon poise for a 16-year-old pregnant girl. For instance, when she pretends to hang herself from a licorice rope, pretends to smoke a pipe, and makes public her reproductive situation at the drugstore where she takes the pregnancy test in the film's opening sequence, Juno is acting in ways we rarely see teenage girls behave in movies and television: unnaturally cool and self-aware. Much of the film's comic tone, especially in its first twenty-three minutes, is archly clever, and the cleverness is almost all Juno's. Her hamburger phone is too cute and her unique, slangy lingo too smart, but we are invited to admire the audacity of these extra doses of quirky sensibility. In typical teen comedy fashion the protagonist is a social outsider, but in this case Juno's taste is represented as a paradigm of pop culture connoisseurship. Every square centimeter of Juno's bedroom walls and school locker interior is covered with some exclusive signifier of superior taste (fig. 6.3). Her favorite music is punk rock, and she has strong opinions about which are the best splatter-gore horror films of the classic exploitation era. Every detail of her attire and behavior and personal space seems calculated to establish that Juno is at once offbeat—a "real character"—and adorable, from the cherries on the underwear she removes before having sex to her use of well-turned phrases like "I need to procure a hasty abortion" and words like "shenanigans."

Juno's indieness is especially evident when the film introduces Mark and Vanessa Loring (Jason Bateman and Jennifer Garner) as the prospective adoptive parents of Juno's baby. The scene in which Juno's family drives to meet them establishes the numbing conformity of their suburban McMansion world in a montage of tracking shots that pass a series of nearly identical houses. The Lorings' upper-class gentility is signaled by their home décor, heavy on the muted earth tones and whites and well appointed with fresh flowers. Vanessa is exceedingly polite, offering Juno and her parents a choice of upscale beverages. Since we have been aligned with Juno throughout the film's first act, we are invited to take her perspective in this first encounter with Mark and Vanessa, and we might imagine that she sees them as typical rich squares, ideals of domestic stability.[53]

Thus we share Juno's surprise when she ventures upstairs to use the bathroom to find that Mark has a room in which he keeps electric guitars. We quickly learn that he had a career as a rocker and that he and Juno share much of their pop culture tastes (fig. 6.4). But now he works for advertisers and composes jingles to sell consumer products, which helps pay for the trappings of haute-bourgeois living. In other words, he is a sellout and Juno can see it (she calls him that), but they have something in common and she feels a connection to him and so finds reasons to drop in unannounced.

As the film progresses we get less of Juno's quirky diction and more scenes of emotional depth. The one in which Juno announces her pregnancy to her parents is less screwball than those preceding it (as when Juno claims to have been turned off the idea of an abortion by the thought of the fetus's fingernails) and more honest and direct. Most importantly, the film switches tones by moving from presenting us mainly with scenes of Juno in dialogue with her friends Leah or Paulie to scenes in which Juno encounters adults like Vanessa Loring who are totally without quirk, who always speak sincerely in standard English in contrast to Juno's ironic lingo.

The sequence of the MacGuffs' visit to the Lorings is presented as a contrast in styles, with Juno's uninhibited hipster talk potentially alarming the buttoned-down affect of the Lorings and their lawyer,

FIGURE 6.4 Juno and Mark find a connection through their common taste.

but now the sincerity of Vanessa's desire for a child and her earnestness and fragility balance Juno's antics as they present a clash of personalities. The film loses some of its arch cleverness, its protective coating of quirky sensibility as Vanessa emerges as a significant character and a foil for Juno. This is nowhere more evident than in the shopping mall scene in which Juno and her friend Leah run into Vanessa and some friends and observe Vanessa playing with a young child. Juno now has a big pregnant belly and complains of the baby's kicking. Vanessa crouches down and speaks to her child-to-be (fig. 6.5). It is in this moment that the film introduces a new tone of sentimentality and invites our full sympathy for Vanessa. More importantly, it introduces a sense of Juno's recognition of Vanessa's desire to be a mother and Juno's empathy and feeling of a connection to the character that seems least like her of any in the film.

Meanwhile, Mark Loring is having second thoughts about becoming a father at all. The film implies that getting to know Juno has reminded him of who he really wants to be: an independent artist liv-

FIGURE 6.5 Vanessa talking to her baby in utero signals a shift in tone.

ing in the city, not the suburbs, creating art rather than selling his talent for a corporate payday, and answering only to himself rather than to a controlling wife who stresses out over which shade of yellow to paint the nursery and allows him a room in his own house in which to keep his stuff. One might expect an indie film that is so effectively performing its own alternativeness to celebrate this character, but actually we are more likely to think he is pathetic for not growing up and accepting adult responsibility. Juno has to decide what to do with her baby now that the adoptive couple has split, and she decides to give it to Vanessa anyway, solidifying a bond with her that substitutes for her connection to Mark. Like the scene in the mall, this moment in which Juno recognizes Vanessa and empathizes with her substitutes sentimentality and emotion for the quirky-clever tone of the earlier portions of the film.

The film also introduces a more emotionally weighty dimension to the love story between Juno and Paulie Bleeker (Michael Cera), the father of her child and love of her life. Whereas earlier in the film their relationship had been casual and distanced, the third act resolves their courtship with a very public kiss, and the movie ends on their duet of "Anyone Else But You." Mark and Vanessa's relationship failure has given Juno the insight that she and Paulie really are meant to be together, that each of them loves the other for who he or she really is. Thus a film that starts out cool warms up and finds a heart. This turn makes its narrative more accessible; like *Little Miss Sunshine*, the ending is affirmative and communal: characters come together. It is both funny and sad, comic and a bit melodramatic. If one marker of indieness is exclusiveness in relation to mainstream cinema and its audience, the form of *Juno* could be seen by the time of the film's ending to be making an appeal to this broad audience. This is especially so in the representation of Vanessa Loring, initially presented as the suburban conformist, as increasingly sympathetic, since much of the film's emotional weight rests on her. It's hard to be cynical and hip in the moment when she first holds her baby. *Juno* comes on indie— or rather as *trying* to be indie—but by the end has shed some of its pretensions.

One other significant element of *Juno*'s indieness is its pop soundtrack. Although the protagonist's favorites tend toward hard rock and punk (the Stooges, Patti Smith, the Runaways), most of the music used in the film is heavy on strummed acoustic guitar, and there are no anguished notes in the often childlike vocals (one closing credits song, "Vampire," is sung by a 12-year-old). Much of this music is by the anti-folk singer-songwriter Kimya Dawson, but songs by Cat Power, the Velvet Underground, and Belle and Sebastian fit the general pattern of acoustic instruments and sincere, often cute or juvenile-sounding vocals. Scoring by Mateo Messina duplicates Dawson's guitar sound, sometimes with her vocal merely humming the melody of a song.[54] One part of the film's perceived quirk and thus its indieness was the "twee" quality of this music (like quirk, twee is a somewhat vague term connoting cuteness, and in reference to music refers to lo-fi, folky indie pop opposed to the masculine aggressiveness of rock and roll and punk),[55] a style that aligns an indie cinema aesthetics with one of indie music.[56]

A *Juno* backlash took shape during the film's theatrical run as it posted huge box office grosses and was lavished with nominations for awards, including four Oscars in major categories.[57] This backlash took a number of forms: dissenting on the film's quality, on its representation of Juno's choice against abortion, on the deservingness of its popularity and its nominations for awards, and on the legitimacy of its claim to be not just an independent film but also a "sleeper" hit that crossed over from the art house to the megaplex to satisfy the demand of a word-of-mouth audience.[58] Seizing on the film's crowd-pleasing potential and critical accolades, Searchlight had followed the standard Hollywood rollout for awards hopefuls, screening the film at many film festivals and industry guild events, as other mini-major studios did that same season with films such as *Atonement* and *No Country for Old Men*.[59] It worked for *Juno*, which found itself on numerous year-end top tens and lists of awards nominees. In the first week of 2008 it was also clear that *Juno* was a hit, far surpassing Fox Searchlight's previous top earner, *Sideways*, which had grossed $73 million.[60] By the end of January the film had become an "indie block-buster," expanding to more than 2,400 screens and passing the $100 million domestic box office benchmark.[61] It would go on to win not only an Oscar for best original screenplay, but several Independent Spirit Awards including best feature, best lead actress, and screenplay. (*No Country for Old Men* and *There Will Be Blood*, distributed like *Juno* by studio specialty divisions and indies by many people's reckoning, were ineligible for surpassing budgetary limits, but were rewarded with more Oscars.)

At the time of *Juno*'s theatrical release in early December, following a period of buzz-building through festival screenings and promotional discourses such as the film's trailer, the influential indieWire site ran a scathing and snooty review, establishing the terms of *Juno*'s refusal of entry in the indie category, i.e., its de-authentication.

> The hype machine is chugging along at full speed for "Juno," and it's amazing what a little festival attention can do. A well-timed Telluride premiere, to an already almost legendarily appreciative audience, was soon followed by Toronto and Austin unveilings, all of which led award pundits and *Entertainment Weekly* columnists to mark it as a Serious Oscar Contender. Fox Searchlight, who proved irritably savvy when it came to promoting its surprise Academy magnet "Little Miss Sunshine" last year, now can position "Juno" as the designated underdog of choice—that "little" movie that seemingly came out of nowhere, that was directed by that guy who had that buzzy debut "Thank You for Smoking," and, did you hear, was written by that ex-stripper, one-time

phone-sex operator, and all-around New Voice in Cinema, Diablo Cody. Shrewd marketing, and Cody's tantalizing, oft trotted-out bio, may make "Juno" the flavor of the season, yet, taking a step back from the hype, it's hard not to feel like this aggressively clever, ultimately sentimental high-school comedy is less true seasonal counter-programming than just another Hollywood wolf in indie sheep clothing.[62]

One indie culture tastemaker, Karina Longworth of the blog Spout, wrote a series of posts in December and January critiquing not so much the movie itself as the narrative of its out-of-nowhere success and the legitimacy of its indieness. In a review from Telluride, Longworth had compared *Juno* favorably with *Knocked Up* and noted that *Juno* is both a crowd-pleaser and tearjerker, establishing its possibility of gaining wide appeal. Her praise had been rather measured: "it does move a few fairly familiar sitcomish situations in exciting directions."[63] (Comparisons with television are rarely flattering in film criticism.) After it had become a hit, Longworth wrote several posts critical of both the positioning of *Juno* as an indie film, and of the credulity of journalists (and presumably of audiences) who accept at face value that the film is a "crossover" hit.

> Tell me again how this film—made by a not-exactly-maverick director for a studio specialty division, starring three known actors and one tabloid staple, targeted at teens and young adults, both thematically and stylistically indebted (or, at the very least, related) to previous hits like *Superbad*, *Ghost World* and *Napoleon Dynamite*—qualifies as a "crossover"?
>
> Yes, Searchlight bought "indie" credibility by taking *Juno* to a bunch of festivals and rolling it out slowly. But we're also talking about a film that's been advertising on NYTimes.com for over three months. This is so clearly a studio film that, in a bit of smart awards season strategy, has been sold by its distributor as an indie. Why are journalists who should know better playing along?[64]

A few days later, Longworth elaborated on the logic of her hostility:

> [T]he idea that *Juno* is "small," that it's some kind of an underdog— either at the box office or within the clusterfuck of award's season—is categorically insane.

It's also somewhat troubling to think that if this kind of market-ing coup works so well once, it'll almost certainly work again, and at some point, there won't be room in the marketplace for actual "small" films that have actually "crossed over," because they'll be pushed out of the conversation by studio films (I don't care how much *Juno* cost to produce—it was paid for by a studio and it has the full benefit of a studio's marketing apparatus) masquerading as "small" "crossovers."[65]

Like Dargis in her division between true and sham indies, Longworth reserves "indie" for the films that rise to a threshold of legitimacy, which would seem to include some combination of an authorial mav-erick quality, distance from the Hollywood marketing machine, and distance as well from the narrative and stylistic qualities that make for a widely appealing film and the audience that turns out to see it.

In addition to the success of the film, a soundtrack recording re-leased by Rhino Records on January 8, 2008, became a hit CD, a #1 on *Billboard*'s 200 chart, and also a hit download, a #1 seller at the iTunes music store.[66] The twee cutesiness of the soundtrack was an additional source of backlash, as music critics could now piled on.[67] If you didn't like the movie, you probably wouldn't like the music either, but evidently many people liked both, as Fox Searchlight exploited the synergistic potential of cross-promotion. The association of this strategy with the standard practices of the media conglomerates could stand as another reason to de-authenticate *Juno*, as had been the case with *Garden State* a few years earlier, another indie romantic comedy with a bestselling and widely loathed indie rock soundtrack.

A number of factors explain the *Juno* backlash in addition to the obvious one of alternative culture looking suspiciously on mas-sive popularity, commercial exploitation, and the "incorporation" of subcultural style by the mainstream media industries. Authenticity in cinema is assigned to the products of sincere and committed *auteurs*, but *Juno* was conspicuously multiply authored. More publicity at-tended the stripper-cum-screenwriter, fresh-new-voice persona of Dia-blo Cody than the comparatively less interesting director, Jason Reit-man. His Hollywood family (his father, Ivan Reitman, is a director of mainstream comedies like *Ghostbusters* [1984], and *Kindergarten Cop* [1990]) does not add indie credibility to Reitman's biographical legend, and his earlier film, *Thank You for Smoking*, had been well received but not terribly high profile. Cody was seen as the source of *Juno*'s most irritating qualities, especially its too-clever dialogue. And she might have seemed to be trying too hard to be cool, with her conspicuous tattoos, her theatrical pseudonym, and her postfeminist, sexualized life story. As well, there could be an ideological dimension to the delegitimation of a film about a teenage girl aimed at girls and women, in a genre like teen romantic comedy that lacks respect. Any unfavorable comparisons with *No Country for Old Men* and *There Will Be Blood*, both of which were widely seen as more appropriate Oscar nominees, would imply an element of gender- and age-based cultural hierarchy.

Finally, once you get past the characters' diction and other elements of quirk, the film's form is actually not all that different from that of a Hollywood comedy. This much is true of many independent films, but when one attains such cultural prominence and attempts to exploit its indieness, the fact of canonical storytelling and conventional appeals is a convenient target. Thus Manohla Dargis can lump *Juno* in with the general trend of those so-called indie films insufficiently challenging of Hollywood, reaffirming the value of the authentic indie as autonomous and oppositional.

> Most of these niche films are nice, polite films of the sort you hear about on National Public Radio in between sob stories and pledge drives. Some are indelible works of art. Most are disposable, and many look, sound and play out, beat for beat, like Hollywood movies with lower budgets. Their provocations are superficial, tiny jabs against putative political correctness, like those of the pregnant teenager in "Juno." These are not films that will ever create a new wave; they barely make a ripple, and intentionally so, since each ripple might threaten possible revenue. Better to make audiences smile than make them squirm, better to reassure them than shake them up, better to stay safe than say, "Sorry, Mr. Murdoch."[68]

Indie cinema has champions in those like Dargis who stand against Mr. Murdoch no matter what, who see art and commerce as opposed in principle and incompatible in practice, and who reserve for themselves the judgment to say what counts as the real alternative. Reading as anti-Hollywood is thus much more than a matter of finding oppositional values in the forms or meanings of texts. This viewing strategy might be just as productive in cases that conform too much to what one expects of Hollywood, and is informed as much by contextual and paratextual reading as it is the encounter with the film itself. Indeed, the encounter with the film can hardly be imagined without the mediation of contexts and paratexts.

Conclusion

Ultimately, then, what is an indie film? In one sense it is not for me to say. This book has not been an effort to define the necessary and sufficient conditions of indieness or to draw firm boundaries around the category. Rather, it has approached indie film culture as a way of thinking about films, as a community with shared knowledge and expectations. The discussions above of the authentication of *Happiness* and the de-authentication of *Juno* are offered as examples of moments in which values of indie culture were recirculated and reaffirmed, which is to say, these were opportunities for indie ways of thinking about indie films to be established and reestablished. But at the same time, the tastemakers are not the only ones empowered to define the category. Fox Searchlight and its ilk, certainly, as well as less vanguardist critics and ordinary moviegoers, also share that power. To an extent, the defensive posture of the tastemakers opposes the larger cultural circulation of indie as a concept and category. The fact that many ordinary moviegoers would identify *Juno* as an indie film (like *Garden State, Napoloeon Dynamite, Sideways, and Little Miss Sunshine* before it) is a testament to that power. At work in the discursive struggles at the heart of this chapter are efforts to negotiate the meaning of indie, which the tastemakers might not likely win. Eventually it might behoove them to conceive of alternative cinema in a new way, with new words and ideas, to better authenticate the works they would champion.

But in a larger sense, I have been authorizing myself to define indie cinema as that which indie culture determines to fit that label. To the extent that that culture can brook disagreement, can be split into factions of differing habits of thought and differing investment in the alternative conception of indie, indie might be inconsistent or contradictory. But I would not have written all this if I did not think there was considerable coherence to the way indie operates as a cultural category. In particular, I have seized on three ways of thinking about movies that I propose indie culture tends to agree about: that indie films invest great significance in characters who are to be read as emblems of their social identities, that their forms are often to be seen as invitations to play, and that our general assumptions about indie films require that we see them in opposition to Hollywood, at least in some ways. It might seem that locating the definition of indieness in the audience slights other explanations of how independent cinema coheres as a category such as economic or political ones. But the economic distinction between Hollywood and its alternatives figures in significantly to the anti-mainstream viewing strategy as we have seen, and the political distinction is often the force motivating prominent social and formal appeals, and more importantly, oppositional ones.

In every period of American film history there has been peripheral cinema. In many periods, it consisted of films made far from Hollywood and its influence. Although it exploits its opposition—or rather, our sense of its opposition—the American independent cinema of the most recent age increasingly has been the product of the major media industries, the conglomerates like News Corp. whose reputation among the culturally savvy is merely that of predatory capitalists. Those who would deny indie cinema's distinction from mainstream culture on the basis of News Corp.'s participation in its production articulate a noble resistance to the incorporation of alternative visions and values by huge multinational corporations eager to profit from consumer preferences for fresh and challenging perspectives. But as a cultural category, indie cinema belongs to a wide community of participants including not only filmmakers, critics, tastemakers, and scholars but also corporations and ordinary film viewers. Ironically, by becoming so visible and vital and commercially significant, for better or worse indie culture has become Hollywood's most prominent alternative to itself. While remaining critical of the independent sector's incorporation by Hollywood, however, we might still appreciate that in many ways indie film, as an alternative to the mainstream of American cinema, holds significant value for those invested in indie culture.

NOTES

Introduction

1. Douglas Gomery, *Shared Pleasures: A History of Movie Presentation in the United States*, 171–96; Barbara Wilinsky, *Sure Seaters: The Emergence of Art House Cinema*.

2. Sarah Thornton, *Club Cultures: Music, Media and Subcultural Capital*.

3. I discuss this tension between resistant and hegemonic functions in Michael Z. Newman, "Indie Culture: In Pursuit of the Authentic Autonomous Alternative," *Cinema Journal* 48.3 (Spring 2009): 16–34.

4. Yannis Tzioumakis, *American Independent Cinema: An Introduction*, argues that throughout the history of the American film industry, industrial and aesthetic innovation has come from outside of the major studio oligopoly in the form of the "top-rank" independent production of the studio era, the exploitation cinema of the 1950s, '60s, and '70s, and the more recent movement of indies. For an argument that innovation in the media industries comes from outside of established firms, see also Ted Turner, "My Beef with Big Media," *Washington Monthly* (July/Aug. 2004), available online at www.washingtonmonthly.com/features (accessed Nov. 23, 2008).

5. Tzioumakis, *American Independent Cinema*.

6. Jason Mittell, *Genre and Television: From Cop Shows to Cartoons in American Culture*, discusses television genres as cultural categories in terms of their clusters of associations.

7. Kaya Oakes, *Slanted and Enchanted: The Evolution of Indie Culture*, covers many of these manifestations of indie culture during the era I am discuss-

ing, including music, publishing, and crafting. On independent bookstores see Laura J. Miller, *Reluctant Capitalists: Bookselling and the Culture of Consumption*. On indie video games see Jason Wilson, "Indie Rocks! Mapping Independent Video Game Design," *Media International Australia incorporating Culture and Policy* 115 (May 2005): 109–122. In a rant against the "quirky indie sensibility," Michael Hirschorn, "Quirked Around," *The Atlantic* (Sept. 2007), includes as examples of what he is discussing the public radio series *This American Life*, the literary magazine *McSweeney's*, the HBO comedy *Flight of the Concords*, novels by Jonathan Lethem and Jonathan Safran Foer, memoirs by Augusten Burroughs, as well as films like *Napoleon Dynamite*, *Rushmore*, *Little Miss Sunshine* and work in several media by Miranda July; available online at www.theatlantic.com/doc/200709/quirk (accessed Nov. 24 2008).

8. Thornton, *Club Cultures*, coined the term "subcultural capital" to describe the forms of knowledge and distinction operating in subcultures, and is also a source for my thinking about "mainstream" as a construct of alternative cultures. "Subcultural capital" plays on the idea of "cultural capital" as employed in Pierre Bourdieu, *Distinction: A Social Critique of the Judgement of Taste*.

9. Alisa Perren, "Sex, Lies, and Marketing: Miramax and the Development of the Quality Indie Blockbuster," *Film Quarterly* 55.2 (Winter 2001–2002): 30–39.

10. David Hedsmondhalgh, "Indie: The Institutional Politics and Aesthetics of a Popular Music Genre," *Cultural Studies* 13.1 (1999): 34–61.

11. Dick Hebdige, *Subculture: The Meaning of Style*, 90–99, uses "incorporation" to refer to the tendency of hegemonic culture to market styles originating in resistant subcultures.

12. Ibid.; Ryan Hibbett, "What Is Indie Rock?" *Popular Music and Society* 28.1 (2005): 55–77.

13. On the Keystone Indie Lounge, *see* www.landmarktheatres.com/market/Indianapolis/KeystoneArtCinema.htm (accessed Nov. 23, 2008). The "INDIES" sign reads, "Favorite independent films chosen for Target by the Independent Film Channel."

14. David Poland, "Defining Indie 2010: Dependents, Full Indies, Mid-Indies, Micro-Indies & House Indies," The Hot Blog, available online at www.mcnblogs.com/thehotblog/archives/2010/02/defining_indie.html (accessed Feb. 10, 2010).

15. As an example of the complexity behind the terms *indie* and *indiewood* as discussed in the popular press, see Lorne Manly, "The Meaning of 'Indie,'" *New York Times*, May 29, 2005, C2.

16. Many writers have remarked on this shift in indie rock. See, for instance, Sasha Frere-Jones, "A Paler Shade of White: How Indie Rock Lost Its Soul," *The New Yorker*, Oct. 22, 2007, 176–81; and Bret Gladstone, "This Is an Essay about Okkervil River. Kinda.," *Village Voice*, Oct. 10, 2007, available online

at www.villagevoice.com/blogs/music/archives/2007/10/this_is_an_essa.php (accessed Nov. 23, 2008).

17. Jessica Winter, *The Rough Guide to American Independent Film*; Jason Wood, 100 *American Independent Films*; Empire, "The 50 Greatest Independent Films: Empire's Ultimate Indie Lineup" (n.d.), available online at www
.empireonline.com/features/50greatestindependent (accessed May 7, 2010).

18. Geoff King, *Indiewood, USA: Where Hollywood Meets Independent Cinema*, considers "indiewood" as a form of niche-marketed cinema.

19. E. Deidre Pribram, *Cinema & Culture: Independent Film in the United States, 1980–2001*, xii, defines independent cinema as a discursive formation, which is similar in concept to a film culture, as both set the job of determining the contours of the category on multiple levels. I stress film culture as the way of understanding indie cinema because it refers to both films as cultural objects, and to communities of filmmakers, critics, and audiences as a cultural formation that constructs films and gives them significance.

20. According to standard usage in film and television studies, indie cinema would not likely be considered a genre. However, if we understand "genre" on a more fundamental level to mean "category of texts," then indie certainly counts. Even if this point seems to strain the term unreasonably, consider that many of the same considerations that go into producing and consuming genres go into producing and consuming independent cinema, whatever kind of category we want to call it.

21. Mittell, *Genre and Television*.

22. Consider this anonymous comment on the indieWire blog: "The notion that 'Sideways,' a $16 million venture, is an independent film is itself a measure of how silly and corrupted this discourse has become" (*see* www.indiewire.com/biz/biz_050228spirit.html; accessed Nov. 23, 2008).

23. The Independent Spirit Awards have been given annually since 1984 by the nonprofit Film Independent organization and have become one of the most visible regular indie film events, in part by being scheduled in Los Angeles during the same weekend as the Academy Awards. See www.spiritawards.com (accessed May 13, 2010).

24. John Pierson, *Spike, Mike, Slackers & Dykes: A Guided Tour Across a Decade of American Independent Cinema*; Peter Biskind, *Down and Dirty Pictures: Miramax, Sundance, and the Rise of Independent Film*; Emmanuel Levy, *The Cinema of Outsiders: The Rise of American Independent Film*; Pribram, *Cinema & Culture*; Geoff King, *American Independent Cinema*. Additional single-authored volumes on independent cinema include King, *Indiewood, USA*; Geoff Andrew, *Stranger Than Paradise: Maverick Film-makers in Recent American Cinema*; Sharon Waxman, *Rebels on the Backlot: Six Maverick Directors and How They Conquered the Hollywood Studio System*; James Mottram, *The Sundance Kids: How the Mavericks Took Back Hollywood*; and D. K. Holm,

Independent Cinema; and Donald Lyons, *Independent Visions: A Critical Intro-duction to Recent American Independent Film.*

25. Chris Holmlund and Justin Wyatt, eds., *American Independent Cinema: From the Margins to the Mainstream*; Chuck Kleinhans, "Independent Features: Hopes and Dreams"; Kim Newman, "Exploitation and the Mainstream"; Wood, 100 *American Independent Films*; Justin Wyatt, "The Formation of the 'Major Independent'"; Tzioumakis, *American Independent Cinema*; and King, *Indiewood, USA.*

26. King, *American Independent Cinema.*

27. King, *Indiewood, USA.*

28. Pribram, *Cinema & Culture.*

29. Jeffrey Sconce, "Irony, Nihilism and the New American 'Smart' Film," *Screen* 43.4 (Winter 2002): 349–69.

30. Ibid., 352.

31. Biskind, *Down and Dirty Pictures*; Levy, *The Cinema of Outsiders*; Lyons, *Independent Visions*; Pierson, *Spike, Mike, Slackers & Dykes*; Waxman, *Rebels on the Backlot*; Mottram, *The Sundance Kids*; Holm, *Independent Cinema.*

32. This is in the same spirit as Rick Altman, *Film/Genre*, 207–215, which calls for a "semantic/syntactic/pragmatic approach to genre." Although independent cinema is not a genre, the same terms would seem to have some purchase in understanding how it functions as a category.

33. Tzioumakis, *American Independent Cinema*, 192–284; Perren, "Sex, Lies, and Marketing"; Wyatt, "The Formation of the 'Major Independent,'" 74–90.

34. Bourdieu, *Distinction.* Geoff King makes a similar point about the taste-culture of niche-oriented indiewood cinema in *Indiewood, USA*, 11–38.

35. "Creative class" is the coinage of Richard Florida, *The Rise of the Creative Class and How It's Transforming Work, Leisure, and Everyday Life* (New York: Basic Books, 2002).

1. Indie Cinema Viewing Strategies

1. Levy, *Cinema of Outsiders*; Owen Glieberman, "A Terrible Twist Ending," *Entertainment Weekly*, Dec. 3, 2004, 25–26.

2. The notion of "viewing strategies" follows David Bordwell's approach to art cinema and James Peterson's approach to the avant-garde, both of which identify reception practices that are suggested by the films and institutionalized in film culture. David Bordwell, "The Art Cinema as a Mode of Film Practice"; James Peterson, *Dreams of Chaos, Visions of Order: Understanding the American Avant-Garde Cinema.*

3. David Bordwell, Janet Staiger, and Kristen Thompson, *The Classical Hollywood Cinema: Film Style and Mode of Production to 1960*; Bordwell, *Narration in the Fiction Film*; Bordwell, "The Art Cinema as a Mode of Film Practice"; Steve Neale, "Art Cinema as Institution"; Murray Smith, "Modernism and the Avant-gardes."

4. King, *American Independent Cinema*, 101–104.

5. The "circuit of culture" is a term offered by Richard Johnson, "What Is Cultural Studies Anyway?" *Social Text* 16 (1986/87), 33–80, to account for the significance of both production and consumption in understanding cultural texts.

6. Edward E. Smith, "Categorization"; Ziva Kunda, *Social Cognition*, 15–52.

7. Kristin Thompson and David Bordwell, *Film History: An Introduction*, 39–42.

8. Robert Sklar, *Movie-Made America: A Cultural History of American Movies*, 33–47.

9. Tzioumakis, *American Independent Cinema*, 19–62; one case study of an American independent producer is Matthew Bernstein, *Walter Wanger: Hollywood Independent*.

10. Thompson and Bordwell, *Film History*, 218, 304.

11. Ibid., 336–39.

12. On exploitation films aimed at the youth market, see Thomas Doherty, *Teenagers and Teenpics: The Juvenilization of American Movies in the 1950s*; on the relation of exploitation films to Hollywood, see Kim Newman, "Exploitation and the Mainstream." For a more general discussion of independent production in the 1960s and 1970s, see Thompson and Bordwell, *Film History*, 530–32.

13. David E. James, *Allegories of Cinema: American Film in the Sixties*, 280–303.

14. King, *American Independent Cinema*, 6, makes a similar point about Cassavetes and *Shadows*.

15. P. Adams Sitney, *Visionary Film: The American Avant-Garde, 1948–1978*, viii.

16. Tzioumakis, *American Independent Cinema*, 192–284, describes this shift.

17. Bordwell, "The Art Cinema as a Mode of Film Practice," 779.

18. In distinguishing classical and art cinema narration, I am relying on Bordwell, *Narration in the Fiction Film*.

19. Jim Hillier, "Introduction," in Hillier, ed., *American Independent Cinema: A Sight and Sound Reader*, ix–xvii; Steven Soderbergh and Richard Lester, *Getting Away with It; Or, The Further Adventures of the Luckiest Bastard You Ever Saw*. See also Levy, *Cinema of Outsiders*; Lyons, *Independent Visions*; and Pierson, *Spike, Mike, Slackers & Dykes*.

20. For an extensive discussion of these discourses and their significance as a context for understanding media, see Ron Becker, *Gay TV and Straight*

America, esp. ch. 4, "The Affordable, Multicultural Politics of Gay Chic," 108–135.

21. Loren King, "The Troubled Inner Child," *Boston Globe*, July 16, 2000, Arts sec., p. 1.

22. On Hollywood characters as one-dimensional, see Thomas Schatz, "The New Hollywood"; on the ancillary-product-promotion function of American movies, see Robert C. Allen, "Home Alone Together: Hollywood and the 'Family Film.'"

23. For example, Biskind, *Down and Dirty Pictures*, 19, writes: "Hollywood favored spectacle, action, and special effects, while indies worked on a more intimate scale, privileging script and emphasizing character and mise-en-scène." (He uses the past tense to contrast the "purist" past conception of this opposition with a more recent one that sees the rise of Miramax and Sundance as a sign of the independent cinema's demise.)

24. Karen Alexander, "*Daughters of the Dust*," in Hillier, ed., *American Independent Cinema*, 40–43.

25. Lyons, *Independent Visions*, 284.

26. Pierson, *Spike, Mike, Slackers & Dykes*.

27. Bordwell, "The Art Cinema as a Mode of Film Practice," 777.

28. Thomas Schatz, *Hollywood Genres: Formulas, Filmmaking, and the Studio System*, 24–36; and Schatz, *Old Hollywood/New Hollywood: Ritual, Art, and Industry*, 67–167.

29. Levy, *Cinema of Outsiders*.

30. Larry Gross, "Antibodies: Larry Gross Talks to *Safe*'s Todd Haynes," *Filmmaker* 3.4 (1995); available online at www.filmmakermagazine.com/summer1995/antibodies.php; Amy Taubin, "Nowhere to Hide," in Hillier, ed., *American Independent Cinema*, 100–107.

31. Bordwell, "The Art Cinema as a Mode of Film Practice," 779.

32. James, *Allegories of Cinema*, 297–303.

33. Andreas Huyssen, *After the Great Divide: Modernism, Mass Culture, Postmodernism*.

34. Levy, *Cinema of Outsiders*, 55–57; for more on claims that certain indie directors such as the Coens and Tarantino are postmodernist, see chapters 5 and 6 (this volume).

35. Noël Carroll, "The Future of Allusion: Hollywood in the Seventies (and Beyond)" *October* 20 (1982): 51–81.

36. For similar characterizations of the indie audience see Levy, *Cinema of Outsiders*, 28–29; Perren, "Sex, Lies and Marketing."

37. These conceptions are well summarized in the chapter "Postmodernism in the Arts," Steven Best and Douglas Kellner, *The Postmodern Turn* (New York: Guilford Press, 1997), 124–94.

38. Michael Z. Newman, "Characterization in American Independent Cinema" (Ph.d. diss., University of Wisconsin-Madison, 2005), 251–72.

39. Peterson, *Dreams of Chaos, Visions of Order*, 28.

40. Levy, *Cinema of Outsiders*, 498.

41. Quoted in ibid., 3.

42. I am not arguing that difference from Hollywood automatically amounts to a critique of Hollywood, only that it is often seen that way. No one would say that foreign-language films are implicitly critical of Hollywood because their dialogue is not in English, which is different from the norm of Hollywood filmmaking. The differences must be seen as relevant to determining the identity of each category for them to amount to an implicit critique.

43. Michael Hirschorn, "Quirked Around," *The Atlantic*, Sept. 2007.

44. Luc Sante, "Mystery Man."

45. Gavin Smith, ed., *Sayles on Sayles*, 44–49.

2. Home Is Where the Art Is: Indie Film Institutions

1. Redford, quoted in John Lombardi, "At the Sundance Institute . . . ," *New York Times Magazine*, Oct. 23, 1983, 48.

2. Vincent Canby, "Rejoice! It's Independents' Day," *New York Times* (hereafter, *NYT*), Oct. 8, 1989.

3. Bordwell, Staiger, and Thompson, *The Classical Hollywood Cinema*, 330–37.

4. Ann Swinton, "Culture in Action: Symbols and Strategies," *American Sociological Review* 51.2 (Apr. 1986): 237–86.

5. Arthur Danto, "The Artworld," *Journal of Philosophy* 61.19 (1964): 571–84; George Dickie, *Art and the Aesthetic: An Institutional Analysis*.

6. Danto, "The Artworld," 580.

7. Howard S. Becker, *Art Worlds*.

8. Richard Linklater, *Slacker* (New York: St. Martin's, 1992), 118–21.

9. Shyon Baumann, *Hollywood Highbrow: From Entertainment to Art*, 54–59.

10. Bazin, quoted in Robert Sklar, "Beyond Hoopla: The Cannes Film Festival and Cultural Significance," *Cineaste* 22.3 (Dec. 1996): 18-20.

11. Marijke de Valck, *Film Festivals: From European Geopolitics to Global Cinephilia*, 24.

12. Thomas Elsaesser, *European Cinema: Face to Face With Hollywood*, 88.

13. De Valck, *Film Festivals*, 38, argues that film festivals "are sites of passage that function as the gateways to cultural legitimation."

14. Ibid., 90.

15. Thompson and Bordwell, *Film History*, 718.

16. Kenneth Turan, *Sundance to Sarajevo: Film Festivals and the World They Made*, 46.

17. Julian Stringer, "Regarding Film Festivals" (Ph.D. diss., Indiana University, 2003), 65.

18. Paul DiMaggio, "Cultural Boundaries and Structural Change: The Extension of the High Culture Model to Theater, Opera and the Dance, 1900–1940."

19. Ibid., 24–25.

20. Ibid., 43. The notion of "sacralization" of culture comes from Lawrence W. Levine, *Highbrow/Lowbrow: The Emergence of Cultural Hierarchy in America.*

21. J. Mark Schuster, *Mapping State Cultural Policy: The State of Washington,* 9, asserts that cultural policy includes both explicit and implicit, intentional and unintentional products of state involvement in culture.

22. Tyler Cowen, *Good and Plenty: The Creative Successes of American Arts Funding,* 34.

23. James Quandt, ed., *Robert Bresson*; and James Quandt, ed., *Shohei Imamura.*

24. "Sundance Group Announces Cinema Intention," *Business Wire,* May 20, 2005, 1.

25. Richard W. Christopherson, "From Folk Art to Fine Art: A Transformation in the Meaning of Photographic Work," *Urban Life and Culture* 3.2 (July 1974), 123–157.

26. Baumann, *Hollywood Highbrow,* 83.

27. Liz Czach, "Film Festivals, Programming, and the Building of a National Cinema," *The Moving Image* 4.1 (2004): 76–88; Luzy Mazdon, "The Cannes Film Festival as Transnational Space," *Post Script* 25.2 (Winter/Spring 2006): 19–30; Lucy Mazdon, "Transnational 'French' Cinema: The Cannes Film Festival," *Modern & Contemporary France* 15.1 (Feb. 2007): 9–20; Owen Evans, "Border Exchanges: The Role of the European Film Festival," *Journal of Contemporary European Studies* 15.2 (Apr. 2007): 23–33; Bill Nichols, "Discovering Form, Inferring Meaning: New Cinemas and the Film Festival Circuit," *Film Quarterly* 47.3 (Spring 1994): 16–30; Bill Nichols, "Global Image Consumption in the Age of Late Capitalism," *East-West Film Journal* 8.1 (1994): 68–85; Alexander Craig, "Dragons and Tigers Take on Leopards and Skunks: The Importance of Film Festivals," *Performing Arts & Entertainment in Canada* 31.2 (Fall 1997): 16ff; Stringer, "Regarding Film Festivals," 58–103.

28. On Venice and Berlin, see Stringer, "Regarding Film Festivals"; and Elsaesser, *European Cinema.* On the origins of Sundance, see Lory Smith, *Party in a Box: The Story of the Sundance Festival.*

29. Czach, "Film Festivals."

30. Vincent Canby, "How Is a Festival Measured?" *NYT,* Sept. 20, 1987.

31. New York Film Festival online archive (*see* www.filmlinc.com/archive/nyff/nyffarchive.html).

32. Thompon & Bordwell, *Film History,* 716.

33. Amy Taubin, "ALL TALK? Supposedly the voice of its generation, the indie film movement known as Mumblecore has had its 15 minutes," *Film Comment* (Nov./Dec. 2007); available online at www.filmlinc.com/fcm/nd07/mumblecore.htm (accessed May 13, 2010).

34. The films included in the *Sundance Film Festival DVD Collection* released by Hart Sharp Video and Sundance Channel Home Entertainment are *sex, lies, and videotape* (1989), *Clerks* (1994), *The Usual Suspects* (1995), *Smoke Signals* (1998), *American Movie* (1999), *Boys Don't Cry* (1999), *In the Bedroom* (2001), *Real Women Have Curves* (2002), *Capturing the Friedmans* (2003), and *American Splendor* (2003).

35. See also Smith, *Party in a Box*; John Anderson, *Sundancing: Hanging Out and Listening at America's Most Important Film Festival*; Benjamin Craig, *Sundance: A Festival Virgin's Guide.*

36. Anderson, *Sundancing*, 2.

37. Ibid., 41.

38. Christine Spines, "25 Years of Sundance," *Entertainment Weekly*, Feb. 3, 2006, 32–34, 36.

39. Tzioumakis, *American Independent Cinema*, 272–75.

40. Todd McCarthy, "Indie Film Festival Grows Up," *Daily Variety*, Jan. 18, 1995.

41. Biskind, *Down and Dirty Pictures*, 25–29.

42. John Powers, "Downhill at Park City," *Film Comment* 23.2 (Mar.–Apr. 1987): 4–6.

43. Aljean Harmetz, "Independent Films Get Better But Go Begging," *NYT*, Feb. 1, 1989.

44. Perren, "Sex, Lies, and Marketing."

45. Smith, *Party in a Box*, 44; Elsaesser, *European Cinema*, 83.

46. Smith, *Party in a Box*, 26.

47. Aljean Harmetz, "Moguls Take to the Slopes for Deals," *NYT*, Mar. 7, 1984, C17.

48. Thompson and Bordwell, *Film History*, 716.

49. Smith, *Party in a Box*, 41.

50. Ibid., 24.

51. Herbert Mitang, "Market for Film Makers Spotlights Independents," *NYT*, Oct. 18, 1984, C19.

52. Smith, *Party in a Box*, 40.

53. Gerald Peary, "Sundance," *American Film* 7.1 (Oct. 1981): 46–51.

54. Lombardi, "At the Sundance Institute."

55. Ibid.

56. Peary, "Sundance," 49.

57. Ibid., 47.

58. Ibid.

59. Smith, *Party in a Box*, 103.

60. Ibid., 98.

61. Ibid., 104.

62. Powers, "Downhill at Park City," 4.

63. Todd McCarthy, "Redford Keeping Sundance Small," *Daily Variety*, Jan. 25, 1993, 1.

64. Todd McCarthy, "Redford Bullish on Indies," *Daily Variety*, Jan. 24, 1994, 1.

65. Tzioumakis, *American Independent Cinema*, 254.

66. Mottram, *The Sundance Kids*; Waxman, *Rebels on the Backlot*.

67. Smith, *Party in a Box*, 185.

68. Canby, "Rejoice! It's Independents' Day."

69. Much of the evidence in support of the points to follow is from the history on the Telluride Film Festival's Web site (*see* http://telluridefilmfestival.org/history.html), accessed May 13, 2010.

70. Grace Lichtenstein, "Telluride Festival in Colorado Forms a Peak for Movie Buffs," *NYT*, Sept. 2, 1975.

71. Jonathan Baumbach, "New York," *American Film* 3.4 (Feb. 1978): 66–67.

72. Vincent Canby, "The New York Film Festival: Why It Thrives" *NYT*, Sept. 21, 1980.

73. This claim is historically inaccurate, as the early years of the New York Film Festival had included screenings of "New American Cinema" programmed by Amos Vogel, its first program director.

74. Vincent Canby, "How Is a Festival Measured?" *NYT*, Sept. 20, 1987.

75. Vincent Canby, "Now We Know: Home Is Where the Art Is," *NYT*, May 21, 1989.

76. At just the moment that the mainstream press was latching onto independent cinema as a new and exciting thing, purists of the alternative filmmaking community denounced the commercialization of their movement. For an example of this contrary rhetoric see Jon Jost, "End of the Indies," *Film Comment* 25.1 (Jan.–Feb. 1989): 42–45.

77. Canby, "Rejoice! It's Independents' Day."

78. See the NYFF online archive (note 31 above).

79. Baumann, *Hollywood Highbrow*, argues that it was around 1960 that Americans began to see film as an art form rather than merely as entertainment, and the art house and the films it showed are among the causes of this shift.

80. Wilinsky, *Sure Seaters*; and Gomery, *Shared Pleasures*, 171–96.

81. Dallas Smythe, Parker B. Lusk, and Charles A. Lewis, "Portrait of an Art-Theater Audience," *Quarterly of Film, Radio, and Television* 8 (Fall 1953): 28–50.

82. Wilinsky, *Sure Seaters*, 114.

83. "Is New York Losing Its Reps?" *Village Voice*, Dec. 3, 1985, 16.

84. "The Last Thalia Picture Show," *NYT*, Sept. 30, 1973; "Thalia, West Side Muse of Reruns, Is Revived," *NYT*, Aug. 12, 1977; "The Thalia, Offbeat Home of Classic Movies, Is Closed, " *NYT*, May 11, 1987; "Three Hurt in Beam Collapse at Theater Under Demolition," *NYT*, July 18, 1987.

85. Michael Buckley, "The Regency: Manhattan's Premier Revival House," *Films in Review* 34 (June–July 1983): 326–28. The theater had since changed to a first-run policy.

86. "Goodbye Gable: Regency Is Mourned," *NYT*, Aug. 24, 1987; "More Than Nostalgia Was Involved in Sale of Regency Theater," *NYT*, Sept. 14, 1987.

87. "Cinema Studio to Close Doors After 30 Years," *NYT*, Mar. 25, 1990.

88. "Goodbye Gable: Regency Is Mourned," *NYT*, Aug. 24, 1987; "More Than Nostalgia Was Involved in Sale of Regency Theater," *NYT*, Sept. 14, 1987.

89. "The Last Picture Shows," *Newsweek*, June 8, 1987, 76–77.

90. Tino Balio, "The Art Film in the New Hollywood," 65.

91. Gomery, *Shared Pleasures*, 195.

92. Leonard Klady, "Summer Drought Hits Specialized Fare," *Variety*, June 9, 1997, 7.

93. Jesse McKinley, "The House Filmgoers Love to Hate," *NYT*, Aug. 10, 2003.

94. "Art House Theaters Also Part of Building Boom," *Star Tribune* (Minneapolis), Feb. 15, 1998; Carolyn T. Geer, "Coming Soon: An Art Theater Near You," *Forbes*, July 6, 1998.

95. Linda Moss, "A Complex Solution: Independent Producer Tries Downtown Cinemas," *Crain's New York Business* , June 19, 1989, 20; Thomas L. Waite, " 'Miracle' in Manhattan; Basement Multiplex," *NYT*, Jan. 8, 1989.

96. "The Screening of Lower Manhattan," *Village Voice*, June 20, 1989, 83–86.

97. Moss, "A Complex Solution."

98. "About the Angelika," available online at http://angelikafilmcenter.com/about_us.asp (accessed May 13, 2010).

99. Christine Vachon, *A Killer Life: How an Independent Film Producer Survives Deals and Disasters in Hollywood and Beyond*, 55.

100. Dan Margolis and Monica Roman, "Exhibs Target Stix for Niche Pix," *Variety*, Mar. 24–30, 1997.

101. Giulia, quoted in Klady, "Summer Drought Hits Specialized Fare."

102. Leonard Klady, "New Fix for Art Pix," *Variety*, Sept. 28, 1998.

103. Andrew Hindes, "Landmark to Launch Gotham Arthouse Multi," *Variety*, Dec. 21, 1998–Jan. 3, 1999.

104. Monica Roman, "Big Apple Art Boom," *Variety*, Nov. 16, 1998.

105. Ian Mohr, "IFC Front and Center," *Daily Variety*, June 14, 2005.

106. Hindes, "Landmark to Launch Gotham Arthouse Multi."

107. Richard Natale, "Theaters Take On Challenge of 'Difficult' Subject Matter," *Daily Variety*, Oct. 19, 1999, A4.

108. Wilinsky, *Sure Seaters*, 122–27.

109. "Sunshine Cinema," available online at www.landmarktheatres.com/market/NewYork/SunshineCinema.htm (accessed Nov. 30, 2008); and "Oriental Theater," online at www.landmarktheatres.com/market/Milwaukee/Oriental Theatre.htm (accessed Nov. 30, 2008).

110. "Kendall Square Cinema," online at www.landmarktheatres.com/market/Boston/KendallSquareCinema.htm (accessed Nov. 30, 2008).

111. "The Magnolia," online at www.landmarktheatres.com/market/Dallas/TheMagnolia.htm (accessed Nov. 30, 2008).

112. Bernard, quoted in Christopher Grove, "New Specialty Film Era: As Audience Ages, Landmark Premieres Lush New Theaters," *Daily Variety*, Oct. 19, 1999.

113. Tom Daykin, "Sundance Premiere: Madison Theater Is First in Chain Led by Robert Redford," *Milwaukee Journal-Sentinel*, May 9, 2007.

3. Indie Realism: Character-Centered Narrative and Social Engagement

1. Tzioumakis, *American Independent Cinema*, 13; Pribram, *Cinema & Culture*, xii.

2. Nathan Rabin, "My Year of Flops, Case File 1: *Elizabethtown*: The Bataan Death March of Whimsy," *The Onion A.V. Club*, Jan. 27, 2007, available online at www.avclub.com/articles/my-year-of-flops-case-file-1-elizabethtown-the-bat,15577/ (accessed Feb. 11, 2010).

3. For instance, John Pierson, a representative for independent filmmakers, notes, "Many of the trendsetting independent films, including some I've been involved in myself, have championed the idea of the character-driven movie" (Graham Fuller, "Summer Movies: Indies," *New York Times*, May 2, 1999, sec. 2A, 44). John Sayles observes that his films "tend to be about characters" (Claudia Dreyfus, "John Sayles," *Progressive* 55.11 [1991]: 30–33). Mark Gill, who was director of marketing at independent distributor Miramax in the 1990s, declared, "Miramax films tend to be more stimulating, more character-driven" (Edward Helmore, "Fast Forward from Art House to Your House," *The Observer*, Sept. 7, 1997, 12). Jim Hillier discusses American independent films as the reemergence of an American film aesthetic of the 1960s and 1970s, exemplified in films such as *Easy Rider*, *Bonnie and Clyde*, *Two-Lane Blacktop*, and *M*A*S*H**, which "are frequently led more by character than plot" ("Introduction," in Hillier, ed., *American Independent Cinema*, viii–xvii, viii; see also Jeff Sipe, "Indie Vets Mull State of the Biz, Then and Now," *Daily Variety*, Aug. 18, 2003, Special Section 1, p. A56).

4. One emblematic statement of this position is Owen Glieberman's "A Terrible Twist Ending," *Entertainment Weekly*, Dec. 3, 2004, 25–26. Glieberman

condemns contemporary Hollywood blockbusters such as *Van Hesling* for being plot-driven and admires *Sideways* in contrast as being character-driven.

5. For example, Peter Biskind, *Down and Dirty Pictures*, 19, writes: "Hollywood favored spectacle, action, and special effects, while indies worked on a more intimate scale, privileging script and emphasizing character and mise-en-scène." (He uses the past tense to contrast the "purist" past conception of this opposition with a more recent one that sees the rise of Miramax and Sundance as a sign of the independent cinema's demise.)

6. Geoff King, *Spectacular Narratives*; Bordwell, *Narration in the Fiction Film*; Warren Buckland, "A Close Encounter with Raiders of the Lost Ark: Notes on Narrative Aspects of the New Hollywood Blockbuster," 166–77; Scott Higgins, "Suspenseful Situations: Melodramatic Narrative and the Contemporary Action Film," *Cinema Journal* 47.2 (Winter 2008): 74–96. Cf. Tom Schatz, "The New Hollywood," a scholarly perspective that assumes the Hollywood blockbuster is a plot-driven narrative form.

7. David Bordwell, *The Way Hollywood Tells It*, 63–71.

8. Some examples in which these titles are discussed are Syd Field, *Screenplay: The Foundations of Screenwriting*; David Howard and Edward Mably, *The Tools of Screenwriting: A Writer's Guide to the Craft and Elements of a Screenplay*; and Jeff Kitchen, *Writing a Great Movie: Key Tools for Successful Screenwriting*.

9. Gina Marchetti, "Action-Adventure as Ideology," 182–97.

10. Roland Barthes, "The Reality Effect," in *The Rustle of Language*, trans. Richard Howard, 141–48; Gerard Genette, "Vraisamblence and Motivation," trans. David Gorman, *Narrative* 9.3 (2001): 239–58; Colin MacCabe, "Realism and the Cinema: Notes on Some Brechtian Theses," *Screen* 15.2 (1974): 7–27.

11. Julia Hallam with Margaret Marshment, *Realism and Popular Cinema*, x.

12. Jeanne Hall, "Realism as a Style in Cinema Verité: A Critical Analysis of *Primary*," *Cinema Journal* 30.4 (Summer, 1991): 24–50.

13. Kristin Thompson, *Breaking the Glass Armor: Neoformalist Film Analysis*, 195–244.

14. Henry James, "The Art of Fiction," 15.

15. The idea of artistic works having a "dominant" comes from Russian Formalism, and its application to cinematic narrative is explained in Bordwell, Staiger and Thompson, *The Classical Hollywood Cinema*, 12.

16. Ibid.

17. David Bordwell, "The Hook: Scene Transitions in Classical Cinema," accessed Dec. 1, 2008, on David Bordwell's Web site on cinema (Jan. 2008).

18. Kristin Thompson, *Storytelling in the New Hollywood: Understanding Classical Narrative Technique*, 16.

19. Bordwell, "The Art Cinema as a Mode of Film Practice."

20. Bordwell, *Narration in the Fiction Film*, 35.

21. Thompson, *Storytelling in the New Hollywood*, 27–36.

22. Danièle M. Klapproth, *Narrative as Social Practice: Anglo-Western and Australian Aboriginal Oral Traditions*, 143.

23. Nancy L. Stein, "The Development of Children's Storytelling Skill," 282–97.

24. Ibid., 284 ff.

25. Sofia Coppola, quoted in Anthony Kaufman, "The Indie Edge," *Daily Variety*, Dec. 18, 2003, Special Section 1, A1.

26. Solondz, quoted in Levy, *Cinema of Outsiders*, 290–91.

27. Thompson, *Breaking the Glass Armor*, 214.

28. Donald Richie, *Ozu*, 25.

29. I develop this argument in more depth in Newman, "Characterization in American Independent Cinema."

30. Bordwell. Staiger, and Thompson, *The Classical Hollywood Cinema*, 44–48.

31. Roland Barthes, *S/Z*, trans. Richard Miller, 17.

32. For a similar point about independent films and episodic narration, see J. J. Murphy, *Me and You and Memento and Fargo: How Independent Screenplays Work*, 22.

33. Bordwell, *The Way Hollywood Tells It*, 63–71.

4. Pastiche as Play: The Coen Brothers

1. William Rodney Allen, *The Coen Brothers Interviews*, 181. The full quote is: "being original and always doing the new thing is incredibly overrated."

2. Richard Corliss, "Same Old Song Blood Simple" *Time*, Jan. 28, 1985.

3. J. Hoberman, "Blood Simple," *Village Voice*, Feb. 5, 2002, in a reappraisal of the film after its release in a director's cut on DVD.

4. Allen, *The Coen Brothers Interviews*, 137.

5. Foster Hirsch, *Detours and Lost Highways: A Map of Neo-Noir*; Richard Dyer, *Pastiche*, 119–30.

6. Dyer, *Pastiche*, 102.

7. Ibid., 104.

8. Pauline Kael, "Plain and Simple," *The New Yorker*, Feb. 25, 1985.

9. For instance, in a career recap David Denby, "Killing Joke: The Coen Brothers' Twists and Turns," *The New Yorker*, Feb. 25 2008, writes: "From the beginning, they have been playing with moviemaking, playing with the audience, the press, the deep-dish interpreters, disappearing behind a façade of mockery."

10. Johan Huizinga, *Homo Ludens*.

11. In this sense, allusive appeals such as those of the Coens function similarly to those of the "smart" cinema discussed by Jeffrey Sconce in "Irony, Nihilism and the New American 'Smart' Film."

12. Jonathan Romney, "In Praise of Goofing Off," *Sight and Sound* (May 1998), reprinted in Hiller, ed., *American Independent Cinema*, 258–60.

13. For instance, Peter Körte and Georg Seesslen, eds., *Joel and Ethan Coen*, 13, write that "play with genre runs through [the Coen brothers'] work as a leitmotif."

14. This position is effectively summarized in Jon Lewis, "The Coen Brothers: Some Notes on Independence and Independents in the New Hollywood."

15. Sonnenfeld, quoted in Körte and Seesslen, eds., *Joel and Ethan Coen*, 71.

16. Noted in John Ashbrook and Ellen Cheshire, "Look in Your Heart: Miller's Crossing Revisited," *Kamera.co.uk* (2000).

17. Julia Kristeva, *Desire in Language: A Semiotic Approach to Literature and Art.*

18. Riffaterre, quoted in Gerard Genette, *Palimpsests: Literature in the Second Degree*, 2.

19. T. Jefferson Kline, *Intertextuality in French New Wave Cinema.*

20. Peter J. Rabinowitz, *Before Reading: Narrative Conventions and the Politics of Interpretation.*

21. Dyer, *Pastiche*, 7–51, clarifies many of these concepts and distinctions.

22. Linda Hutcheon, *A Theory of Parody*, 6, characterizes parody as "a form of imitation," which is further characterized by "ironic inversion."

23. Ibid., 84–99; Dyer, *Pastiche*, 1–3, defines pastiche as "imitation that you are meant to know is an imitation" and notes that it requires "particular competencies on the part of audiences."

24. I am using *paratext* to designate a text alongside another text functioning to establish and anchor its meanings, including anything from a book jacket to a review to a publicity appearance by a text's author to an extra feature on a DVD. Metatexts are a category of paratexts that explicitly describe or interpret a text.

25. Linda Hutcheon, *Irony's Edge: The Theory and Politics of Irony*, makes a similar argument about irony being enabled by discursive communities and social contexts. My points about allusion having a communal function should dovetail with this approach to the aesthetics of ironic texts, including the significance of "getting it."

26. Barbara Klinger, *Beyond the Multiplex: Cinema, New Technologies, and the Home*, 228.

27. Allen, *The Coen Brothers Interviews*, 180.

28. Dyer, *Pastiche*, 40 ff.; Simon Dentith, *Parody*, 9, defines parody as "polemical allusive imitation."

29. Henry Jenkins, *Convergence Culture: Where Old and New Media Collide.*

30. Luminosity discusses this work in Logan Hill, "The Vidder," *New York* (Nov. 12, 2007), available online at http://nymag.com/movies/features/videos/40622 (accessed July 3, 2008).

31. Fredric Jameson, *Postmodernism; Or, The Cultural Logic of Late Capitalism*, 279–96.

32. Noël Carroll, "The Future of Allusion: Hollywood in the Seventies (and Beyond)" *October* 20 (1982): 51–81.

33. On postmodernism and the Coens, see Joseph Natoli, "Joel and Ethan Coen," 88–92; and R. Barton Palmer, *Joel and Ethan Coen*. On belatedness, see Bordwell, *The Way Hollywood Tells It*, 23–26.

34. Michiko Kakutani, "In the Coen Brothers' Off-Kilter World, the Only Certainty Is Uncertainty," *New York Times* (hereafter, *NYT*), Nov. 5, 2000.

35. Franz Lidz, "Brothers Who Practice the Art of the Put-On," *NYT*, July 2, 2000.

36. Dyer, *Pastiche*, 131.

37. Steve Neale, "Melo Talk: On the Meaning and Use of the Term 'Melodrama' in the American Trade Press," *The Velvet Light Trap* 32 (Fall 1993).

38. Ulrich Kriest, "Raising Arizona," in Körte and Seesslen, eds., *Joel and Ethan Coen*, 65.

39. Vincent Canby, "Film: 'Raising Arizona,' Coen Brothers Comedy" *NYT*, Mar. 11, 1987.

40. Roger Ebert, "Raising Arizona," *Chicago Sun-Times*, Mar. 20, 1987.

41. Brian Ford Sullivan, "On the futon with . . . 'My Name Is Earl' creator Greg Garcia," TheFutonCritic.com (Oct. 30, 2006), available online at www.thefutoncritic.com/rant.aspx?id=20061030 (accessed Dec. 1, 2008).

42. Körte and Seesslen, eds., *Joel and Ethan Coen*, 65.

43. Carolyn R. Russell, *The Films of Joel and Ethan Coen*, 28.

44. Mottram, *The Sundance Kids*, 40–41.

45. Ibid., 41.

46. Russell, *The Films of Joel and Ethan Coen*, 41.

47. Ibid., 43–44.

48. Wikipedia, "Raising Arizona," available online at http://en.wikipedia.org/wiki/Raising_Arizona (accessed Nov. 30, 2008).

49. Todd McCarthy, "The Hudsucker Proxy," *Variety*, Jan. 31, 1994.

50. Janet Maslin, "Sniffing Out the Truth About Instant Success," *NYT*, Mar. 11, 1994.

51. Bill Green, Ben Peskoe, Will Russell, and Scott Shuffitt, *I'm a Lebowski, You're a Lebowski: Life, "The Big Lebowski," and What Have You* (New York: Bloomsbury, 2007).

52. *Noir* is often a background against which *Fargo* is read, e.g., Hirsch, *Detours and Lost Highways*, 247, calls *Fargo* a "film blanc" in the way it "revers[es] noir's customary shadowy world."

53. Allen, *The Coen Brothers Interviews*, 120.

54. Russell, *The Films of Joel and Ethan Coen*, 66.

55. Ibid., 68.

56. James Naremore, *More Than Night: Film Noir in Its Contexts*, 214.

57. Denby, "Killing Joke."

58. Naremore, *More Than Night*, 214–15.

59. Esther Sonnet and Peter Stanfield, " 'Good Evening Gentlemen, Can I Check Your Hats Please?': Masculinity, Dress and the Retro Gangster Cycle of the 1990s," 163–84.

60. Ibid., 166.

61. Neil Steinberg, *Hatless Jack: The President, the Fedora, and the History of American Style*.

62. Sonnet and Stanfield, " 'Good Evening Gentlemen," 172.

63. See for instance Kristin Thompson, "The Concept of Cinematic Excess," 130–42.

64. Harold Bloom, *The Anxiety of Influence: A Theory of Poetry*.

65. Palmer, *Joel and Ethan Coen*, 30.

66. In accepting the 2007 Academy Award for best directing for *No Country for Old Men*, Joel Coen said: "Ethan and I have been making stories with movie cameras since we were kids. In the late '60s when Ethan was 11 or 12, he got a suit and a briefcase and we went to the Minneapolis International Airport with a Super 8 camera and made a movie about shuttle diplomacy called 'Henry Kissinger, Man on the Go.' And honestly, what we do now doesn't feel that much different from what we were doing then. There are too many people to thank for this. We're really thrilled to have received it, and we're very thankful to all of you out there for letting us continue to play in our corner of the sandbox, so thank you very much." Transcribed at www.mahalo.com/Coen_brothers_oscar _acceptance_speech (accessed July 3, 2008).

5. Games of Narrative Form: *Pulp Fiction* and Beyond

1. James Wood, "Pulp Fiction: 'You're sayin' a foot massage don't mean nothin', and I'm sayin' it does.' " *The Guardian* (UK), Nov. 19, 1994.

2. "The New Classics," *Entertainment Weekly*, June 16, 2008, available online at www.ew.com/ew/article/0,,20207387_20207063,00.html (accessed Nov. 14, 2008).

3. Levy, *Cinema of Outsiders*, 125.

4. Ibid., 126–27.

5. Dana Polan, *Pulp Fiction*, 7.

6. Ibid., 26.

7. Ibid., 32.

8. Ibid., 81.

9. Anthony Kaufman, *Steven Soderbergh Interviews*, 122.

10. Ibid., xiv.

11. King, *American Independent Cinema*, 97.

12. Ibid., 98.

13. Kaufman, *Steven Soderbergh Interviews*, 133.

14. King, *American Independent Cinema*, 96.

15. André Bazin, "Bicycle Thief," 58.

16. Charles Ramirez Berg, "A Taxonomy of Alternative Plots in Recent Films: Classifying the 'Tarantino Effect'" *Film Criticism* 31.1–2 (Fall/Winter 2006): 8.

17. Kaufman, *Steven Soderbergh Interviews*, 121.

18. See "The View: Has Charlie Kaufman Lost the Plot?" available online at www.guardian.co.uk/film/filmblog/2008/jun/06/theviewhaveifallenoutoflovewith charliekaufman (accessed Nov. 21, 2008); movie review from *Time Out New York*, online at www.timeout.com/film/newyork/reviews/82935/November.html (accessed Nov. 21, 2008). A Google search for "synecdoche new york mindfuck" returned about 1,840 results (Nov. 21, 2008), including a large number of blogs and other Web sites about film and popular culture describing the film with this term.

19. For instance, see the untitled Web site www.freeweb.hu/neuwanstein/primer_timeline.html (accessed Nov. 21, 2008). See also "Primer," kottke.org (May 31, 2005), available online at http://kottke.org/05/05/primer (accessed Nov. 22, 2008).

20. Susan Sontag, *Styles of Radical Will*, 126.

21. Tarantino identifies his storytelling style with that of the novel. See Bordwell, *The Way Hollywood Tells It*, 91.

22. Berg, "A Taxonomy of Alternative Plots in Recent Films," is one example of such a taxonomy.

23. Bordwell, *The Way Hollywood Tells It*, 72–103, discusses network narratives, puzzle films, and multiple-draft narratives, and in *Poetics of Cinema* devotes a chapter each to network narratives and forking-paths films; King, *American Independent Film*, 84–104, refers to multistrand narratives, which he also calls "multi-thread"; many of these terms are cataloged in Jan Simons, "Complex Narratives," *New Review of Film and Television Studies* 6.2 (Aug. 2008): 111–26; and Berg, "A Taxonomy of Alternative Plots." See also Warren Buckland, ed., *Puzzle Films: Complex Storytelling in Contemporary Cinema*.

24. Berg, "A Taxonomy of Alternative Plots."

25. Jason Mittell, "Narrative Complexity in Contemporary American Television," *The Velvet Light Trap* 58 (Fall 2006): 29–40, uses the term "narrative complexity." I argue against restricting the notion of complex narration to certain kinds of plotting in Michael Z. Newman, "Character and Complexity in American Independent Cinema: 21 *Grams* and *Passion Fish*," *Film Criticism* 31.1–2 (Fall-Winter 2006): 89–106.

26. Bordwell, *The Way Hollywood Tells It*, 73.

27. Field, *Screenplay*, 136; Kathleen Atwell Herbert, *Writing Scripts Hollywood Will Love*, 62.

28. J. J. Murphy, *Me and You and Memento and Fargo*, 144–45.

29. Polan, *Pulp Fiction*, 78.

30. Edward Branigan, *Narrative Comprehension and Film*, 21.

31. Paul Thagard, *Coherence in Thought and Action*.

32. Alisa Quart, "Networked: Dysfunctional Families, Reproductive Acts, and Multitasking Minds Make for Happy Endings," *Film Comment* (July/Aug. 2005): 48–51. The term appears to have spread into popular usage when it appeared in Roger Ebert, "Syriana," *Chicago Sun-Times*, Dec. 9, 2005. See "Hyperlink cinema," *Wikipedia*, available online at http://en.wikipedia.org/wiki/Hyperlink_Cinema (accessed Nov. 21, 2008).

33. Quart, "Networked," 51.

34. Bordwell, *Narration in the Fiction Film*, 49–53, distinguishes between two orderings of narrative: the *syuzhet*, the presentation of the events in the order the audience encounters them, and *fabula*, those same events in the natural order in which they occur in the world of the story.

35. Murray Smith, "Parallel Lines," 155–61.

36. King, *American Independent Cinema*, 59–104.

37. On *Tout va bien* and Brechtian cinema, see Thompson, *Breaking the Glass Armor*, 110–31; on the classic realist text see Colin MacCabe, "Theory and Film: Principles of Realism and Pleasure," 179–97.

38. Bourdieu, *Distinction*, 3, 29.

39. Mittell, "Narrative Complexity."

40. Neil Harris, *Humbug: The Art of P. T. Barnum*, 59–90.

41. Tom Gunning, "The Cinema of Attractions," *Wide Angle* 8.3–4 (1986): 63–70.

42. Schatz, "The New Hollywood"; Bordwell summarizes this position and indicates its inadequacies in *The Way Hollywood Tells It*, 5–12.

43. Bordwell, *The Way Hollywood Tells It*; Thompson, *Storytelling in the New Hollywood*.

44. Bordwell, *The Way Hollywood Tells It*, 121–38.

45. Nick Dawson, "John August, *The Nines*," *Filmmaker* (Aug. 31, 2007), available online at www.filmmakermagazine.com/directorinterviews/2007/08/john-august-nines.php (accessed Nov. 21, 2008).

46. Tarentino, quoted in Berg, "A Taxonomy of Alternative Plots," 5.

47. Sergei Eisenstein, "Griffith, Dickens, and the Film Today," *Film Form: Essays in Film Theory*, trans. Jay Leyda, 195–256.

48. Thompson, *Breaking the Glass Armor*, 16–21.

49. King, *Indiewood, USA*, 111–35, offers an extensive analysis of *Kill Bill* as an instance of the indiewood "mainstreaming of cult." On *Donnie Darko*'s

cult appeals, see Geoff King, *Donnie Darko*. Barbara Klinger, "Becoming Cult: *The Big Lebowski*, Replay Culture, and Male Fans," *Screen* 51.1 (2010): 1–20, considers *The Big Lebowski* as a cult film in the context of contemporary "replay culture."

50. Klinger, "Becoming Cult," argues that television and DVD viewing have become essential to the creation of new cult films.

51. Matt Hills, "Media Fandom, Neoreligiosity, and Cult(ural) Studies," 133–48.

52. Thornton, *Club Cultures*.

53. Scott Tobias, "The New Cult Canon: *Donnie Darko*" *The Onion* (Feb. 22, 2008), available online at www.avclub.com/content/feature/the_new_cult_canon_donnie_darko (accessed Nov. 21, 2008).

54. King, *Donnie Darko*, 5–6.

55. Mark Jancovich, "Cult Fictions: Cult Movies, Subcultural Capital, and the Production of Cultural Distinctions," 149–62.

56. Jonathan Rosenbaum and J. Hoberman, *Midnight Movies*.

57. See Richard Kelly, *The Donnie Darko Book*, and supplementary materials on the "director's cut" DVD release.

58. Scott Macaulay, "Tech Support," *Filmmaker* (Spring 2004), available online at www.filmmakermagazine.com/spring2004/features/tech_support.php (accessed Nov. 21, 2008).

59. Rosenbaum and Hoberman, *Midnight Movies*.

60. Joanne Hollows, "The Masculinity of Cult," 41–42.

61. Klinger, "Becoming Cult."

62. King, *Donnie Darko*, 23–24, argues for the centrality of ambiguity and interpretability to *Donnie Darko*'s cult status.

63. Klinger, *Beyond the Multiplex*, 156–64.

6. Indie Opposition: *Happiness* vs. *Juno*

1. King, *American Independent Cinema*, 104.

2. Andrew O'Hehir, "Hooray for Indiewood!" *Salon.com* (Dec. 28, 2006), available online at www.salon.com/ent/movies/feature/2006/12/28/best_indies (accessed Nov. 24, 2008).

3. Manohla Dargis, "The Revolution Is Dead, Long Live the Revolution," *New York Times* (hereafter, *NYT*), Sept. 4, 2008.

4. Mark Polish, Michael Polish, and Jonathan Sheldon, *The Declaration of Independent Filmmaking: An Insider's Guide to Making Movies Outside of Hollywood*; Vincent Canby, "Rejoice! It's Independents' Day," *NYT*, Oct. 8, 1989.

5. Philip Auslander, *Liveness: Performance in a Mediatized Culture*, 66.

6. In making this point Auslander quotes Simon Frith, *Performing Rites: On the Value of Popular Music*, 71.

7. Mottram, *The Sundance Kids*, xix.

8. Waxman, *Rebels on the Backlot*, xix.

9. Andrew, *Stranger Than Paradise*, 5.

10. Ibid., 6.

11. Auslander, *Liveness*, 67.

12. Ibid., 72.

13. Kleinhans, "Independent Features," 308.

14. Stephen Duncombe, "'I'm a Loser, Baby': Zines and the Creation of Underground Identity," 245–47.

15. Auslander, *Liveness*, 70.

16. Michael Z. Newman, "Indie Culture," 16–34.

17. Michael Atkinson, "Autonomy Lessons: Paying the Price of Independence," *Village Voice*, Apr. 14–20, 1999.

18. Biskind, *Down and Dirty Pictures*, 334.

19. Howard Feinstein, "A Tender Comedy About Child Abuse? What Is Todd Solondz Up To?" *Guardian* (UK), Mar. 26, 1999.

20. Dan Cox, "'Happiness' Over at October Films," *Variety*, July 2, 1998.

21. David Edelstein, "Bleak Houses," *Slate*, Oct. 18, 1998.

22. For example, Janet Maslin, "'Happiness': Music Is Easy Listening and Dessert Is Hard to Take," *NYT*, Oct. 9, 1998.

23. Todd McCarthy, "Dark Side of 'Happiness' Explores Sexual Taboos," *Variety*, May 18, 1998.

24. J. Hoberman, "Kin Flicks," *Village Voice*, Oct. 7–13, 1998.

25. Berney, quoted in Andrew Hindes, "'Happiness at B.O.: Gotham Venues Embrace Controversial Pic," *Variety*, Oct. 13, 1998.

26. Andrew Gumbel, "Letter from Hollywood: How 'Happiness' Won," *The Independent* (UK), Oct. 25, 1998, 16.

27. Schmidt, quoted in Dan Cox, "October Axes 'Happiness'; Good Steps In," *Variety*, July13–July 19, 1998, 18.

28. Biskind, *Down and Dirty Pictures*, 336.

29. David Rosen, *Off Hollywood: The Making and Marketing of Independent Films*, 273, is the source of the phrase "undercapitalized business venture."

30. Atkinson, "Autonomy Lessons."

31. Pribram, Cinema & Culture, 38.

32. On the box office revenue see Biskind, *Down and Dirty Pictures*, 336; on the film's New York opening, see Hindes, "Happiness at B.O."

33. Vachon with Bunn, *A Killer Life*, 92.

34. "Mixed Bag for the Rest of the Indies," *The Hollywood Reporter*, Jan. 7, 1999.

35. Monica Roman and Andrew Hindes, "'Happiness' for Duo: Vets Berney, Kalish Handle Distrib'n for Pic," *Daily Variety*, July 23, 1998.

36. Andrew Hindes, "'Elizabeth' Rules: Art Films Bow Big as Oscar Season Nears," *Daily Variety*, Nov. 9, 1998.

37. Biskind, *Down and Dirty Pictures*, 336, is the source of the phrase "under the table"; on the possibility of Universal profiting from the film, see Nigel Andrews, "Make Way for the Originals," *The Independent* (UK), Apr. 15, 2000, 8.

38. Gumbel, "Letter from Hollywood."

39. Bourdieu, *Distinction*, 6.

40. Patrick Goldstein, "'Juno' Born of a Talent Mandate," *Los Angeles Times*, Feb. 5, 2008, E–1.

41. "Juno (2007)—Daily Box Office Results," Box Office Mojo, *see* www.boxofficemojo.com/movies/?page=daily&id=Juno.htm (accessed Nov. 26, 2008).

42. "Juno (2007)—International Box Office Results," Box Office Mojo, *see* www.boxofficemojo.com/movies/?page=intl&id=Juno.htm (accessed Nov. 26, 2008).

43. Perren, "Sex, Lies, and Marketing," 30–39.

44. Winter Miller, "Indie Spirits Wade into the Mainstream," *Variety*, Mar. 10–Mar. 16, 2008, 53.

45. Roger Ebert, "Toronto #5: Great Performances, Strong Stories," *Chicago Sun-Times*, Sept. 9, 2007.

46. Scott Weinberg, "TIFF Review: Juno" *Cinematical* (Sept. 10, 2007).

47. Ebert, "Toronto #5."

48. Peter Sciretta, "TIFF Movie Review: Juno" *Slashfilm* (Sept. 7, 2007).

49. Juno production notes, 2, available online at www.sadibey.com/dosyalar/Basin_Bultenleri/Juno_06.doc (accessed Nov. 28, 2008).

50. Todd McCarthy, "A Bun in the Oven, but Tongue in Cheek," *Variety*, Sept. 10–Sept. 16, 2007, 83.

51. Stephanie Zacharek, "Toronto Film Festival," Salon.com (Sept. 11, 2007), available online at www.salon.com/ent/movies/review/2007/09/11/toronto4 (accessed Nov. 25, 2008).

52. On quirk as a comical tone in American films of the 1990s and 2000s, see James MacDowell, "Notes on Quirky," *Movie: A Journal of Film Criticism* 1, available online at www2.warwick.ac.uk/fac/arts/film/movie/contents/notes_on_quirky.pdf (accessed Sept. 13, 2010).

53. The idea of alignment with character is from Murray Smith, *Engaging Characters: Fiction, Emotion, and the Cinema*.

54. Todd Martens, "The Quirks in 'Juno's' Score . . . with Audio," Extended Play blog, *Los Angeles Times* online (Dec. 18, 2007), *see* http://latimesblogs.latimes.com/extendedplay/2007/12/the-quirks-in-j.html (accessed Nov. 27, 2008).

55. Joey Sweeney, "We're the Younger Generation," Salon.com (Aug. 31, 2000), *see* http://archive.salon.com/ent/music/feature/2000/08/31/kindercore/index.html (accessed Nov. 27, 2008).

56. Ben Myers, "The Return of Indie Twee Music," Music Blog, Guardian.co.uk (Feb. 8, 2008), *see* www. Guardian.co.uk/music/musicblog/2008/feb/08/thereturnoftweeindiemusic (accessed Nov. 27, 2008).

57. Dana Stevens, "Hating Juno," *Slate* (Feb. 8, 2008), *see* www.slate.com/
id/2183937 (accessed Nov. 27, 2008); David Carr, "'Juno' Laid Low By Success,"
The Carpetbagger Blog, nytimes.com (Jan. 30, 2008), *see* http://carpetbagger
.blogs.nytimes.com/2008/01/30/juno-laid-low-by-success/?hp (accessed Nov. 28,
2008).

58. An extensive collection of links to online sites can be found at "The Juno
Backlash," BuzzFeed (n.d.), *see* www.buzzfeed.com/buzz/The_Juno_Backlash (accessed Nov. 27, 2008).

59. Anne Thompson, "Studios Try Slower Pace to Kudos Race," *Variety*,
Oct. 22–Oct. 28, 2007, 12.

60. Carl DiOrio, "'Treasure' Tops as 'Juno' Jumps," *The Hollywood Reporter*, Jan. 7, 2008.

61. "Juno (2007)—Daily Box Office Results."

62. Michael Koresky, "Attitude Adjustment: Jason Reitman's Juno," *IndieWire* (Dec. 3, 2007), *see* www.indiewire.com/movies/2007/12/attitude_adjust
.html (accessed Nov. 27, 2008).

63. Karina Longworth, "Telluride 2007: Juno," SpoutBlog (Sept. 4, 2007),
see http://blog.spout.com/2007/09/04/telluride-2007-juno (accessed Nov. 27,
2008).

64. Karina Longworth, "Where Is JUNO Crossing Over from Exactly?"
SpoutBlog (Dec. 31, 2007), *see* http://blog.spout.com/2007/12/31/where-is-juno-
crossing-over-from-exactly (accessed Nov. 27, 2008).

65. Karina Longworth, "More on JUNO and the 'Crossover' Issue," Spout-
Blog (Jan. 3, 2008), *see* http://blog.spout.com/2008/01/03/more-on-juno-and-the-
crossover-issue (accessed Nov. 28, 2008).

66. Erik Pedersen, "What a Week for 'Juno,'" *The Hollywood Reporter*,
Jan. 31, 2008.

67. For instance, J. Freedom du Lac, "'Juno' Soundtrack More Goo-Goo
Than Gaga," *Washington Post*, Jan. 23, 2008, calls the film "evil," and the recording "horribly precious," "cheese to the movie's macaroni," and "insufferably
twee."

68. Dargis, "The Revolution Is Dead, Long Live the Revolution."

BIBLIOGRAPHY

Allen, Robert C. "Home Alone Together: Hollywood and the 'Family Film.'" In Melvyn Stokes and Richard Maltby, eds., *Identifying Hollywood's Audiences: Cultural Identity and the Movies*, 109–113. London: BFI, 1999.

Allen, William Rodney. *The Coen Brothers Interviews*. Jackson: UP of Mississippi, 2006.

Altman, Rick. *Film/Genre*. London: BFI, 1999.

Anderson, John. *Sundancing: Hanging Out and Listening at America's Most Important Film Festival*. New York: Avon, 2000.

Andrew, Geoff. *Stranger Than Paradise: Maverick Film-makers in Recent American Cinema*. New York: Limelight, 1999.

Ashbrook, John and Ellen Cheshire. "Look in Your Heart: Miller's Crossing Revisited." *Kamera.co.uk* (2000), available online at www.kamera.co.uk/features/millerscrossing.html (accessed Nov. 30, 2008).

Auslander, Philip. *Liveness: Performance in a Mediatized Culture*. New York: Routledge, 1999.

Balio, Tino. "The Art Film in the New Hollywood." In Geoffrey Nowell-Smith and Steven Ricci, eds., *Hollywood and Europe: Economics, Culture, National Identity, 1945–95*, 63–73. London: BFI, 1998.

Barthes, Roland. "The Reality Effect." In *The Rustle of Language*, 141–48. Trans. Richard Howard. New York: Hill and Wang, 1986.

———. *S/Z*. Trans. Richard Miller. New York: Hill & Wang, 1974.

Baumann, Shyon. *Hollywood Highbrow: From Entertainment to Art*. Princeton: Princeton UP, 2007.

Bazin, André. *What Is Cinema?* Vol. 2. Trans. Hugh Gray. Berkeley: U of California P, 1971.

Becker, Howard S. *Art Worlds*. Berkeley: U of California P, 1982.

Becker, Ron. *Gay TV and Straight America*. New Brunswick, N.J.: Rutgers UP, 2006.

Berg, Charles Ramirez. "A Taxonomy of Alternative Plots in Recent Films: Classifying the 'Tarantino Effect'" *Film Criticism* 31.1–2 (Fall/Winter 2006): 5–61.

Bernstein, Matthew. *Walter Wanger: Hollywood Independent*. Berkeley: U of California P, 1994.

Biskind, Peter. *Down and Dirty Pictures: Miramax, Sundance, and the Rise of Independent Film*. New York: Simon & Schuster, 2004.

Bloom, Harold. *The Anxiety of Influence: A Theory of Poetry*. Oxford: Oxford UP, 1975.

Bordwell, David. "The Art Cinema as a Mode of Film Practice." In Leo Braudy and Marshall Cohen, eds., *Film Theory and Criticism*, 774–82. 6th ed. New York: Oxford UP, 2004.

———. "The Hook: Scene Transitions in Classical Cinema." See David Bordwell's Web site on cinema (Jan. 2008), www.davidbordwell.net/essays/hook.php.

———. *Narration in the Fiction Film*. Madison: U of Wisconsin P, 1988.

———. *Poetics of Cinema*. New York: Routledge, 2007.

———. *The Way Hollywood Tells It: Story and Style in Modern Movie*. Berkeley: U of California P, 2006.

Bordwell, David, Janet Staiger, and Kristen Thompson, *The Classical Hollywood Cinema: Film Style and Mode of Production to 1960*. New York: Columbia UP, 1985.

Bourdieu, Pierre. *Distinction: A Social Critique of the Judgement of Taste*. Trans. Richard Nice. Cambridge: Harvard UP, 1984.

Branigan, Edward. *Narrative Comprehension and Film*. New York: Routledge, 1992.

Buckland, Warren. "A Close Encounter with Raiders of the Lost Ark: Notes on Narrative Aspects of the New Hollywood Blockbuster." In Steve Neale and Murray Smith, eds., *Contemporary Hollywood Cinema*, 166–77. New York: Routledge, 1998.

Buckland, Warren, ed. *Puzzle Films: Complex Storytelling in Contemporary Cinema*. London: Blackwell, 2009.

Christopherson, Richard W. "From Folk Art to Fine Art: A Transformation in the Meaning of Photographic Work." *Urban Life and Culture* 3.2 (July 1974): 123–57.

Cowen, Tyler. *Good and Plenty: The Creative Successes of American Arts Funding*. Princeton: Princeton UP, 2006.

Craig, Alexander. "Dragons and Tigers Take on Leopards and Skunks: The Importance of Film Festivals." *Performing Arts & Entertainment in Canada* 31.2 (Fall 1997): 16–17.

Craig, Benjamin. *Sundance: A Festival Virgin's Guide.* London: Cinemagine Media, 2005.

Czach, Liz. "Film Festivals, Programming, and the Building of a National Cinema." *The Moving Image* 4.1 (2004): 76–88.

Danto, Arthur. "The Artworld." *Journal of Philosophy* 61.19 (1964): 571–84.

Dentith, Simon. *Parody.* London: Routledge, 2000.

De Valck, Marijke. *Film Festivals: From European Geopolitics to Global Cinephilia.* Amsterdam: U of Amsterdam P, 2007.

Dickie, George. *Art and the Aesthetic: An Institutional Analysis.* Ithaca: Cornell UP, 1974.

DiMaggio, Paul. "Cultural Boundaries and Structural Change: The Extension of the High Culture Model to Theater, Opera and the Dance, 1900–1940." In Michele Larmont and Marcel Fourner, eds., *Cultivating Differences: Symbolic Boundaries and the Making of Inequality,* 21–57. Chicago: U of Chicago P, 1992.

Doherty, Thomas. *Teenagers and Teenpics: The Juvenilization of American Movies in the 1950s.* Boston: Unwin Hyman, 1988.

Duncombe, Stephen. " 'I'm a Loser, Baby': Zines and the Creation of Underground Identity." In Henry Jenkins, Tara McPherson, and Jane Shattuc, eds., *Hop on Pop: The Politics and Pleasures of Popular Culture,* 227–50. Durham, N.C.: Duke UP, 2002.

Dyer, Richard. *Pastiche.* London: Routledge, 2007.

Eisenstein, Sergei. *Film Form: Essays in Film Theory.* Trans. Jay Leyda. New York: Harcourt, 1977.

Elsaesser, Thomas. *European Cinema: Face to Face with Hollywood.* Amsterdam: U of Amsterdam P, 2005.

Evans, Owen. "Border Exchanges: The Role of the European Film Festival." *Journal of Contemporary European Studies* 15.2 (Apr. 2007): 23–33.

Field, Syd. *Screenplay: The Foundations of Screenwriting.* 3d ed. New York: Dell, 1994.

Frith, Simon. *Performing Rites: On the Value of Popular Music.* Cambridge: Harvard UP, 1996.

Genette, Gerard. *Palimpsests: Literature in the Second Degree.* Lincoln: U of Nebraska P, 1997.

———. "Vraisamblence and Motivation." Trans. David Gorman. *Narrative* 9.3 (2001): 239–58.

Gomery, Douglas. *Shared Pleasures: A History of Movie Presentation in the United States.* Madison: U of Wisconsin P, 1992.

Gunning, Tom. "The Cinema of Attractions." *Wide Angle* 8.3–4 (1986): 63–70.

Hall, Jeanne. "Realism as a Style in Cinema Verité: A Critical Analysis of Primary." *Cinema Journal* 30.4 (Summer 1991): 24–50.

Hallam, Julia with Margaret Marshment. *Realism and Popular Cinema*. Manchester: Manchester UP, 2000.

Harris, Neil. *Humbug: The Art of P. T. Barnum*. Boston: Little, Brown, 1973.

Hebdige, Dick. *Subculture: The Meaning of Style*. London: Routledge, 1979.

Hedsmondhalgh, David. "Indie: The Institutional Politics and Aesthetics of a Popular Music Genre," *Cultural Studies* 13.1 (1999): 34–61.

Herbert, Kathleen Atwell. *Writing Scripts Hollywood Will Love*. New York: Watson-Guptill, 2000.

Hibbett, Ryan. "What Is Indie Rock?" *Popular Music and Society* 28.1 (2005): 55–77.

Hillier, Jim, ed. *American Independent Cinema: A Sight and Sound Reader*. London: BFI, 2001.

Hills, Matt. "Media Fandom, Neoreligiosity, and Cult(ural) Studies." In Mathijs and Mendik, eds., *The Cult Film Reader*, 133–48. New York: McGraw-Hill, 2008.

Hirsch, Foster. *Detours and Lost Highways: A Map of Neo-Noir*. New York: Limelight Editions, 1999.

Hirschorn, Michael. "Quirked Around." *The Atlantic*, Sept. 2007, 142–47.

Hollows, Joanne. "The Masculinity of Cult." In Mark Jancovich, Antonio Lázaro Reboll, Julian Stringer, and Andy Willis, eds., *Defining Cult Movies: The Cultural Politics of Oppositional Taste*, 41–42. Manchester: Manchester UP, 2003.

Holm, D. K. *Independent Cinema*. London: Oldcastle, 2007.

Holmlund, Chris and Justin Wyatt, eds. *American Independent Cinema: From the Margins to the Mainstream*. London: Routledge, 2004.

Howard, David and Edward Mably. *The Tools of Screenwriting: A Writer's Guide to the Craft and Elements of a Screenplay*. New York: St. Martin's, 1993.

Huizinga, Johan. *Homo Ludens*. Boston, Beacon P, 1955.

Hutcheon, Linda. *Irony's Edge: The Theory and Politics of Irony*. London: Routledge, 1994.

———. *A Theory of Parody*. New York: Methuen, 1985.

Huyssen, Andreas. *After the Great Divide: Modernism, Mass Culture, Postmodernism*. Bloomington: Indiana UP, 1986.

James, David E. *Allegories of Cinema: American Film in the Sixties*. Princeton: Princeton UP, 1989.

James, Henry. "The Art of Fiction." In Leon Edel, ed., *The Future of the Novel*, 3–27. New York: Vintage, 1965.

Jameson, Fredric. *Postmodernism; Or, The Cultural Logic of Late Capitalism*. Durham: Duke UP, 1991.

Jancovich, Mark. "Cult Fictions: Cult Movies, Subcultural Capital, and the Production of Cultural Distinctions." In Mathijs and Mendik, eds., *The Cult Film Reader*, 149–62. New York: McGraw-Hill, 2008.

Jenkins, Henry. *Convergence Culture: Where Old and New Media Collide*. New York: New York UP, 2006.

Johnson, Richard. "What Is Cultural Studies Anyway?" *Social Text* 16 (1986/87): 33–80.

Johnson, Trevor. "Sayles Talk." In Jim Hillier, ed., *American Independent Cinema: A Sight and Sound Reader*, 215–19. London: BFI, 2001.

Kaufman, Anthony. *Steven Soderbergh Interviews*. Jackson: UP of Mississippi, 2002.

Kelly, Richard. *The Donnie Darko Book*. London: Faber & Faber, 2003.

King, Geoff. *American Independent Cinema*. Bloomington: Indiana UP, 2005.

——. *Donnie Darko*. London: Wallflower, 2007.

——. *Indiewood, USA: Where Hollywood Meets Independent Cinema*. London: I. B. Tauris, 2009.

——. *Spectacular Narratives: Hollywood in the Age of the Blockbuster*. London: I. B. Tauris, 2001.

Kitchen, Jeff. *Writing a Great Movie: Key Tools for Successful Screenwriting*. New York: Lone Eagle, 2006.

Klapproth, Danièle M. *Narrative as Social Practice: Anglo-Western and Australian Aboriginal Oral Traditions*. Berlin: Mouton, 2004.

Kleinhans, Chuck. "Independent Features: Hopes and Dreams." In Jon Lewis, ed., *The New American Cinema*, 307–327. Durham: Duke UP, 1998.

Kline, T. Jefferson. *Intertextuality in French New Wave Cinema*. Baltimore: Johns Hopkins UP, 2002.

Klinger, Barbara. "Becoming Cult: *The Big Lebowski*, Replay Culture, and Male Fans." *Screen* 51.1 (2010), 1–20.

——. *Beyond the Multiplex: Cinema, New Technologies, and the Home*. Berkeley: U of California P, 2006.

Körte, Peter and Georg Seesslen, eds. *Joel and Ethan Coen*. New York: Limelight, 2004.

Kristeva, Julia. *Desire in Language: A Semiotic Approach to Literature and Art*. New York: Columbia UP, 1980.

Kuhn, Annette. "Women's Genres: Melodrama, Soap Opera and Theory." *Screen* 25.1 (1984): 18–28.

Kunda, Ziva. *Social Cognition: Making Sense of People*. Cambridge: MIT Press, 2002.

Levine, Lawrence W. *Highbrow/Lowbrow: The Emergence of Cultural Hierarchy in America*. Cambridge: Harvard UP, 1988.

Levy, Emmanuel. *The Cinema of Outsiders: The Rise of American Independent Film*. New York: New York UP, 1999.

Lewis, Jon. "The Coen Brothers: Some Notes on Independence and Independents in the New Hollywood." In Yvonne Tasker, ed., *Fifty Contemporary Filmmakers*, 108–117. New York: Routledge, 2002.

Lyons, Donald. *Independent Visions: Critical Introduction to Recent Independent American Film*. New York: Ballantine, 1994.

MacCabe, Colin. "Realism and the Cinema: Notes on Some Brechtian Theses." *Screen* 15.2 (1974): 7–27.

———. "Theory and Film: Principles of Realism and Pleasure." In Philip Rosen, ed., *Narrative, Apparatus, Ideology*, 179–97. New York: Columbia UP, 1986.

Marchetti, Gina. "Action-Adventure as Ideology." In Ian Angus and Sut Jhally, eds., *Cultural Politics in Contemporary America*, 182–97. New York: Routledge, 1989.

Mathijs, Ernest and Xavier Mendik, eds., *The Cult Film Reader*. New York: McGraw-Hill, 2008.

Mazdon, Luzy. "The Cannes Film Festival as Transnational Space." *Post Script* 25.2 (Winter/Spring 2006): 19–30.

———. "Transnational 'French' Cinema: The Cannes Film Festival." *Modern & Contemporary France* 15.1 (Feb. 2007): 9–20.

Miller, Laura J. *Reluctant Capitalists: Bookselling and the Culture of Consumption*. Chicago: U of Chicago P, 2006.

Mittell, Jason. *Genre and Television: From Cop Shows to Cartoons in American Culture*. New York: Routledge, 2004.

———. "Narrative Complexity in Contemporary American Television," *The Velvet Light Trap* 58 (Fall 2006): 29–40.

Mottram, James. *The Sundance Kids: How the Mavericks Took Back Hollywood*. New York: Faber & Faber, 2006.

Murphy, J. J. *Me and You and Memento and Fargo: How Independent Screenplays Work*. New York: Continuum, 2007.

Naremore, James. *More Than Night: Film Noir in Its Contexts*. Berkeley: U of California P, 1998.

Natoli, Joseph. "Joel and Ethan Coen." In Hans Bertens and Joseph Natoli, eds., *Postmodernism: The Key Figures*, 88–92. Malden, Mass.: Blackwell, 2002.

Neale, Steve. "Art Cinema as Institution." *Screen* 22.1 (1981): 11–39.

———. "Melo Talk: On the Meaning and Use of the Term 'Melodrama' in the American Trade Press." *The Velvet Light Trap* 32 (Fall 1993): 66–89.

Newman, Kim. "Exploitation and the Mainstream." In Geoffrey Nowell-Smith, ed., *The Oxford History of World Cinema*, 509–515. Oxford: Oxford UP, 1996.

Newman, Michael Z. "Character and Complexity in American Independent Cinema: 21 *Grams* and *Passion Fish*." *Film Criticism* 31.1–2 (Fall-Winter 2006): 89–106.

———. "Characterization in American Independent Cinema." Ph.D. diss., University of Wisconsin-Madison, 2005.

———. "Indie Culture: In Pursuit of the Authentic Autonomous Alternative." *Cinema Journal* 48.3 (Spring 2009): 16–34.

Nichols, Bill. "Discovering Form, Inferring Meaning: New Cinemas and the Film Festival Circuit." *Film Quarterly* 47.3 (Spring 1994): 16–30.

———. "Global Image Consumption in the Age of Late Capitalism." *East-West Film Journal* 8.1 (1994): 68–85.

Oakes, Kaya. *Slanted and Enchanted: The Evolution of Indie Culture.* New York: Holt, 2009.

Palmer, R. Barton. *Joel and Ethan Coen.* Urbana: U of Illinois P, 2004.

Perren, Alisa. "Sex, Lies, and Marketing: Miramax and the Development of the Quality Indie Blockbuster." *Film Quarterly* 55.2 (Winter 2001–202): 30–39.

Peterson, James. *Dreams of Chaos, Visions of Order: Understanding the American Avant-Garde Cinema.* Detroit: Wayne State UP, 1994.

Pierson, John. *Spike, Mike, Slackers & Dykes: A Guided Tour Across a Decade of American Independent Cinema.* New York: Hyperion, 1995.

Polan, Dana. *Pulp Fiction.* London: BFI, 2000.

Polish, Mark, Michael Polish, and Jonathan Sheldon. *The Declaration of Independent Filmmaking: An Insider's Guide to Making Movies Outside of Hollywood.* New York: Harcourt, 2006.

Pribram, E. Deidre. *Cinema & Culture: Independent Film in the United States, 1980–2001.* New York: Peter Lang, 2002.

Quandt, James, ed. *Robert Bresson.* Toronto: Cinémathèque Ontario, 1998.

———, ed. *Shohei Imamura.* Toronto: Cinémathèque Ontario, 1997.

Quart, Alisa. "Networked: Dysfunctional Families, Reproductive Acts, and Multitasking Minds Make for Happy Endings." *Film Comment* (July/Aug. 2005): 48–51.

Rabinowitz, Peter J. *Before Reading: Narrative Conventions and the Politics of Interpretation.* Itaca: Cornell UP, 1987.

Richie, Donald. *Ozu.* Berkeley: U of California P, 1974.

Rosen, David. *Off Hollywood: The Making and Marketing of Independent Films.* New York: Grove Weidenfeld, 1990.

Rosen, Philip, ed. *Narrative, Apparatus, Ideology: A Film Theory Reader.* New York: Columbia UP, 1986.

Rosenbaum, Jonathan and J. Hoberman. *Midnight Movies.* New York: Harper & Row, 1983.

Russell, Carolyn R. *The Films of Joel and Ethan Coen.* Jefferson, N.C.: McFarland, 2001.

Sante, Luc. "Mystery Man." In Ludvig Hertzberg, ed., *Jim Jarmusch Interviews*, 87–98. Jackson: U of Mississippi P, 2001.

Schatz, Thomas. *Hollywood Genres: Formulas, Filmmaking, and the Studio System.* New York: McGraw-Hill, 1981.

———. "The New Hollywood." In Jim Collins, Hillary Radner, and Ava Preacher Collins, eds., *Film Theory Goes to the Movies*, 8–36. New York: Routledge, 1993.

———. *Old Hollywood/New Hollywood: Ritual, Art, and Industry*. Ann Arbor: UMI Research Press, 1983.

Schuster, J. Mark. *Mapping State Cultural Policy: The State of Washington*. University of Chicago Cultural Policy Center, 2003.

Sconce, Jeffrey. "Irony, Nihilism and the New American 'Smart' Film." *Screen* 43.4 (Winter 2002): 349–69.

Simons, Jan. "Complex Narratives." New Review of Film and Television Studies 6.2 (Aug. 2008): 111–26.

Singer, Ben. *Melodrama and Modernity: Early Sensational Cinema and Its Contexts*. New York: Columbia UP, 2001.

Sitney, P. Adams. *Visionary Film: The American Avant-Garde, 1948–1978*. 2d ed. New York: Oxford UP, 1979.

Sklar, Robert. "Beyond Hoopla: The Cannes Film Festival and Cultural Significance." *Cineaste* (June 1996): 18–20.

———. *Movie-Made America: A Cultural History of American Movies*. Rev. ed. New York: Vintage, 2004.

Smith, Edward E. "Categorization." In Daniel N. Osherson and Edward E. Smith, eds., *An Invitation to Cognitive Science*, vol. 3: *Thinking*, 33–53. Cambridge: MIT Press, 1990.

Smith, Gavin, ed. *Sayles on Sayles*. Boston: Faber & Faber, 1998.

Smith, Lory. *Party in a Box: The Story of the Sundance Festival*. Salt Lake City: Gibbs Smith, 1999.

Smith, Murray. *Engaging Characters: Fiction, Emotion, and the Cinema*. Oxford: Oxford UP, 1995.

———. "Modernism and the Avant-gardes." In John Hill and Pamela Gibson, eds., *The Oxford Guide to Film Studies*, 399–412. New York: Oxford UP, 1998.

———. "Parallel Lines." In Hillier, ed., *American Independent Cinema*, 155–61. London: BFI, 2001.

Smythe, Dallas, Parker B. Lusk, and Charles A. Lewis, "Portrait of an Art-Theater Audience." *Quarterly of Film, Radio, and Television* 8 (Fall 1953): 28–50.

Soderbergh, Steven and Richard Lester. *Getting Away with It; Or, The Further Adventures of the Luckiest Bastard You Ever Saw*. London: Faber & Faber, 2000.

Sonnet, Esther and Peter Stanfield, " 'Good Evening Gentlemen, Can I Check Your Hats Please?': Masculinity, Dress and the Retro Gangster Cycle of the 1990s." In Lee Grieveson, Esther Sonnet, and Peter Stanfield, eds., *Mob Culture: Hidden Histories of the American Gangster Film*, 163–84. New Brunswick, N.J.: Rutgers UP, 2005.

Sontag, Susan. *Styles of Radical Will*. New York: Picador, 1966.

Stein, Nancy L. "The Development of Children's Storytelling Skill." In Margery B. Franklin and Sybil S. Barten, eds., *Child Language: A Reader*, 282–97. New York: Oxford UP, 1988.

Steinberg, Neil. *Hatless Jack: The President, the Fedora, and the History of American Style*. New York: Plume, 2004.

Stokes, Melvyn and Richard Maltby, eds. *Hollywood Spectatorship: Changing Perceptions of Cinema Audiences*. London: BFI, 2001.

——, eds. *Identifying Hollywood's Audiences: Cultural Identity and the Movies*. London: BFI, 1999.

Swinton, Ann. "Culture in Action: Symbols and Strategies." *American Sociological Review* 51.2 (Apr. 1986): 237–86.

Stringer, Julian. "Regarding Film Festivals." Ph.D. diss., Indiana University, 2003.

Taubin, Amy. "ALL TALK? Supposedly the voice of its generation, the indie film movement known as Mumblecore has had its 15 minutes." *Film Comment* (Nov./Dec. 2007). Also available online at www.filmlinc.com/fcm/nd07/mumblecore.htm.

Thagard, Paul. *Coherence in Thought and Action*. Cambridge: MIT Press, 2002.

Thompson, Kristin. *Breaking the Glass Armor: Neoformalist Film Analysis*. Princeton: Princeton UP, 1988.

——. "The Concept of Cinematic Excess." In Philip Rosen, ed., *Narrative, Apparatus, Ideology*, 130–42. New York: Columbia UP, 1986.

——. *Storytelling in the New Hollywood: Understanding Classical Narrative Technique*. Cambridge: Harvard UP, 1999.

Thompson, Kristin and David Bordwell. *Film History: An Introduction*. 2d ed. New York: McGraw-Hill, 2003.

Thornton, Sarah. *Club Cultures: Music, Media and Subcultural Capital*. Middletown, Conn.: Wesleyan UP, 1996.

Turan, Kenneth. *Sundance to Sarajevo: Film Festivals and the World They Made*. Berkeley: U of California P, 2002.

Tzioumakis, Yannis. *American Independent Cinema: An Introduction*. New Brunwick, N.J.: Rutgers UP, 2007.

Vachon, Christine with Austin Bunn. *A Killer Life: How an Independent Producer Survives Deals and Disasters in Hollywood and Beyond*. New York: Simon & Schuster, 2006.

Waxman, Sharon. *Rebels on the Backlot: Six Maverick Directors and How They Conquered the Hollywood Studio System*. New York: HarperCollins, 2005.

Wilinsky, Barbara. *Sure Seaters: The Emergence of Art House Cinema* (Minneapolis: U of Minnesota P, 2001).

Wilson, Jason. "Indie Rocks! Mapping Independent Video Game Design." *Media International Australia incorporating Culture and Policy* 115 (May 2005): 109–122.

Winter, Jessica. *The Rough Guide to American Independent Film*. London: Rough Guides, 2006.

Wood, Jason. 100 *American Independent Films*. London: BFI, 2004.

Wyatt, Justin. "The Formation of the 'Major Independent': Miramax, New Line and the New Hollywood." In Steve Neal and Murray Smith, eds., *Contemporary Hollywood Cinema*, 74–90. London: Routledge, 1998.

INDEX

Initial articles in all languages (A, An, El, The) are ignored in sorting. Page numbers followed by f indicate figures, and *n* indicates note.